The Recognition of Ralph Waldo Emerson

Ralph Waldo Emerson
From a painting by Alfred E.
Smith, after a daguerreotype

The
Recognition
of
Ralph Waldo Emerson

Selected Criticism Since 1837

Edited by

MILTON R. KONVITZ

Ann Arbor

THE UNIVERSITY OF MICHIGAN PRESS

ACKNOWLEDGMENTS

For permission to reprint copyrighted materials, grateful acknowledgment is made to the following authors and publishers:

The Atlantic Monthly

James Truslow Adams, "Emerson Re-read," reprinted from *Atlantic Monthly,* October, 1930.

Harvard University Press

Jonathan Bishop, *Emerson on the Soul.* Reprinted by permission of the publishers, Cambridge, Mass. Copyright 1964, by the President and Fellows of Harvard College.

William C. Brownell, *American Prose Masters,* edited by Howard Mumford Jones. Reprinted by permission of The Belknap Press of Harvard University Press, Cambridge, Mass. Copyright 1963 by the President and Fellows of Harvard College.

Macmillan

John Morley, *Miscellanies,* Volume I. London and Basingstoke: Macmillan, 1886.

The Macmillan Company

Theodore L. Gross, *The Heroic Ideal in American Literature.* Reprinted with permission of The Macmillan Company. Copyright © 1971 by Theodore L. Gross.

Robert E. Spiller, "Ralph Waldo Emerson: Man Thinking," from *Literary History of the United States,* edited by Robert E. Spiller, Willard Thorp, Thomas H. Johnson, Henry S. Canby. Reprinted with permission of The Macmillan Company. Copyright © The Macmillan Company 1946, 1947, 1948, 1953, 1959, 1963.

George Edward Woodberry, *Ralph Waldo Emerson.* Copyright, 1907, by The Macmillan Company.

Lewis Mumford
  Lewis Mumford, *The Golden Day*. Boni & Liveright, 1926; Beacon Press, 1957.
Laurence Pollinger Ltd.
  D. H. Lawrence, *Phoenix*. Published by William Heinemann Ltd. Reprinted by permission of Lawrence Pollinger Ltd. and the Estate of the late Frieda Lawrence Ravagli.
Charles Scribner's Sons
  Stuart Sherman, *Americans*. Reprinted by permission of Charles Scribner's Sons. Copyright 1922 Charles Scribner's Sons; renewal copyright 1950.
The Viking Press, Inc.
  Phoenix: The Posthumous Papers of D. H. Lawrence, edited by Edward D. McDonald. Copyright 1936 by Frieda Lawrence, copyright renewed 1964 by the Estate of the late Frieda Lawrence Ravagli. Reprinted by permission of The Viking Press, Inc.

For my son Josef

"The blessings of your father
Surpass the blessings of my ancestors,
To the utmost bounds of the eternal hills.
May they rest on the head of Josef—"

Genesis 49:26

Preface

Among American thinkers, Emerson holds a unique place, for in any listing of American philosophers, he must be mentioned along with Jonathan Edwards, Charles S. Peirce, William James, Josiah Royce, and John Dewey. At the same time, in any study of American literature, Emerson's work looms large for its interest and influence. No similar claim can be made for any other American writer.

Recognition did not come to Emerson belatedly. With his first publication, *Nature* (1836), he immediately entered the mainstream of American culture, and he has remained there. From Thomas Carlyle, Margaret Fuller, and Theodore Parker, to Walt Whitman, Matthew Arnold, Henry James, and D. H. Lawrence, and to our own day, most major writers and critics in America and England have had to come to terms with Emerson. Even the few who felt compelled to reject him could not by-pass him indifferently.

"We are very near to greatness: one step and we are safe: can we not take the leap?" Emerson asked in his Journals. There have always been those who were sure that Emerson took the leap and that he reached greatness with strength and grace. Hyatt H. Waggoner in his massive work, *American Poets from the Puritans to the Present* (1968), claims that Emerson is "the central figure in American poetry, essential both as spokesman and as catalyst, not only the founder of the chief 'line' in our poetry but essential for an understanding of those poets not numbered among his poetic sons." He confirms Leslie Fiedler's statement that it was Emerson who brought to "full consciousness" the unbroken line of poetic development that has run from Edward Taylor through Robert Frost and beyond. Waggoner asserts that Emerson's essays "The Poet" and "Circles" are "the greatest prose statements ever made about the relation between American poetry and American life," and that without Emerson, Walt Whitman, Emily Dickinson, Edwin Arlington Robinson, and Robert Frost "would have written very differently, or perhaps not at all."

There have also been those—relatively few in number—who have claimed that Emerson fell far short in his presumptuous leap to greatness, and that his fall was disastrous to others as well as to himself. Yvor Winters, in *Maule's Curse* (1938), charged Emerson with being "a fraud and a sentimentalist," and he thought that in a comparison with Jones Very—whose *Essays and Poems* Emerson edited in 1839—Emerson would come out as the lesser of the two. In his extreme denigration of Emerson, Winters went so far as to say that Emerson "could not think clearly or coherently."

More recently, Quentin Anderson, in his widely-noted book, *The Imperial Self: an Essay in American Literary and Cultural History* (1971), finds that Emerson was the prophet of a movement more radical than anarchism or communism—for they seek to destroy only particular kinds of political or economic organization, whereas Emerson attacked society itself. In proclaiming the primacy of the individual, Emerson pushed the sovereign claims of the Self to the point where the individual alone had spiritual reality. Emerson represented the idea of "secular incarnation"—"incarnation from the human point of view: that God can be manifest only in that which is a particular, not in generic humanity. . . ." The individual man incorporates the world and images the world. The Emersonian individual is "The Imperial Self," and "our [American] dreams of [an American] empire have had to do with imperial selves"; and it was Emerson who "helped to make the overextension of the significance of individual claims seem a positive value. . . ." Because the "outward becomes the mere acting out of the inward," Emerson found no congenial place for society or community: only the individual consciousness, only "secular incarnation" was left to "shoulder the burden." In Emerson, in his great years, says Anderson, "was the social voice stilled." Emerson imposed upon his contemporary Christians, and even more on his immediately post-Christian audience, the "fantasy" that "the road to transcendence lay through self-absorption, [that] one had to take possession of the imperium of one's own consciousness," "his fantasy of the primacy of the imperial self."

By finding that Emerson denied the authority of society, religion, and history, and instead absorbed the world into himself, Anderson had no difficulty in identifying Allen Ginsberg, Henry Miller, and Norman O. Brown among the heirs of Emerson—all of them afflicted with the same disease, "hypertrophy of the self." In "the long run," Anderson says, Emerson's influence has been greater than that of evangelical revivalism, with which he associates Emerson's thought, of course to its detriment.

Indeed, Emerson has had his adversaries or detractors from the beginning. When his Divinity School Address (1838) was printed in three hundred copies by the members of the class that had invited him, the chief Unitarian journal blasted the publication, remarking that its notions, "so far as they are intelligible," were "utterly distasteful" to the faculty of Harvard Divinity School and to the Unitarian clergy, to whom they are "neither good divinity nor good sense". A Presbyterian journal denounced Emerson's "nonsense and impiety" and Emerson himself as "an infidel and an atheist." Attacks of this kind are included in the present collection, as are later negative appraisals by D. H. Lawrence, James Truslow Adams, and Theodore Gross.

Much more typical of the critical responses to Emerson is the essay by Theodore Parker, the first important comprehensive study of his thought, written in 1850. By that time Emerson had published *Essays, First Series* (1841), *Essays, Second Series* (1844), *Poems* (1847), *Nature, Addresses and Lectures* (1849), and *Representative Men* (1849). Parker did not permit, as he put it, "private and foolish friendship to hinder us from speaking of his faults." "We sincerely lament," he wrote, "the want of logic in his method, and his exaggeration of the intuitive powers. . . . In Emerson's poetry there is often a ruggedness and want to finish which seems wilful . . ." Yet, he continued, "spite of these defects, Mr. Emerson on the whole speaks with a holy power which no other man possesses who now writes the English tongue."

This objective spirit, which sees beyond Emerson's faults to his greatness, is to be found in the essays by Morley, Chapman, Brownell, and Henry James, as well as in other essays in this collection. A striking example of this characteristic approach is the essay by Matthew Arnold. Emerson was not, said Arnold, "one of the legitimate poets," nor could he be ranked among the great men of letters. Neither was Emerson a great philosophical writer—he could not be placed with "the Platos and Spinozas." And yet Arnold found Emerson's relation to us of an "even superior importance" for, like Marcus Aurelius, "he is the friend and aider of those who would live in the spirit." Arnold thought that just as Wordsworth's poetry was the most important English verse written in the nineteenth century, so Emerson's essays were "the most important work done in prose."

He found it possible to link Emerson only with Benjamin Franklin as the "most distinctively and honorably American . . . writers," and "the most original and the most valuable." Arnold paid tribute to Emerson's "dignity, delicacy, severity, elevation," and he concluded with the admonition: "You cannot prize him too much. . . ."

Although Emerson's reputation has, as we have seen, been challenged by some twentieth-century critics, interest in him continues to run strong. His essays are available in at least a dozen paperback editions; essays and books on Emerson have been published in a steady stream; scholarly editions of his works have been published, and additional ones are in preparation. But there has been a shift in at least one important way in which scholars and critics approach Emerson and his work. Until recently he was read and studied as if his thought had undergone no evolutionary process; as if the dates of composition or publication were irrelevant. The most notable departure from this static view of Emerson was made in the influential book, *Freedom and Fate: an Inner Life of Ralph Waldo Emerson*, by the late Stephen E. Whicher. According to Whicher's biographical-developmental view, Emerson at about 1840 entered a period when his essays and journals "betray his disturbed awareness that the pattern of his convictions is undergoing an unforeseen modification." Whicher saw the new mood in the essay "Circles" from *Essays, First Series* (1841). While the "promise of the Soul remained," Emerson was no longer willing to discard experience and its evidence of limits on the Self's potentiality. "He recognized his empirical limitations but, like a deposed monarch, gave up none of his pretensions to sovereignty. . . ." The essay "Experience," in *Essays, Second Series* (1844), claims that the author's faith in the Soul, which rests on intuition, was not shaken by contradictory experience, yet the essay is a "chief testament" of the "newly empirical Emerson."

"For some reason," wrote Whicher, Emerson's "anxiety visibly lessens in the 1840's, and he comes to terms with the outside world." In his early thought, which might be termed revolutionary, Emerson's Self could aim for the best. His later thought, as in the case of Plato, was "characteristically an affirmation of a *second best.*" Whicher found the cause of the shift from egocentrism to "a trust in the tendency of things as they are," the shift "from a subjective toward an objective idealism," in Emerson's "new way of conceiving nature, the general idea of evolution." This new way of seeing nature began to take effect in 1841, and from then on his egocentric transcendentalism is thrown into a new perspective. *The Conduct of Life* (1860), begun as a series of lectures in 1851, and revised and enlarged during the 1850's, was "the finest product of his later thought." Emerson's "ethics of Self-reliance fell off to an ethics of vocation; he replaced his hopes of performance with acquiescence and optimism. . . . His final optimism took him to a wise and balanced empiricism, a detached report on the human condition, and a genuinely humanist ethics." Yet, Whicher concluded, "it meant a defeat of his first unworldly protest against the world, a defeat that laid a shadow of promise unfulfilled across his later serenity."

Jonathan Bishop, in *Emerson On the Soul* (1964), a book dedicated to the memory of Whicher, makes more specific the connections between Emerson's inner life and certain events. He places the beginning of the creative portion of Emerson's life in the early and middle 1830's, and finds that his first creative period largely coincided with the life of his first-born son, Waldo (1836–1842). Bishop describes the year of Waldo's death as "a watershed," and comments that Waldo's death "seems to have been the end of something essential in Emerson. . . . Emerson began to work on 'Experience' within three months of Waldo's death." Bishop admits that Emerson "did not change all at once or change totally. The shift is one of emphasis." The particulars are minute, but they do accumulate "and become decisive by the close of the 1840's. By that time, the moments when some part of the original doctrine is reasserted often (though by no means always) ring false."

Studies such as those by Whicher and Bishop have opened up new and significant lines of inquiry which have become indispensable for a more comprehensive appreciation of Emerson the man and Emerson the thinker and the connections between them. These inquiries intensify the need to read and study the essays, poems, lectures, and journals, and they contribute immeasurably to the value and pleasure derived. They reenforce Emerson's own insight that thought is the basic key to man.

Two months after the death of Waldo, Emerson wrote in his Journal: "I am *Defeated* all the time; yet to Victory I am born." That men continue to read him, and that he has stood out, across almost a century and a half of American intellectual and literary history, massive, pervasive, and alive, is indeed the vindication of his claim to his birthright.

Contents

CONTEMPORANEOUS CRITICISM

CRITICISM

1837-1882

FRANCIS BOWEN (1811–1890) was professor of natural religion, moral philosophy, and civil polity at Harvard for thirty-six years. For over ten years he was editor of *North American Review*. His most important work was *Modern Philosophy, from Descartes to Schopenhauer and Hartmann* (1877). The first part of Bowen's review of *Nature* appeared in the January 1837 issue of *The Christian Examiner*, a Unitarian publication. The second part appeared in the November issue.

Emerson's *Nature*

FRANCIS BOWEN

We find beautiful writing and sound philosophy in this little work; but the effect is injured by occasional vagueness of expression, and by a vein of mysticism, that pervades the writer's whole course of thought. The highest praise that can be accorded to it, is, that it is a *suggestive* book, for no one can read it without tasking his faculties to the utmost, and relapsing into fits of severe meditation. But the effort of perusal is often painful, the thoughts excited are frequently bewildering, and the results to which they lead us, uncertain and obscure. The reader feels as in a disturbed dream, in which shows of surpassing beauty are around him, and he is conversant with disembodied spirits, yet all the time he is harassed by an uneasy sort of consciousness, that the whole combination of phenomena is fantastic and unreal.

In point of taste in composition, some defects proceed from over anxiety to avoid common errors. The writer aims at simplicity and directness, as the ancient philosopher aimed at humility, and showed his pride through the tatters of his cloak. He is in love with the Old Saxon idiom, yet there is a spice of affectation in his mode of using it. He is sometimes coarse and blunt, that he may avoid the imputation of sickly refinement, and writes bathos with malice prepense, because he abhors forced dignity and unnatural elevation . . .

It belongs to a class, and may be considered as the latest representative of that class. . . .

The writers of whom we speak, openly avow their preference of such indistinct modes of reflection, and justify loose and rambling speculations, mystical forms of expression, and the utterance of truths that are but half perceived, on the same principle, it would seem, that influences the gambler, who expects by a number of random casts to obtain at last the desired combination . . .

Dogmatism and the spirit of innovation go hand in hand . . . Both the means and the ends, which other philosophers have proposed to themselves, are rejected by the new sect of hierophants. They are among men, but not of men. From the heights of mystical speculation, they look down with a ludicrous self-complacency and pity on the mass of mankind, on the ignorant and the educated, the learners and the teachers, and should any question the grounds on which such feelings rest, they are forthwith branded with the most opprobrious epithets, which the English or the Transcendental language can supply. It is not going too far to say, that to the bitterness and scorn, with which Coleridge and some of his English adherents have replied to modest doubts and fair arguments, no parallel can be found, save in the scholastic controversies of the Middle Ages . . .

The aim of the Transcendentalists is high. They profess to look not only beyond facts, but without the aid of facts, to principles. What is this but Plato's doctrine of innate, eternal, and immutable ideas, on the consideration of which all science is founded? . . . Again, they are busy in the inquiry (to adopt their own phraseology), after the Real and the Absolute, as distinguished from the Apparent. Not to repeat the same doubt as to their success, we may at least request them to beware lest they strip Truth of its relation to Humanity, and deprive it of its usefulness. Granted that we are imprisoned in matter, why beat against the bars in a fruitless attempt to escape, when a little labor might convert the prison to a palace, or at least render the confinement more endurable. The frame of mind which longs after the forbidden fruit of knowledge in subjects placed beyond the reach of the human faculties, as it is surely indicative of a noble temperament, may also, under peculiar circumstances, conduce to the happiness of the individual. But if too much indulged, there is danger lest it waste its energies in mystic and unprofitable dreams, and despondency result from frequent failure, till at last, disappointment darkens into despair . . .

Arrogance and self-sufficiency are no less absurd in philosophy, than criminal in morals; and we cannot but think, that these qualities are displayed by men who censure indiscriminately the objects which the wise and good have endeavored to attain, and the means which they have employed in the pursuit. A fair and catholic spirit will ever incline to eclecticism in its inquiries and systems; while it is the mark of a narrow mind to consider novelty as a mark of truth, or to look upon the difficulties of a question as evincing the importance of its solution. To regard Franklin as a greater name than that of Plato, might be unjust, were not the comparison itself fanciful and improper; but we may safely assert, that there are few, very few, who would not do better to look at the American rather than the Grecian sage, as their model of the philosophical character.

Second installment

If the alteration regard the dress more than the substance, if the transcendental philosophy as yet be a manner rather than a creed, still the departures from the old method are real, and involve important consequences. But we believe, that the change is more sweeping in its nature. It is proposed, not to alter and enlarge, but to construct the fabric anew . . . It is a matter worthy of all inquiry, whether the present revolution be like that effected by Lord Bacon, an evidence of intellectual progress, an epoch in the history of man, or whether it be the mere reaction of mind pushed too far to one extreme, the recoil of systems too much depreciated, and too long forgotten . . .

The arrogant tone has been too quickly assumed, for the new philosophy wants even the first recommendation to notice. There is *prima facie* evidence against it. It is abstruse in its dogmas, fantastic in its dress, and foreign in its origin. It comes from Germany, and is one of the first fruits of a diseased admiration of every thing from that source, which has been rapidly gaining ground of late, till in many individuals it amounts to sheer midsummer madness . . .

We judge the tree by its fruits, when we assert, that the study of such writings tends to heat the imagination, and blind the judgment —that it gives a dictatorial tone to the expression of opinion, and a harsh, imperious, and sometimes flippant manner to argumentative discussion—that it injures the generous and catholic spirit of speculative philosophy by raising up a sect of such a marked and distinctive character that it can hold no fellowship either with former laborers in the cause, or with those, who, at the present time, in a different line of inquiry, are aiming at the same general objects. The difference in the mode of philosophizing between the old and new schools is radical. Either one party or the other is entirely in the wrong. To come over to the new system, we must read our former lessons backwards, give up the old tests of correctness and sincerity, and rely no longer on meek and gentle features without, as indications of truth and goodness dwelling within . . .

Whatever course, therefore, tends to rive the philosophical world into parties, to inflame discussion between them beyond all discreet bounds, to remove the objects of thought still farther from the common pursuits and interests of mankind, is so far positively pernicious and wrong. Let the Transcendentalists look to this point. Their efforts hitherto have tended to undermine the only foundation, on which they could safely rest. They have deepened the gulf between speculative and practical men, and by their innovations in language, they are breaking down the only bridge that spans the chasm. Let them succeed in this end, and they perish by isolation . . .

Originality has become the cant of the day—the magic sign, whose worshippers would fain persuade themselves of the worthlessness of every thing, save that which is too strange, too wild, and fantastical, to have entered human thought before. In such a doctrine as this we have no share. There is that in Truth, which prevents the labors of the humblest of her admirers from becoming degrading or useless to himself or mankind . . . There are mysteries in nature, which human power cannot penetrate; there are problems which the philosopher cannot solve. He may form theories, but his theories will be mere dreams—the futile attempts of human intellect to scan the designs of that Being, "whose judgments are unsearchable, and His way past finding out." Even in that field of discovery, which is open to the philosopher, he must seek to gratify his thirst for further knowledge only by persevering labor and humble trust. That eager self-confidence, which would fain grasp at conclusions, without first examining the premises, which would reach the pinnacle without the previous toil of ascending the steps, must be restrained. Truth would lose its proper estimation, if it were a pearl that could be obtained without price. It can be purchased only by patient observation, by deep and thorough reflection. In the words of Bacon, "*Homo, naturae minister et interpres, tantum facit et intelligit, quantum de naturae ordine re vel mente observaverit; nil amplius scit aut potest.*"

ANDREWS NORTON (1786–1853) was professor of sacred literature at Harvard Divinity School from 1819 to 1830. In his time he was best known for the three-volume work, *The Evidences of the Genuineness of the Gospels* (1837, 1844), a history of the New Testament canon based on evidence outside the Bible. This was one of the first critical works on the Bible published in the United States. Norton attacked Emerson's Divinity School Address in lectures and in the press. The following is taken from Norton's letter published in *The Boston Daily Advertiser*, August 27, 1838.

On the Divinity School Address

ANDREWS NORTON

There is a strange state of things existing about us in the literary and religious world, of which none of our larger periodicals has yet taken notice. It is the result of that restless craving for notoriety and excitement, which in one way or another, is keeping our community in a perpetual stir. . . .

The characteristics of this school are the most extraordinary assumption, united with great ignorance, and incapacity for reasoning. There is indeed a general tendency among its disciples to disavow learning and reasoning as sources of their higher knowledge.—The mind must be its own unassisted teacher. It discerns transcendental truths by immediate vision, and these truths can no more be communicated to another by addressing his understanding, than the power of clairvoyance can be given to one not magnetized. They announce themselves as the prophets and priests of a new future, in which all is to be changed, all old opinions done away, and all present forms of society abolished. But by what process this joyful revolution is to be effected we are not told; nor how human happiness and virtue is to be saved from the universal wreck, and regenerated in their Medea's caldron. There are great truths with which they are laboring, but they are unutterable in words to be understood by common minds. To such minds they seem nonsense, oracles as obscure as those of Delphi.

The rejection of reasoning is accompanied with an equal contempt for good taste. All modesty is laid aside. The writer of an article for an obscure periodical, or a religious newspaper, assumes a tone as if he were one of the chosen enlighteners of a dark age.— He continually obtrudes himself upon his reader, and announces his own convictions, as if from their having that character, they were necessarily indisputable. . . .

The state of things described might seem a matter of no great concern, a mere insurrection of folly, a sort of Jack Cade rebellion, which in the nature of things must soon be put down, if those engaged in it were not gathering confidence from neglect, and had not proceeded to attack principles which are the foundation of human society and human happiness. "Silly women," it has been said, and silly young men, it is to be feared, have been drawn away from their Christian faith, if not divorced from all that can properly be called religion. The evil is becoming, for the time, disastrous and alarming; and of this fact there could hardly be a more extraordinary and ill boding evidence, than is afforded by a publication, which has just appeared, entitled, an "Address, delivered before the Senior Class in Divinity College, Cambridge," upon the occasion of that class taking leave of the Institution—"By Ralph Waldo Emerson."

It is not necessary to remark particularly on this composition. It will be sufficient to state generally, that the author professes to reject all belief in Christianity as a revelation, that he makes a general attack upon the Clergy, on the ground that they preach what he calls "Historical Christianity," and that if he believe in God in the proper sense of the term, which one passage might have led his hearers to suppose, his language elsewhere is very ill-judged and indecorous. But what *his* opinions may be is a matter of minor concern; the main question is how it has happened, that religion has been insulted by the delivery of these opinions in the Chapel of the Divinity College of Cambridge, as the last instruction which those were to receive, who were going forth from it, bearing the name of Christian preachers. This is a question in which the community is deeply interested. No one can doubt for a moment of the disgust and strong disapprobation with which it must have been heard by the highly respectable officers of that Institution. They must have felt it not only as an insult to religion, but as personal insult to themselves. But this renders the fact of its having been so delivered only the more remarkable. We can proceed but a step in accounting for it. The preacher was invited to occupy the place he did, not by the officers of the Divinity College, but by the members of the graduating class. These gentlemen, therefore, have become accessories, perhaps innocent accessories, to the commission of a great offence; and the public must be desirous of learning what exculpation or excuse they can offer.

It is difficult to believe that they thought this incoherent rhapsody a specimen of fine writing, that they listened with admiration, for instance, when they were told that the religious sentiment "is myrrh, and storax and chlorine and rosemary;" or that they wondered at the profound views of their present Teacher, when he announced to them that "the new Teacher," for whom he is looking, would "see the identity of the law of gravitation with purity of heart;" or that they had not some suspicion of inconsistency, when a new Teacher was talked of, after it had been declared to them, that religious truth "is an intuition," and "cannot be received at second hand."

But the subject is to be viewed under a far more serious aspect. The words God, Religion, Christianity, have a definite meaning, well understood. They express conceptions and truths of unutterable moment to the present and future happiness of man. We well know how shamefully they have been abused in modern times by infidels and pantheists; but their meaning remains the same; the truths which they express are unchanged and unchangeable. The community know what they require when they ask for a Christian Teacher; and should any one approving the doctrines of this discourse assume that character, he would deceive his hearers; he would be guilty of a practical falsehood for the most paltry of temptations; he would consent to live a lie, for the sake of being maintained by those whom he had cheated. It is not, however, to be supposed that his vanity would suffer him long to keep his philosophy wholly to himself. This would break out in obscure intimations, ambiguous words, and false and mischievous speculations. But should such preachers abound, and grow confident in their folly, we can hardly overestimate the disastrous effect upon the religion and moral state of the community.

ORESTES A. BROWNSON (1803–1876) started out as a Presbyterian; then he became a Universalist minister, but soon found even that denomination too conservative and restrictive. He became an independent minister, identifying himself with workers and their interests, and in 1836 organized his own church for the working men of Boston. He attacked both Roman Catholicism and Protestantism, and became a popular figure for his writings and speeches. For some years he was close to Thoreau and other Transcendentalists, and he sent his son to join the Brook Farm colony. In 1844 he shocked New England by converting to Roman Catholicism, and for the next thirty years he attacked all enemies of the Church. The following article on the Divinity School Address was published in the October 1838 issue of the *Boston Quarterly Review*, which Brownson had established earlier that year.

On the Divinity School Address

ORESTES A. BROWNSON

This is in some respects a remarkable address,—remarkable for its own character and for the place where and the occasion on which it was delivered. It is not often, we fancy, that such an address is delivered by a clergyman in a Divinity College to a class of young men just ready to go forth into the churches as preachers of the Gospel of Jesus Christ. Indeed it is not often that a discourse teaching doctrines like the leading doctrines of this, is delivered by a professedly religious man, anywhere or on any occasion.

We are not surprised that this address should have produced some excitement and called forth some severe censures upon its author; for we have long known that there are comparatively few who can hear with calmness the utterance of opinions to which they do not subscribe. Yet we regret to see the abuse which has been heaped upon Mr. Emerson. We ought to learn to tolerate all opinions, to respect every man's right to form and to utter his own opinions whatever they may be. If we regard the opinions as unsound, false, or dangerous, we should meet them calmly, refute them if we can; but be careful to respect, and to treat with all Christian meekness and love, him who entertains them . . .

In dismissing this address, we can only say that we have spoken of it freely, but with no improper feeling to its author. We love bold speculation; we are pleased to find a man who dares tell us what and precisely what he thinks, however unpopular his views may be. We have no disposition to check his utterance, by giving his views a bad name, although we deem them unsound. We love progress, and progress cannot be effected without freedom. Still we wish to see a certain sobriety, a certain reserve in all speculations, something like timidity about rushing off into an unknown universe, and some little regret in departing from the faith of our fathers.

Nevertheless, let not the tenor of our remarks be mistaken. Mr. Emerson is the last man in the world we should suspect of conscious hostility to religion and morality. No one can know him or read his productions without feeling a profound respect for the singular purity and uprightness of his character and motives. The great object he is laboring to accomplish is one in which he should receive the hearty coöperation of every American scholar, of every friend of truth, freedom, piety, and virtue. Whatever may be the character of his speculations, whatever may be the moral, philosophical, or theological system which forms the basis of his speculations, his real object is not the inculcation of any new theory on man, nature, or God; but to induce men to think for themselves on all subjects, and to speak from their own full hearts and earnest convictions. His object is to make men scorn to be slaves to routine, to custom, to established creeds, to public opinion, to the great names of this age, of this country, or of any other. He cannot bear the idea that a man comes into the world to-day with the field of truth monopolized and foreclosed. To every man lies open the whole field of truth, in morals, in politics, in science, in theology, in philosophy. The labors of past ages, the revelations of prophets and bards, the discoveries of the scientific and the philosophic, are not to be regarded as superseding our own exertions and inquiries, as impediments to the free action of our own minds, but merely as helps, as provocations to the freest and fullest spiritual action of which God has made us capable.

This is the real end he has in view, and it is a good end. To call forth the free spirit, to produce the conviction here implied, to provoke men to be men, self-moving, self-subsisting men, not mere puppets, moving but as moved by the reigning mode, the reigning dogma, the reigning school, is a grand and praiseworthy work, and we should reverence and aid, not abuse and hinder him who gives himself up soul and body to its accomplishment. So far as the author of the address before us is true to this object, earnest in executing this work, he has our hearty sympathy, and all the aid we, in our humble sphere, can give him. In laboring for this object, he proves himself worthy of his age and his country, true to religion and to morals. In calling, as he does, upon the literary men of our community, in the silver tones of his rich and eloquent voice, and above all by the quickening influence of his example, to assert and maintain their independence throughout the whole domain of thought, against every species of tyranny that would encroach upon it, he is doing his duty; he is doing a work the effects of which will be felt for good far and wide, long after men shall have forgotten the puerility of his conceits, the affectations of his style, and the unphilosophical character of his speculations. The doctrines he puts forth, the positive instructions, for which he is now censured, will soon be classed where they belong: but the influence of his free spirit, and free utterance, the literature of this country will long feel and hold in grateful remembrance.

J. W. ALEXANDER, ALBERT DOD, and CHARLES HODGE were three leading theologians at Princeton Theological Seminary. They wrote two articles for the January 1839 issue of *The Biblical Repertory and Princeton Review,* in which they analyzed critically the state of theology in New England. The following passages attack Emerson and his Divinity School Address.

Transcendentalism of the Germans and of Cousin and Its Influence on Opinion in This Country

J. W. ALEXANDER, ALBERT DOD, AND CHARLES HODGE

We have another alarming symptom of its progress among us, in the Address delivered in July last, by the Rev. Ralph Waldo Emerson, before the Senior Class in Divinity, at Harvard University. This Address is before us. We have read it, and we want words with which to express our sense of the nonsense and impiety which pervade it. It is a rhapsody, obviously in imitation of Thomas Carlyle, and possessing as much of the vice of his mannerism as the author could borrow, but without his genius. The interest which it possesses for us arises from its containing the application of the Transcendental Philosophy in the form of instruction to young men, about to go forth as preachers of Christianity. The principles upon which Mr. Emerson proceeds, so far as he states them, are the same with those of M. Cousin. We find the same conception of the Deity as the substratum of all things, the same attributes assigned to the reason, and the same claim of inspiration for every man. But here we have a somewhat more distinct avowal of the results to which these principles lead, in their application to Christianity, than M. Cousin has seen fit to give us. What we had charged upon the system, before reading this pamphlet, as being fairly and logically involved in its premises, we have here found avowed by one of its own advocates. Thus we have said, that if the notion which it gives us of God is correct, then he who is concerned in the production of any phenomenon, who employs his agency in any manner, in kindling a fire or uttering a prayer, does thereby manifest the Deity and render to him religious worship. This consequence is frankly avowed and taught by Mr. Emerson. Speaking of the "religious sentiment," he says, "It is mountain air" . . . He even admonishes us, that the time is coming when men shall be taught to believe in "the identity of the law of gravitation with purity of heart" . . . He complains grievously of this want of faith in the infinitude of the soul; he cries out because "man is ashamed of himself, and skulks and sneaks through the world" . . . Miracles, in the proper sense of the word, are of course discarded . . . There is not a single truth or sentiment in this whole Address that is borrowed from the Scriptures. And why should there be? Mr. Emerson, and all men, are as truly inspired as the penmen of the sacred volume. Indeed, he expressly warns the candidates for the ministry, whom he was addressing, to look only into their own souls for the truth. He has himself succeeded thus in discovering many truths, that are not to be found in the Bible . . . The present mode of interpreting Christianity, even under the form of Unitarianism, he abhors as utterly repugnant to reason, and insufficient for the wants of our nature; he stigmatizes it as an historical, traditional Christianity, that has its origin in past revelations, instead of placing its faith in new ones . . . He treats Christianity as a Mythos, like the creeds of Pagan Greece and Rome, and does not even pay it sufficient respect, under this aspect, to be at the trouble of interpreting for us more than a few of the hidden meanings, that lie concealed under its allegorical forms. We have at least to thank him, on behalf of those whose eyes might not otherwise have been opened, for giving us so distinct and ample an illustration of the kind of service which M. Cousin professes himself willing to render to Christianity by means of his philosophy. We would call public attention to this Address, as the first fruits of transcendentalism in our country. We hold it up as a warning evidence of the nature of the tree which has produced it . . .

We pretend not, as we have said, to comprehend these dogmas. We know not what they are; but we know what they are *not* . . . No one, who has ever heard such avowals, can forget the touching manner in which pious as well as celebrated German scholars have sometimes lamented their still lingering doubts as to the personality of God. But while these systems rob us of our religious faith, they despoil us of our reason. Let those who will, rehearse to us the empty babble about reason as a faculty of immediate insight of the infinite; we will trust no faculty, which, like Eastern princes, mounts the throne over the corpses of its brethren. We cannot sacrifice our understanding. If we are addressed by appeals to consciousness, to intuition, we will try those appeals. If we are addressed by reasoning, we will endeavour to go along with that reasoning. But in what is thus offered, there is no ratiocination; there is endless assertion, not merely of unproved, but of unreasonable, of contradictory, of absurd propositions. And if any overcome by the *prestige* of the new philosophy, as transatlantic, or as new, are ready to repeat dogmas which neither they, nor the inventors of them, can comprehend, and which approach the dialect of Bedlam, we crave to be exempt from the number, and will contentedly abstain for life from "the high *priori* road." The more we have looked at it, the more we have been convinced of its emptiness and fatuity. It proves nothing; it determines nothing; or, where it seems to have results, they are hideous and godless. Moreover, we think we speak the sentiment of a large body of scholars in our country, when we say, that if we must have a transatlantic philosophy, we desire to have it in its native robustness and freshness. We do not wish to have it through the medium of French declaimers, or of the French language, than which no tongue is less fit to convey the endless distinctions of the German . . . We learn with pain, that, among the Unitarians of Boston and its vicinity, there are those who affect to embrace the pantheistic creed. The time may not be far off, when some new Emerson shall preach pantheism under the banner of a self-styled Calvinism; or when, with formularies as sound as those of Germany, some author among ourselves may, like Dinter, address his reader thus, *O thou Son of God!* For the tendency of German philosophizing is towards impious temerity. We have long deplored the spread of Socinianism, but there is no form of Socinianism, or of rational Deism, which is not immeasurably to be preferred to the German insanity. In fine, we cleave with more tenacity than ever to the mode of philosophizing which has for several generations prevailed among our British ancestors; and especially to that Oracle in which we read, what the investigation of this subject has impressed on us with double force, that God will destroy the wisdom of the wise, and bring to nothing the understanding of the prudent; that the foolishness of God is wiser than men, and that, when men change the truth of God into a lie, he will give them over to a reprobate mind.

RICHARD MONCKTON MILNES, LORD HOUGHTON (1809–1885) is best known
for his biography of John Keats (1848). He was probably the first writer
who publicly championed Keats as a great poet. He was a friend of
Tennyson and Thackeray. For the following review in the March 1840
issue of the *Westminster Review*, Milnes had read Emerson's *Nature*, the
American Scholar Address, the Divinity School Address, and several other
writings.

American Philosophy — Emerson's Works

RICHARD MONCKTON MILNES

The writings of Mr. Carlyle have already received our criticism and
commendation, and it may not be unpleasing to our readers to receive some supplementary notice of a mind cognate to his, however
inferior in energies and influences, and to us especially significant
as the eldest palpable and perspicuous birth of American Philosophy. The utterances of Mr. Carlyle are in the streets and schools
of experienced and studious Europe, but this voice has come to us
over the broad Atlantic, full of the same tender complaint, the same
indignant exhortation, the same trust and distrust, faith and incre-
dulity, yet all sufficiently modified by circumstances of personality
and place to show that the plant is assimilated to the climate and
the soil, although the seed may have been brought from elsewhere.

It is with no disrespect to Mr. Emerson that we would say that
there is little in such of his works as have reached us (and we have
read all that we could find), which would be new to the competent
student of European Philosophy; for we must couple this with the
assertion that to the general English reader there is much that
would appear extravagantly, absurdly original; and we believe that
no one, however well read, would feel anything but gratification at
reading thoughts already familiar to him, arrayed in language so
freshly vigorous, so eloquently true. . . .

The Philosophy of Mr. Emerson is an Idealistic Pantheism. It
would hardly be fair to pronounce it superficial on merely negative
proof, for these writings are in nowise of a controversial character;
and the exposition and illustration of his system, as far as it is given,
is as earnest and sincere as if the soul of the very man were laid
bare before us. But, at the same time, we cannot but regard the confidence with which he invests his conclusions, and the solemnity
with which he urges his hearers to act them out fully and immediately, as evidence that he has not probed the depth of the ground

on which he is standing, but that, knowing it to be strong enough to bear himself at that moment, he has believed it capable of supporting the world. All religious philosophy has perhaps a basis of pantheism, but here there is little or no superstructure. The identity of man with nature, the primary duty of 'a wise passiveness' to the superincumbent spirit, the 'occult relation between man and the vegetable,' the creed 'I am nothing—I see all—the currents of the Universal Being circulate through me—I am part or particle of God' . . . have been uttered often before, and in many senses; but here they are all-in-all, and they are propounded as if they lay on the surface of truth and within the grasp of all men, and contained not problems, or parts of problems, in the solution of which the lives of thoughtful men have gone by, leaving the giant contradictions of our moral being just as they were, standing face to face, irreconcilable.

The first look of such a system as Mr. Emerson's has assuredly much that is attractive for assertors of the democratic principle in general, and for a people so circumstanced as the Americans in particular. The 'vox populi vox Dei,' assumes a very special import when the 'vox populi' does not merely mean an historical utterance, but an expression of the universal Spirit, which is at once the Thought of God and the Instinct of Man: the sense of the majority is no longer a sum of separate wills and passions, but an absolute and transcending power, only not supernatural because it is the most perfect development of nature.

We would ask Mr. Emerson just to bring before his fancy what, in all probability, would be the result, if this indiscriminate self-reliance was generally adopted as the sole regulating principle of life. We find no barrier that shall prevent its falling into that moral state of imperfect sympathies which especially distinguishes the lower animals from man. The habitual dependence on instinct, which is the characteristic of their organization, seems of itself to exclude any interest in the pleasures and pains, hopes and fears, of others of their kind, except in reference to their own perceptions; and it is only in exceptions to this rule, in rare cases of affection and sympathy (and these, singularly enough, far more frequently manifested in relation to man, the higher creature, than to individuals of their own species or level in nature), that we perceive any presence of a purer intelligence.

What a battle field for enthusiasms would the world become, did men once believe that they are not speaking, but spoken from! What a range for every fancy-fuddled and passion-puzzled man to wander through, proclaiming his own Messias-ship, and abjuring all other divinity! What a premium on the worst, because wilful, ignorance,—on the worst, because uneasy, idleness! What a discord of obstinate and irresponsible wills to drown the voice of conscience and opinion!

Reading and reflection will soon lead Mr. Emerson to 'believe the past,' as far as it ought to be believed: the Present is nothing more than the convergence of the Past and Future, and unless we have experience of the one, and such imperfect vision as we can get of the other, we cannot call this Present our own.

THOMAS CARLYLE (1795–1881), essayist, social critic, and historian, is best known for *Sartor Resartus,* an account of the author's spiritual crisis. This work first appeared in 1833–1834 in *Fraser's Magazine.* Emerson then arranged for its publication as a book in the United States, and it was published in Boston in 1836. The work did not appear as a book in England until 1838. Carlyle's *The French Revolution* was published in 1837. In 1841 Carlyle returned the compliment to Emerson by writing the Preface to the English edition of *Essays, First Series,* from which the following passage is taken.

Preface to *Essays, First Series*

THOMAS CARLYLE

He has not written a line which is not conceived in the interest of mankind. He never writes in the interest of a section, of a party, of a church, or a man, always in the interest of mankind. Hence comes the ennobling literature of the times; and, while his culture joins him to the history of man, Emerson's writings and speakings amount to something:—and yet hitherto, as seems to me, this Emerson is perhaps far less notable for what he has spoken or done, than for the many things he has not spoken, and has forborne to do. With uncommon interest, I have learned that this, and in such a never-resting locomotive country too, is one of those rare men who have withal the invaluable talent of sitting still! . . . What Emerson's talent is, we will not altogether estimate by this book. The utterance is abrupt, fitful; the great idea not yet embodied struggles towards an embodyment. Yet everywhere there is the true heart of a man; which is the parent of all talent; which without much talent cannot exist. A breath as of the green country,—all the welcomer that it is *New* England country, not second-hand but first-hand country,— meets us wholesomely everywhere in these "essays:" the authentic green Earth is there, with her mountains, rivers, with her mills and farms. Sharp gleams of insight arrest us by their pure intellectuality; here and there, in heroic rusticism, a tone of modest manfulness, of mild invincibility, low-voiced but lion-strong, makes us too, thrill with a noble pride.

MARGARET FULLER (1810–1850) was a member of Emerson's circle on a level of equality with Thoreau and Alcott, and was a friend of James Freeman Clarke, William Henry Channing, and Frederic Hedge. Her "conversations," which attracted women from Boston's intellectual circle, were famous. Her *Woman in the Nineteenth Century* (1845) was a pioneering statement on women's rights. Together with Emerson and George Ripley, she edited *The Dial*. In her own lifetime, however, she achieved fame mainly for her writing while on the staff of Horace Greeley's *New York Daily Tribune*. Her following article on Emerson appeared in the issue of December 7, 1844.

Emerson's *Essays*

MARGARET FULLER

At the distance of three years this volume follows the first series of essays, which have already made to themselves a circle of readers attentive, thoughtful, more and more intelligent, and this circle is a large one if we consider the circumstances of this country and of England also, at this time.

In England it would seem there are a larger number of persons waiting for an invitation to calm thought and sincere intercourse than among ourselves. Copies of Mr. Emerson's first-published little volume, called *Nature*, have there been sold by thousands in a short time, while one edition has needed seven years to get circulated here. Several of his orations and essays from the *Dial* have also been republished there, and met with a reverent and earnest response.

We suppose that while in England the want of such a voice is as great as here, a larger number are at leisure to recognize that want; a far larger number have set foot in the speculative region and have ears refined to appreciate these melodious accents.

Our people, heated by a partisan spirit, necessarily occupied in these first stages by bringing out the material resources of the land, not generally prepared by early training for the enjoyment of books that require attention and reflection, are still more injured by a large majority of writers and speakers who lend all their efforts to flatter corrupt tastes and mental indolence, instead of feeling it their prerogative and their duty to admonish the community of the danger and arouse it to nobler energy. The aim of the writer or lecturer is not to say the best he knows in as few and well-chosen words as he can, making it his first aim to do justice to the subject. Rather he seeks to beat out a thought as thin as possible, and to consider what the audience will be most willing to receive.

The result of such a course is inevitable. Literature and art must become daily more degraded; philosophy cannot exist. A man who has within his mind some spark of genius or a capacity for the exercises of talent should consider himself as endowed with a sacred commission. He is the natural priest, the shepherd of the people. He must raise his mind as high as he can toward the heaven of truth, and try to draw up with him those less gifted by nature with ethereal lightness. If he does not so, but rather employs his powers to flatter them in their poverty, and to hinder aspiration by useless words and a mere seeming of activity, his sin is great: he is false to God and false to man.

Much of this sin indeed is done ignorantly. The idea that literature calls men to the genuine hierarchy is almost forgotten. One who finds himself able uses his pen as he might a trowel solely to procure himself bread, without having reflected on the position in which he thereby places himself.

Apart from the troop of mercenaries, there is one still larger of those who use their powers merely for local and temporary ends, aiming at no excellence other than may conduce to these. Among these, rank persons of honor and the best intentions but they neglect the lasting for the transient, as a man neglects to furnish his mind that he may provide the better for the house in which his body is to dwell for a few years.

When these sins and errors are prevalent and threaten to become more so, how can we sufficiently prize and honor a mind which is quite pure from such? When as in the present case we find a man whose only aim is the discernment and interpretation of the spiritual laws by which we live and move and have our being, all whose objects are permanent, and whose every word stands for a fact?

If only as a representative of the claims of individual culture in a nation which tends to lay such stress on artificial organization and external results, Mr. Emerson would be invaluable here. History will inscribe his name as a father of the country, for he is one who pleads her cause against herself.

If New England may be regarded as a chief mental focus of the New World, and many symptoms seem to give her this place, as to other centers the characteristics of heart and lungs to the body politic; if we may believe, as the writer does believe, that what is to be acted out in the country at large is most frequently first indicated there, as all the phenomena of the nervous system in the fantasies of the brain, we may hail as an auspicious omen the influence Mr.

Emerson has there obtained, which is deep-rooted, increasing, and over the younger portion of the community far greater than that of any other person.

His books are received there with a more ready intelligence than elsewhere, partly because his range of personal experiences and illustration applies to that region, partly because he has prepared the way for his books to be read by his great powers as a speaker.

The audience that waited for years upon the lectures, a part of which is incorporated into these volumes of essays, was never large, but it was select and it was constant. Among the hearers were some who, attracted by the beauty of character and manner, though they were willing to hear the speaker through, always went away discontented. They were accustomed to an artificial method whose scaffolding could easily be retraced, and desired an obvious sequence of logical inferences. They insisted there was nothing in what they had heard, because they could not give a clear account of its course and purport. They did not see that Pindar's odes might be very well arranged for their own purpose, and yet not bear translating into the methods of Mr. Locke.

Others were content to be benefited by a good influence without a strict analysis of its means. "My wife says it is about the elevation of human nature, and so it seems to me," was a fit reply to some of the critics. Many were satisfied to find themselves excited to congenial thought and nobler life, without an exact catalogue of the thoughts of the speaker.

Those who believed no truth could exist unless encased by the burrs of opinion went away utterly baffled. Sometimes they thought he was on their side, then presently would come something on the other. He really seemed to believe there were two sides to every subject, and even to intimate higher ground from which each might be seen to have an infinite number of sides or bearings, an impertinence not to be endured! The partisan heard but once and returned no more.

But some there were, simple souls, whose life had been perhaps without clear light yet still a search after truth for its own sake, who were able to receive what followed on the suggestion of a subject in a natural manner as a stream of thought. These recognized beneath the veil of words the still small voice of conscience, the vestal fires of lone religious hours, and the mild teachings of the summer woods.

The charm of the elocution too was great. His general manner was that of the reader, occasionally rising into direct address or invocation in passages where tenderness or majesty demanded more energy. At such times both eye and voice called on a remote future to give a worthy reply. A future which shall manifest more largely the universal soul as it was then to this soul. The tone of the voice was a grave body-tone, full and sweet rather than sonorous, yet flexible and haunted by many modulations, as even instruments of wood and brass seem to become after they have been long played on with skill and taste; how much more so the human voice! In the more expressive passages it uttered notes of silvery clearness, winning yet still more commanding. The words uttered in those tones floated awhile above us, then took root in the memory like winged seed.

In the union of an even rustic plainness with lyric inspirations, religious dignity with philosophic calmness, keen sagacity in details with boldness of view, we saw what brought to mind the early poets and legislators of Greece—men who taught their fellows to plow and avoid moral evil, sing hymns to the gods and watch the metamorphoses of nature. Here in civic Boston was such a man—one who could see man in his original grandeur and his original childishness, rooted in simple nature, raising to the heavens the brow and eyes of a poet.

And these lectures seemed not so much lectures as grave didactic poems, theogonies perhaps, adorned by odes when some Power was in question whom the poet had best learned to serve, and with eclogues wisely portraying in familiar tongue the duties of man to man and "harmless animals."

Such was the attitude in which the speaker appeared to that portion of the audience who have remained permanently attached to him. They value his words as the signets of reality; receive his influence as a help and incentive to a nobler discipline than the age in its general aspect appears to require; and do not fear to anticipate the verdict of posterity in claiming for him the honors of greatness and in some respects of a master.

In New England he thus formed for himself a class of readers who rejoice to study in his books what they already know by heart. For though the thought has become familiar, its beautiful garb is always fresh and bright in hue.

A similar circle of like-minded the books must and do form for themselves, though with a movement less directly powerful, as more distant from its source.

The essays have also been obnoxious to many charges. To that of obscurity, or want of perfect articulation. Of "Euphuism," as an excess of fancy in proportion to imagination, and an inclination at times to subtlety at the expense of strength, has been styled. The human heart complains of inadequacy, either in the nature or experience of the writer, to represent its full vocation and its deeper needs. Sometimes it speaks of this want as "underdevelopment" or a want of expansion which may yet be remedied; sometimes doubts whether "in this mansion there be either hall or portal to receive the loftier of the passions." Sometimes the soul is deified at the expense of nature, then again nature at that of man, and we are not quite sure that we can make a true harmony by balance of the statements. This writer has never written one good work, if such a work be one where the whole commands more attention than the parts, if such an one be produced only where, after an accumulation of materials, fire enough be applied to fuse the whole into one new substance. This second series is superior in this respect to the former, yet in no one essay is the main stress so obvious as to produce on the mind the harmonious effect of a noble river or tree in full leaf. Single passages and sentences engage our attention too much in proportion. These essays, it has been justly said, tire like a string of mosaics or a house built of medals. We miss what we expect in the work of the great poet or the great philosopher, the liberal air of all the zones: the glow, uniform yet various in tint, which is given to a body by free circulation of the heart's blood from the hour of birth. Here is undoubtedly the man of ideas, but we want the ideal man also; want the heart and genius of human life to interpret it, and here our satisfaction is not so perfect. We doubt this friend raised himself too early to the perpendicular and did not lie along the ground long enough to hear the secret whispers of our parent life. We could wish he might be thrown by conflicts on the lap of mother earth, to see if he would not rise again with added powers.

All this we may say, but it cannot excuse us from benefiting by the great gifts that have been given and assigning them their due place. . . .

Two high claims our writer can vindicate on the attention of his contemporaries. One from his *sincerity*. You have his thought just as it found place in the life of his own soul. Thus, however near or relatively distant its approximation to absolute truth, its action on you cannot fail to be healthful. It is a part of the free air.

He belongs to that band of whom there may be found a few in every age, and who now in known human history may be counted by hundreds, who worship the one God only, the God of Truth. They worship not saints nor creeds nor churches nor relics nor idols in any form. The mind is kept open to truth, and life only valued as a tendency toward it. This must be illustrated by acts and words of love, purity, and intelligence. Such are the salt of the earth; let the minutest crystal of that salt be willingly by us held in solution.

The other is through that part of his life which, if sometimes obstructed or chilled by the critical intellect, is yet the prevalent and the main source of his power. It is that by which he imprisons his hearer only to free him again as a "liberating God" (to use his own words). But indeed let us use them altogether, for none other, ancient or modern, can worthily express how, making present to us the courses and destinies of nature, he invests himself with her serenity and animates us with her joy. . . .

Thus have we in a brief and unworthy manner indicated some views of these books. The only true criticism of these or any good books may be gained by making them the companions of our lives. Does every accession of knowledge or a juster sense of beauty make us prize them more? Then they are good indeed, and more immortal than mortal. Let that test be applied to these; essays which will lead to great and complete poems—somewhere.

THEODORE PARKER (1810–1860) graduated from Harvard Divinity School in 1836 and warmly welcomed Emerson's Divinity School Address two years later. He became a friend of Emerson, Alcott, and the Channings, and found himself discarding beliefs in orthodoxy and miracles for intuitionism and idealism. His famous sermon on "The Transient and Permanent in Christianity" in 1841 showed Emerson's influence, and estranged him from almost all clergymen and churches. His friends, however, procured for him a "pulpit" in the Music Hall of Boston, where he spoke on moral and social problems. In 1847 Parker founded *The Massachusetts Quarterly Review;* it lasted only three years. In the March 1850 issue Parker wrote a comprehensive essay on Emerson which remains one of the best critical writings on Emerson and the Transcendentalist movement.

The Writings of Ralph Waldo Emerson

THEODORE PARKER

It is now almost fourteen years since Mr. Emerson published his first book, Nature. A beautiful work it was, and will be deemed for many a year to come. In this old world of literature, with more memory than wit, with much tradition and little invention, with more fear than love, and a great deal of criticism upon very little poetry, there came forward this young David, a shepherd, but to be a king, "with his garlands and singing robes about him;" one note upon his new and fresh-strung lyre was "worth a thousand men." Men were looking for something original, they always are; when it came some said it thundered, others that an angel had spoke. How men wondered at the little book! It took nearly twelve years to sell the five hundred copies of Nature. Since that time Mr. Emerson has said much, and if he has not printed many books, at least has printed much; some things far surpassing the first essay, in richness of material, in perfection of form, in continuity of thought; but nothing which has the same youthful freshness, and the same tender beauty as this early violet, blooming out of Unitarian and Calvinistic sand or snow. Poems and Essays of a later date are there, which show that he has had more time and woven it into life; works which present us with thought deeper, wider, richer, and more complete, but not surpassing the simplicity and loveliness of that maiden flower of his poetic spring.

We know how true it is that a man cannot criticise what he cannot comprehend, nor comprehend either a man or a work greater than himself. Let him get on a Quarterly never so high, it avails him nothing; "pyramids are pyramids in vales," and emmets are emmets even in a Review. Critics often afford an involuntary proof of this adage, yet grow no wiser by the experience. Few of our tribe can make the simple shrift of the old Hebrew poet, and say, "we have not exercised ourselves in great matters, nor in things too high for us." Sundry Icarian critics have we seen wending their wearying way on waxen wing to overtake the eagle flight of Emerson; some of them have we known getting near enough to see a fault, to overtake a feather falling from his wing, and with that tumbling to give name to a sea, if one cared to notice to what depth they fell.

Some of the criticisms on Mr. Emerson, transatlantic and cisatlantic, have been very remarkable, not to speak more definitely. "What of this new book?" said Mr. Public to the reviewer, who was not "seized and tied down to judge," but of his own free will stood up and answered: "Oh! 'tis out of all plumb, my lord, quite an irregular thing! not one of the angles at the four corners is a right angle. I had my rule and compasses, my lord, in my pocket. And for the poem (your lordship bid me look at it), upon taking the length, breadth, height, and depth of it, and trying them at home upon an exact scale of Bossu's, they are out, my lord, in every one of their dimensions." . . .

We are warned by the fate of our predecessors, when their example does not guide us; we confess not only our inferiority to Mr. Emerson, but our consciousness of the fact, and believe that they should "judge others who themselves excel," and that authors, like others on trial, should be judged by their peers. So we will not call this a criticism which we are about to write on Mr. Emerson, only an attempt at a contribution towards a criticism, hoping that, in due time, some one will come and do faithfully and completely what it is not yet time to accomplish, still less within our power to do.

All of Mr. Emerson's literary works, with the exception of the Poems, were published before they were printed; delivered by word of mouth to audiences. In frequently reading his pieces he had an opportunity to see any defect of form to amend it. Mr. Emerson has won by his writings a more desirable reputation than any other man of letters in America has yet attained. It is not the reputation which brings him money or academic honors, or membership of learned societies; nor does it appear conspicuously in the literary journals as yet. But he has a high place among thinking men on both sides of the water; we think no man who writes the English tongue has now so much influence in forming the opinions and character of young men and women. His audience steadily increases, at home and abroad, more rapidly in England than America. It is now with him as it was, at first, with Dr. Channing, the fairest criticism has come from the other side of the water; the reason is that he, like his predecessor, offended the sectarian and party spirit, the personal prejudices of the men about him; his life was a reproach to them, his words an offense, or his doctrines alarmed their sectarian, their party, or their personal pride, and they accordingly condemned the man. A writer who should bear the same relation to the English mind as Emerson to ours, for the same reason would be more acceptable here than at home. Emerson is neither a sectarian nor a partisan, no man less so; yet few men in America have been visited with more hatred,—private personal hatred, which the authors poorly endeavored to conceal, and perhaps did hide from themselves. The spite we have heard expressed against him by men of the common morality would strike a stranger with amazement, especially when it is remembered that his personal character and daily life are of such extraordinary loveliness. This hatred has not proceeded merely from ignorant men, in whom it could easily be excused; but more often from men who have had opportunities of obtaining as good a culture as men commonly get in this country. Yet while he has been the theme of vulgar abuse, of sneers and ridicule in public and in private; while critics, more remarkable for the venom of their poison than the strength of their bow, have shot at him their little shafts, barbed more than pointed, he has also drawn about him some of what old Drayton called "the idle smoke of praise." Let us see what he has thrown into the public fire to cause this incense, what he has done to provoke the immedicable rage of certain other men; let us see what there is in his works, of old or new, true or false, what American and what cosmopolitan; let us weigh his works with such imperfect scales as we have, weigh them by the universal standard of beauty, truth and love, and make an attempt to see what he is worth. . . .

Mr. Emerson is the most American of our writers. The idea of America, which lies at the bottom of our original institutions, appears in him with great prominence. We mean the idea of personal freedom, of the dignity and value of human nature, the superiority of a man to the accidents of a man. Emerson is the most republican of republicans, the most protestant of the dissenters. Serene as a July sun, he is equally fearless. He looks everything in the face modestly, but with earnest scrutiny, and passes judgment upon its merits. Nothing is too high for his examination, nothing too sacred. On earth only one thing he finds which is thoroughly venerable, and that is the nature of man; not the accidents, which make a man rich or famous, but the substance, which makes him a man. The man is before the institutions of man, his nature superior to his history. All finite things are only appendages of man, useful, convenient, or beautiful. Man is master, and nature his slave, serving for many a varied use. The results of human experience—the state, the church, society, the family, business, literature, science, art—all of these are subordinate to man; if they serve the individual, he is to foster them, if not, to abandon them and seek better things. He looks at all things, the past and the present, the state and the church, Christianity and the markethouse, in the daylight of the intellect. Nothing is allowed to stand between him and his manhood. Hence there is an apparent irreverence; he does not bow to any hat which Gessler has set up for public adoration, but to every man, canonical or profane, who bears the mark of native manliness. He eats showbread, if he is hungry. While he is the most American, he is almost the most cosmopolitan of our writers, the least restrained and belittled by the popular follies of the nation or the age.

In America writers are commonly kept in awe and subdued by fear of the richer class, or that of the mass of men. Mr. Emerson has small respect for either; would bow as low to a lackey as a lord, to a clown as a scholar, to one man as a million. He spurns all constitutions but the law of his own nature, rejecting them with manly scorn. The traditions of the churches are no hindrances to his thought; Jesus or Judas were the same to him, if either stood in his way and hindered the proportionate development of his individual life. The forms of society and the ritual of scholarship are no more effectual restraints. His thought of today is no barrier to freedom of thought to-morrow, for his own nature is not to be subordinated, either to the history of man or his own history. "To-morrow to fresh fields and pastures new," is his motto.

Yet, with all this freedom, there is no wilful display of it. He is so confident of his freedom, so perfectly possessed of his rights, that he does not talk of them. They appear, but are not spoken of. With the hopefulness and buoyant liberty of America, he has none of our ill-mannered boasting. He criticises America often, he always appreciates it; he seldom praises, and never brags of our country. The most democratic of democrats, no disciple of the old régime is better mannered, for it is only the vulgar democrat or aristocrat who flings his follies in your face. While it would be difficult to find a writer so uncompromising in his adhesion to just principles, there is not in all his works a single jeer or ill-natured sarcasm. None is less addicted to the common forms of reverence, but who is more truly reverential?

While his idea is American, the form of his literature is not less so. It is a form which suits the substance, and is modified by the institutions and natural objects about him. You see that the author lives in a land with free institutions, with town-meetings and ballot-boxes, in the vicinity of a decaying church, amongst men whose terrible devils are poverty and social neglect, the only devils whose damnation is much cared for. His geography is American. Katskill and the Alleghanies, Monadnoc, Wachusett, and the uplands of New Hampshire appear in poetry or prose; Contocook and Agiochook are better than the Ilyssus, or Pactolus, or "smooth-sliding Mincius, crowned with vocal reeds." New York, Fall River, and Lowell have a place in his writings where a vulgar Yankee would put Thebes or Pæstum. His men and women are American, John and Jane, not Coriolanus and Persephone. He tells of the rhodora, the club-moss, the blooming clover, not of the hibiscus and the asphodel. He knows the humblebee, the blackbird, the bat and the wren, and is not ashamed to say or sing of the things under his own eyes. He illustrates his high thought by common things out of our plain New-England life—the meeting in the church, the Sunday school, the dancing-school, a huckleberry party, the boys and girls hastening home from school, the youth in the shop, beginning an un-unconscious courtship with his unheeding customer, the farmers about their work in the fields, the bustling trader in the city, the cattle, the new hay, the voters at a town-meeting, the village brawler in a tavern full of tipsy riot, the conservative who thinks the nation is lost if his ticket chance to miscarry, the bigot worshipping the knot hole through which a dusty beam of light has looked in upon his darkness, the radical who declares that nothing is good if established, and the patent reformer who screams in your ears that he can finish the world with a single touch,—and out of all these he makes his poetry or illustrates his philosophy. Now and then he wanders off to other lands, reports what he has seen, but it is always an American report of what an American eye saw. Even Mr. Emerson's recent exaggerated praise of England is such a panegyric as none but an American could bestow. . . .

Yet with this indomitable nationality he has a culture quite cosmopolitan and extraordinary in a young nation like our own. Here is a man familiar with books, not with many but the best books, which he knows intimately. He has kept good company. Two things impress you powerfully and continually—the man has seen nature, and been familiar with books. His literary culture is not a varnish on the surface, not a mere polish of the outside; it has penetrated deep into his consciousness. The salutary effect of literary culture is more perceptible in Emerson than in any American that we know, save one, a far younger man, and of great promise, of whom we shall speak at some other time. . . .

With Emerson all is very different; his literary culture is of him, and not merely on him. His learning appears not in his quotations, but in his talk. It is the wine itself, and not the vintner's brand on the cask, which shows its quality. In his reading and his study he is still his own master. He has not purchased his education with the loss of his identity, nor of his manhood; nay, he has not forgotten his kindred in getting his culture. He is still the master of himself, no man provokes him even into a momentary imitation. He keeps his individuality with maidenly asceticism, and with a conscience rarely found amongst literary men. Virgil Homerizes, Hesiodizes, and plays Theocritus now and then. Emerson plays Emerson, always Emerson. He honors Greece and is not a stranger with her noblest sons, he pauses as a learner before the lovely muse of Germany, he bows low with exaggerating reverence before the practical skill of England; but no one, nor all of these, have power to subdue that serene and upright intellect. He rises from the oracle he stooped to consult just as erect as before. His reading gives a certain richness to his style, which is more literary than that of any American writer that we remember; as much so as that of Jeremy Taylor. He takes much for granted in his reader, as if he were addressing men who had read everything, and wished to be reminded of what they had read. In classic times there was no reading public, only a select audience of highly cultivated men. It was so in England once, the literature of that period indicates the fact. Only religious and dramatic works were designed for pit, box, and gallery. Nobody can speak more clearly and more plainly than Emerson, but take any one of his essays or orations and you see that he does not write in the language of the mass of men more than Thucydides or Tacitus. His style is allusive as an ode of Horace or Pindar, and the allusions are to literature which is known to but few. Hence, while his thought is human in substance and American in its modifications, and therefore easily grasped, comprehended, and welcomed by men of the commonest culture, it is but few who understand the entire meaning of the sentences which he writes. His style reflects American scenery, and is dimpled into rare beauty as it flows by, and so has a pleasing fascination; but it reflects also the literary scenery of his own mind, and so half of his thought is lost on half his readers. Accordingly no writer or lecturer finds a readier access for his thoughts to the mind of the people at large, but no American author is less intelligible to the people in all his manifold meaning and beauty of allusion. He has not completely learned to think with the sagest sages and then put his thoughts into the plain speech of plain men. Every word is intelligible in the massive speech of Mr. Webster and has its effect, while Emerson has still something of the imbecility of the scholar as compared to the power of the man of action, whose words fall like the notes of the wood-thrush, each in its time and place, yet without picking and choosing. "Blacksmiths and teamsters do not trip in their speech," says he, "it is a shower of bullets. It is Cambridge men who correct themselves, and begin again at every half sentence; and moreover, will pun and refine too much, and swerve from the matter to the expression." But of the peculiarities of his style we shall speak again.

Emerson's works do not betray any exact scholarship, which has a certain totality as well as method about it. It is plain to see that his favorite authors have been Plutarch, especially that outpouring of his immense common-place book, his "Moral Writings," Montaigne, Shakespeare, George Herbert, Milton, Wordsworth, Coleridge, and Carlyle. Of late years his works contain allusions to the ancient oriental literature from which he has borrowed some hard names and some valuable thoughts, but is occasionally led astray by its influence, for it is plain that he does not understand that curious philosophy he quotes from. Hence his oriental allies are brought up to take a stand which no man dreamed of in their time, and made to defend ideas not known to men till long after these antediluvian sages were at rest in their graves.

In Emerson's writings you do not see indications of exact mental discipline, so remarkable in Bacon, Milton, Taylor, and South, in Schiller, Lessing, and Schleiermacher; neither has he the wide range of mere literature noticeable in all other men. He works up scientific facts in his writings with great skill, often penetrating beyond the fact, and discussing the idea out of which it and many other kindred facts seem to have proceeded; this indicates not only a nice eye for facts, but a mind singularly powerful to detect latent analogies, and see the one in the many. Yet there is nothing to show any regular and systematic discipline in science which appears so eminently in Schiller and Hegel. He seems to learn his science from occasional conversation with men of science, or from statements of remarkable discoveries in the common Journals, not from a careful and regular study of facts or treatises.

With all his literary culture he has an intense love of nature, a true sight and appreciation thereof; not the analytic eye of the naturalist, but the synthetic vision of the poet. A book never clouds his sky. His figures are drawn from nature, he sees the fact. No chart of nature hangs up in his windows to shut out nature herself. . . .

Most writers are demonized or possessed by some one truth, or perhaps some one whim. Look where they will, they see nothing but that. Mr. Emerson holds himself erect, and no one thing engrosses his attention, no one idea; no one intellectual faculty domineers over the rest. Sensation does not dim reflection, nor does his thought lend its sickly hue to the things about him. Even Goethe, with all his boasted equilibrium, held his intellectual faculties less perfectly in hand than Emerson. He has no hobbies to ride; even his fondness for the ideal and the beautiful does not hinder him from obstinately looking real and ugly things in the face. He carries the American idea of freedom into his most intimate personality, and keeps his individuality safe and sacred. He cautions young men against stooping their minds to other men. He knows no master. Sometimes this is carried to an apparent excess, and he underrates the real value of literature, afraid lest the youth become a bookworm and not a man thinking. . . .

To us the effect of Emerson's writings is profoundly religious; they stimulate to piety, the love of God, to goodness as the love of man. We know no living writer in any language who exercises so powerful a religious influence as he. Most young persons, not ecclesiastical, will confess this. We know he is often called hard names on pretence that he is not religious. We remember once being present at a meeting of gentlemen, scholarly men some of them, after the New England standard of scholarship, who spent the evening in debating "Whether Ralph Waldo Emerson was a Christian." The opinion was quite generally entertained that he was not, for "discipleship was necessary to Christianity." "And the essence of Christian discipleship" was thought to consist in "sitting at the feet of our blessed Lord (pronounced Laawd!) and calling him Master, which Emerson certainly does not do." . . .

Mr. Emerson's writings are eminently religious; Christian in the best sense of that word. This has often been denied for two reasons: because Mr. Emerson sets little value on the mythology of the Christian sects, no more perhaps than on the mythology of the Greeks and the Scandinavians, and also because his writings far transcend the mechanical morality and formal pietism commonly recommended by gentlemen in pulpits. Highly religious, he is not at all ecclesiastical or bigoted. He has small reverence for forms and traditions; a manly life is the only form of religion which he recognizes, and hence we do not wonder at all that he also has been deemed an infidel. It would be very surprising if it were not so. Still it is not religion that is most conspicuous in these volumes; that is not to be looked for except in the special religious literature, yet we must confess that any one of Emerson's works seems far more religious than what are commonly called "good books," including the class of sermons. . . .

Mr. Emerson takes man for his point of departure, he means to take the whole man; man with his history, man with his nature, his sensational, intellectual, moral, affectional and religious instincts and faculties. With him man is the measure of all things, of ideas and of facts; if they fit man they are accepted, if not, thrown aside. This appears in his first book and in his last. . . .

In this Emerson is more American than America herself, and is himself the highest exponent in literature of this idea of human freedom and the value of man. Channing talks of the dignity of human nature, his great and brilliant theme; but he commonly, perhaps always subordinates the nature of man to some of the accidents of his history. This Emerson never does; no, not once in all his works, not in all his life. Still we think it is not the whole of man from which he starts, that he undervalues the logical, demonstrative, and historical understanding, with the results thereof, and also undervalues the affections. Hence his man, who is the measure of all things, is not the complete man. This defect appears in his ethics, which are a little cold, the ethics of marble men; and in his religious teachings, the highest which this age has furnished, full of reverence, full of faith, but not proportionately rich in affection.

Mr. Emerson has a method of his own as plainly marked as that of Lord Bacon or Descartes, and as rigidly adhered to. It is not the inductive method, by which you arrive at a general fact from many particular facts, but never reach a universal law; it is not the deductive method, whereby a minor law is derived from a major, a special from a general law; it is neither inductive nor deductive demonstration. But Emerson proceeds by the way of intuition, sensational or spiritual. Go to the fact and look for yourself, is his command; a material fact you cannot always verify and so for that must depend on evidence, a spiritual fact you can always legitimate for yourself. . . .

He is sometimes extravagant in the claims made for his own method, and maintains that ecstacy is the natural and exclusive mode of arriving at new truths, while it is only one mode. Ecstacy is the state of intuition in which the man loses his individual self-consciousness. Moments of this character are few and rare even with men like the St. Victors, like Tauler, and Böhme and Swedenborg. The writings of all these men, especially of the two last, who most completely surrendered themselves to this mode of action, show how poor and insufficient it is. All that mankind has learned in this way is little compared with the results of reflection, of meditation, and careful, conscientious looking after truth; all the great benefactors of the world have been patient and continuous in their work. . . .

Mr. Emerson says books are only for one's idle hours; he discourages hard and continuous thought, conscious modes of argument, of discipline. Here he exaggerates his idiosyncracy into a universal law. The method of nature is not ecstasy, but patient attention. Human nature avenges herself for the slight he puts on her, by the irregular and rambling character of his own productions. The vice appears more glaring in the Emersonidæ, who have all the agony without the inspiration, who affect the unconscious, write even more ridiculous nonsense than their "genius" requires; are sometimes so child-like as to become mere babies, and seem to forget that the unconscious state is oftener below the conscious than above it, and that there is an ecstasy of folly as well as of good sense.

Some of these imbeciles have been led astray by this extravagant and one-sided statement. What if books have hurt Mr. Oldbuck, and many fine wits lie "sheathed to the hilt in ponderous tomes," sheathed and rusted in so that no Orson could draw the blade,—we need not deny the real value of books, still less the value of the serious and patient study of thoughts and things. Michael Angelo and Newton had some genius; Socrates is thought not destitute of philosophical power; but no dauber of canvas, no sportsman with marble, ever worked like Angelo; the two philosophers wrought by their genius, but with an attention, an order, a diligence, and a terrible industry and method of thought, without which their genius would have ended in nothing but guess-work. Much comes by spontaneous intuition, which is to be got in no other way; but much is to precede that, and much to follow it. There are two things to be considered in the matter of inspiration, one is the Infinite God from whom it comes, the other the finite capacity which is to receive it. If Newton had never studied, it would be as easy for God to reveal the calculus to his dog Diamond as to Newton. . . .

If we put Emerson's conclusions into five great classes representing respectively his idea of man, of God, and of nature; his idea of self-rule, the relation of man's consciousness to his unconsciousness; his idea of religion, the relation of men to God; of ethics, the relation of man to man; and of economy, the relation of man to nature, we find him in the very first rank of modern science. No man in this age is before him. He demonstrates nothing, but assumes his position far in advance of mankind. This explains the treatment he has met with.

Then in his writings there appears a love of beauty in all its forms—in material nature, in art, literature, and above all, in human life. He finds it everywhere. . . .

Few men have had a keener sense for this in common life, or so nice an eye for it in inanimate nature. His writings do not disclose a very clear perception of the beauty of animated nature; it is still life that he describes, in water, plants, and the sky. He seldom refers to the great cosmic forces of the world, that are everywhere balanced into such systematic proportions, the perception of which makes the writings of Alexander von Humboldt so attractive and delightful.

In all Emerson's works there appears a sublime confidence in man; a respect for human nature which we have never seen surpassed, never equalled. Man is only to be true to his nature, to plant himself on his instincts, and all will turn out well. . . .

He has also an absolute confidence in God. He has been foolishly accused of pantheism, which sinks God in nature; but no man is further from it. He never sinks God in man, he does not stop with the law, in matter or morals, but goes back to the Lawgiver; yet probably it would not be so easy for him to give his definition of God as it would be for most graduates at Andover or Cambridge. With this confidence in God he looks things fairly in the face, and never dodges, never fears. Toil, sorrow, pain,—these are things which it is impious to fear. Boldly he faces every fact, never retreating behind an institution or a great man. In God his trust is complete; with the severest scrutiny he joins the highest reverence.

Hence come his calmness and serenity. He is evenly balanced and at repose. A more tranquil spirit cannot be found in literature.

Nothing seems to fret or jar him, and all the tossings of the literary world never jostle him into anger or impatience. He goes on like the stars above the noise and dust of earth, as calm yet not so cold. No man says things more terribly severe than he on many occasions; few in America have encountered such abuse, but in all his writings there is not a line which can be referred to ill-will. Impudence and terror are wasted on him; "upstart wealth's averted eye," which blasts the hope of the politician, is powerless on him as on the piles of granite in New Hampshire hills. Misconceived and misreported, he does not wait to "unravel any man's blunders; he is again on his road, adding new powers and honors to his domain, and new claims on the heart." He takes no notice of the criticism from which nothing but warning is to be had, warning against bigotry and impudence; and goes on his way, his only answer a creative act. Many shafts has he shot, not an arrow in self-defence; not a line betrays that he has been treated ill. This is small praise, but rare; even cool egotistic Goethe treated his "Philistine" critics with haughty scorn, comparing them to dogs who bark in the court-yard when the master mounts to ride. . . .

He lacks the power of orderly arrangements to a remarkable degree. Not only is there no obvious logical order, but there is no subtle psychological method by which the several parts of an essay are joined together; his deep sayings are jewels strung wholly at random. This often confuses the reader; this want appears the greatest defect of his mind. Of late years there has been a marked effort to correct it, . . .

Then he is not creative like Shakespeare and Goethe, perhaps not inventive like many far inferior men; he seldom or never undertakes to prove anything. He tells what he sees, seeing things by glimpses, not by steady and continuous looking, he often fails of seeing the whole object; he does not always see all of its relations with other things. Hence comes an occasional exaggeration. But this is commonly corrected by some subsequent statement. Thus he has seen books imprison many a youth, and speaking to men, desirous of warning them of their danger, he undervalues the worth of books themselves. But the use he makes of them in his own writings shows that this statement was an exaggeration which his practical judgment disapproves. Speaking to men whose chief danger was that they should be bookworms, or mechanical grinders at a logic-mill, he says that ecstasy is the method of nature, but himself never utters anything "poor and extemporaneous;" what he gets in his ecstatic moments of inspiration he examines carefully in his cool, reflective hours, and it is printed as reflection, never as the simple result of ecstatic inspiration, having not only the stamp of Divine truth, but the private mark of Emerson. He is never demonized by his enthusiasm; he possesses the spirit, it never possesses him; if "the God" comes into his rapt soul "without bell," it is only with due consideration that he communicates to the world the message that was brought. Still he must regret that his extravagant estimate of ecstasy, intuitive unconsciousness, has been made and has led some youths and maids astray.

This mode of looking at things, and this want of logical order, make him appear inconsistent. There are actual and obvious contradictions in his works. . . .

Thus a certain twofoldness appears in his writings here and there, but take them all together they form a whole of marvellous consistency; take them in connection with his private character and life, we may challenge the world to furnish an example of a fairer and more consistent whole.

With the exceptions above stated there is a remarkable balance of intellectual faculties, of creative and conservative, of the spontaneous and intuitive, and the voluntary and reflective powers. He is a slave to neither, all are balanced into lovely proportions and intellectual harmony. In many things Goethe is superior to Emerson— in fertility of invention, in a wide acquaintance with men, in that intuitive perception of character which seems an instinct in some men, in regular discipline of the understanding, in literary and artistic culture; but in general harmony of the intellectual powers, and the steadiness of purpose which comes thereof, Emerson is incontestably the superior even of the many-sided Goethe. He never wastes his time on trifles; he is too heavily fraught, and lies so deep in the sea that a little flaw of wind never drives him from his course. If we go a little further and inquire how the other qualities are blended with the intellectual, we find that the moral power a little outweighs the intellectual, and the religious is a little before the moral, as it should be, but the affections seem to be less developed than the intellect. There is no total balance of all the faculties to correspond with the harmony of his intellectual powers. This seems to us the greatest defect in his entire being, as lack of logical power is the chief defect in his intellect; there is love enough for almost any man, not enough to balance his intellect, his conscience, and his faith in God. Hence there appears a certain coldness in his ethics. He is a man running alone, and would lead others to isolation, not society. Notwithstanding his own intense individuality and his theoretic and practical respect for individuality, still persons seem of small value to him, of little value except as they represent or help develop an idea of the intellect. In this respect in his writings he is one-sided, and while no one mental power has subdued another, yet his intellect and conscience seem to enslave and belittle the affections. Yet he never goes so far in this as Goethe, who used men, and women too, as cattle to ride, as food to eat. In Emerson's religious writings there appears a worship of the infinite God far transcending all we find in Taylor or Edwards, in Fénelon or Channing; it is reverence, it is trust, the worship of the conscience, of the intellect; it is obedience, the worship of the will; it is not love, the worship of the affections.

No writer in our language is more rich in ideas, none more suggestive of noble thought and noble life. . . .

His works abound also with the most genial wit; he clearly sees and sharply states the halfnesses of things and men, but his wit is never coarse, and wholly without that grain of malice so often the accompaniment thereof.

Let us now say a word of the artistic style and rhetorical form of these remarkable books. Mr. Emerson always gravitates towards first principles, but never sets them in a row, groups them into a system, or makes of them a whole. Hence the form of all his prose writings is very defective, and much of his rare power is lost. He never fires by companies, nor even by platoons, only man by man; nay, his soldiers are never ranked into line, but stand scattered, sundered and individual, each serving on his own account, and "fighting on his own hook." Things are huddled and lumped together; diamonds, pearls, bits of chalk and cranberries, thrown pell-mell together. . . . Here is a specimen of the Lucretian "fortuitous concourse of atoms," for things are joined by a casual connection, or else by mere caprice. This is so in the Orations, which were designed to be heard, not read, where order is the more needful. His separate thoughts are each a growth. Now and then it is so with a sentence, seldom with a paragraph; but his essay is always a piece of composition, carpentry, and not growth.

Take any one of his volumes, the first series of Essays, for example, the book does not make an organic whole by itself, and so produce a certain totality of impression. The separate essays are not arranged with reference to any progress in the reader's mind, or any consecutive development of the author's ideas. Here are the titles of the several papers in their present order:—History, Self-Reliance, Compensation, Spiritual Laws, Love, Friendship, Prudence, Heroism, The Over-Soul, Circles, Intellect, Art. In each essay there is the same want of organic completeness and orderly distribution of the parts. There is no logical arrangement of the separate thoughts, which are subordinate to the main idea of the piece. They are shot together into a curious and disorderly mass of beauty, like the colors in a kaleidoscope, not laid together like the gems in a collection; still less grown into a whole like the parts of a rose, where beauty of form, fragrance, and color make up one whole of loveliness. The lines he draws do not converge to one point; there is no progress in his drama. Towards the end the interest deepens, not from an artistic arrangement of accumulated thoughts, but only because the author finds his heart warmed by his efforts, and beating quicker. . . .

His love of individuality has unconsciously deprived him of the grace of order; his orations or essays are like a natural field; here is common grass, only with him not half so common as wild roses and violets, for his common grasses are flowers—and then rocks, then trees, brambles, thorns, now flowers, now weeds, here a decaying log with raspberry-bushes on the one side and strawberry-vines on the other, and potentillas creeping among them all. There are emmets and wood-worms, earth-worms, slugs, grass-hoppers, and, more obvious, sheep and oxen, and above and about them, the brown thrasher, the hen-hawk, and the crow, making a scene of beautiful and intricate confusion which belongs to nature, not to human art.

His marked love of individuality appears in his style. His thoughts are seldom vague, all is distinct; the outlines are sharply drawn, things are always discrete from one another. He loves to particularize. He talks not of flowers, but of the violet, the clover, the cowslip and anemone; not of birds, but the nuthatch, and the wren; not of insects, but of the Volvex Globator; not of men and maids, but of Adam, John, and Jane. Things are kept from things, each surrounded by its own atmosphere. This gives great distinctness and animation to his works, though latterly he seems to imitate himself a little in this respect. It is remarkable to what an extent this individualization is carried. The essays in his books are separate, and stand apart from one another, only mechanically bound by the lids of the volume; his paragraphs in each essay are distinct and disconnected or but loosely bound to one another, it is so with sentences in the paragraph, and propositions in the sentence. Take for example his essay on Experience; it is distributed into seven parts, which treat respectively of illusion, temperament, succession, surface, surprise, reality, and subjectiveness. These seven brigadiers are put in one army with as little unity of action as any seven Mexican officers; not subject to one head, nor fighting on the same side. The subordinates under these generals are in no better order and discipline, sometimes the corporal commands the king. But this very lack of order gives variety of form. You can never anticipate him. One half of the essay never suggests the rest. If he have no order, he never sets his method a going, and himself with his audience goes to sleep, trusting that he, they, and the logical conclusion will all come out alive and waking at the last. He trusts nothing to the discipline of his camp; all to the fidelity of the individual soldiers.

His style is one of the rarest beauty; there is no affectation, no conceit, no effort at effect. He alludes to everybody and imitates nobody. No writer that we remember, except Jean Paul Richter, is so rich in beautiful imagery; there are no blank walls in his building. But Richter's temple of poesy is a Hindoo pagoda,—rich, elaborate, of costly stone, adorned with costly work, but as a whole, rather grotesque than sublime, and more queer than beautiful; you wonder how any one could have brought such wealth together, and still more that any one could combine things so oddly together. Emerson builds a rambling Gothic church with an irregular outline, a chapel here, and a tower there, you do not see why; but all parts are beautiful, and the whole constrains the soul to love and trust. His manifold images come from his own sight, not from the testimony of other men. His words are pictures of the things daguerreotyped from nature. Like Homer, Aristotle, and Tacitus, he describes the thing, and not the effect of the thing. This quality he has in common with the great writers of classic antiquity, while his wealth of sentiment puts him with the classics of modern times. Like Burke he lays all literature under contribution, and presses the facts of every-day life into his service. He seems to keep the sun and moon as his retainers, and levy black-mail on the cricket and the titmouse, on the dawdling preacher and the snow-storm which seemed to rebuke his unnatural whine. His works teem with beauty. . . .

Emerson is a great master of language; therewith he sculptures, therewith he paints; he thunders and lightens in his speech, and in his speech also he sings. In Greece, Plato and Aristophanes were mighty masters of the pen, and have not left their equals in ancient literary art; so in Rome were Virgil and Tacitus; four men so marked in individuality, so unlike and withal so skilful in the use of speech, it were not easy to find; four mighty masters of the art to write. In later times there have been in England Shakespeare,

Bacon, Milton, Taylor, Swift, and Carlyle; on the Continent, Voltaire, Rousseau, and Goethe; all masters in this art, skilful to work in human speech. Each of them possessed some qualities which Emerson has not. In Bacon, Milton, and Carlyle, there is a majesty, a dignity and giant strength, not to be claimed for him. Yet separating the beautiful from what men call sublime, no one of all that we have named, ancient or modern, has passages so beautiful as he. From what is called sublime if we separate what is simply vast, or merely grand, or only wide, it is in vain that we seek in all those men for anything to rival Emerson. . . .

JAMES RUSSELL LOWELL (1819–1891) in his time was the most highly respected American man of letters—poet, essayist, critic, translator, editor. As editor of the first four volumes of the *Atlantic Monthly* (1857–1861), Lowell brought together in that periodical's pages the writings of Emerson, Whittier, Longfellow, Holmes, and Hawthorne. The essay that follows is taken from *My Study Windows* (1871).

Emerson the Lecturer

JAMES RUSSELL LOWELL

It is a singular fact, that Mr. Emerson is the most steadily attractive lecturer in America. Into that somewhat cold-waterish region adventurers of the sensational kind come down now and then with a splash, to become disregarded King Logs before the next season. But Mr. Emerson always draws. A lecturer now for something like a third of a century, one of the pioneers of the lecturing system, the charm of his voice, his manner, and his matter has never lost its power over his earlier hearers, and continually winds new ones in its enchanting meshes. What they do not fully understand they take on trust, and listen, saying to themselves, as the old poet of Sir Philip Sidney,—

> "A sweet, attractive, kind of grace,
> A full assurance given by looks,
> Continual comfort in a face,
> The lineaments of gospel books."

We call it a singular fact, because we Yankees are thought to be fond of the spread-eagle style, and nothing can be more remote from that than his. We are reckoned a practical folk, who would rather hear about a new air-tight stove than about Plato; yet our favorite teacher's practicality is not in the least of the Poor Richard variety. If he have any Buncombe constituency, it is that unrealized commonwealth of philosophers which Plotinus proposed to establish; and if he were to make an almanac, his directions to farmers would be something like this: "OCTOBER: Indian Summer; now is the time to get in your early Vedas." What, then, is his secret? Is it not that he out-Yankees us all? that his range includes us all? that he is equally at home with the potato-disease and original sin, with pegging shoes and the Over-soul? that, as we try all trades, so has he tried all cultures? and above all, that his mysticism gives us a counterpoise to our super-practicality?

43

There is no man living to whom, as a writer, so many of us feel and thankfully acknowledge so great an indebtedness for ennobling impulses,—none whom so many cannot abide. What does he mean? ask these last. Where is his system? What is the use of it all? What the deuce have we to do with Brahma? I do not propose to write an essay on Emerson at this time. I will only say that one may find grandeur and consolation in a starlit night without caring to ask what it means, save grandeur and consolation; one may like Montaigne, as some ten generations before us have done, without thinking him so systematic as some more eminently tedious (or shall we say tediously eminent?) authors; one may think roses as good in their way as cabbages, though the latter would make a better show in the witness-box, if cross-examined as to their usefulness; and as for Brahma, why, he can take care of himself, and won't bite us at any rate.

The bother with Mr. Emerson is, that, though he writes in prose, he is essentially a poet. If you undertake to paraphrase what he says, and to reduce it to words of one syllable for infant minds, you will make as sad work of it as the good monk with his analysis of Homer in the "Epistolæ Obscurorum Virorum." We look upon him as one of the few men of genius whom our age has produced, and there needs no better proof of it than his masculine faculty of fecundating other minds. Search for his eloquence in his books and you will perchance miss it, but meanwhile you will find that it has kindled all your thoughts. For choice and pith of language he belongs to a better age than ours, and might rub shoulders with Fuller and Browne,—though he does use that abominable word *reliable*. His eye for a fine, telling phrase that will carry true is like that of a backwoodsman for a rifle; and he will dredge you up a choice word from the mud of Cotton Mather himself. A diction at once so rich and so homely as his I know not where to match in these days of writing by the page; it is like homespun cloth-of-gold. The many cannot miss his meaning, and only the few can find it. It is the open secret of all true genius. It is wholesome to angle in those profound pools, though one be rewarded with nothing more than the leap of a fish that flashes his freckled side in the sun and as suddenly absconds in the dark and dreamy waters again. There is keen excitement, though there be no ponderable acquisition. If we carry nothing home in our baskets, there is ample gain in dilated lungs and stimulated blood. What does he mean, quotha? He means inspiring hints, a diving-rod to your deeper nature. No doubt, Emerson, like all original men, has his peculiar audience, and yet I know none that can hold a promiscuous crowd in pleased attention so long as he. As in all original men, there is something for every palate. "Would you know," says Goethe, "the ripest cherries? Ask the boys and the blackbirds."

The announcement that such a pleasure as a new course of lectures by him is coming, to people as old as I am, is something like those forebodings of spring that prepare us every year for a familiar novelty, none the less novel, when it arrives, because it is familiar. We know perfectly well what we are to expect from Mr. Emerson, and yet what he says always penetrates and stirs us, as is apt to be the case with genius, in a very unlooked-for fashion. Perhaps genius is one of the few things which we gladly allow to repeat itself,—one of the few that multiply rather than weaken the force of their impression by iteration? Perhaps some of us hear more than the mere words, are moved by something deeper than the thoughts? If it be so, we are quite right, for it is thirty years and more of "plain living and high thinking" that speak to us in this altogether unique lay-preacher. We have shared in the beneficence of this varied culture, this fearless impartiality in criticism and speculation, this masculine sincerity, this sweetness of nature which rather stimulates than cloys, for a generation long. If ever there was a standing testimonial to the cumulative power and value of Character (and we need it sadly in these days), we have it in this gracious and dignified presence. What an antiseptic is a pure life! At sixty-five (or two years beyond his grand climacteric, as he would prefer to call it) he has that privilege of soul which abolishes the calendar, and presents him to us always the unwasted contemporary of his own prime. I do not know if he seem old to his younger hearers, but we who have known him so long wonder at the tenacity with which he maintains himself even in the outposts of youth. I suppose it is not the Emerson of 1868 to whom we listen. For us the whole life of the man is distilled in the clear drop of every sentence, and behind each word we divine the force of a noble character, the weight of a large capital of thinking and being. We do not go to hear what Emerson says so much as to hear Emerson. Not that we perceive any falling-off in anything that ever was essential to the charm of Mr. Emerson's peculiar style of thought or phrase. The first lecture, to be sure, was more disjointed even than common. It was as if, after vainly trying to get his paragraphs into sequence and order, he had it last tried the desperate expedient of *shuffling* them. It was chaos come again, but it was a chaos full of shooting-stars, a jumble of creative forces. The second lecture, on "Criticism and Poetry,"

was quite up to the level of old times, full of that power of strange-
ly-subtle association whose indirect approaches startle the mind into
almost painful attention, of those flashes of mutual understanding
between speaker and hearer that are gone ere one can say it lightens. The vice of Emerson's criticism seems to be, that while no man
is so sensitive to what is poetical, few men are less sensible than he
of what makes a poem. He values the solid meaning of thought
above the subtler meaning of style. He would prefer Donne, I
suspect, to Spenser, and sometimes mistakes the queer for the
original.

To be young is surely the best, if the most precarious, gift of
life; yet there are some of us who would hardly consent to be young
again, if it were at the cost of our recollection of Mr. Emerson's first
lectures during the consulate of Van Buren. We used to walk in
from the country to the Masonic Temple (I think it was), through
the crisp winter night, and listen to that thrilling voice of his, so
charged with subtle meaning and subtle music, as shipwrecked men
on a raft to the hail of a ship that came with unhoped-for food and
rescue. Cynics might say what they liked. Did our own imaginations
transfigure dry remainder-biscuit into ambrosia? At any rate, he
brought us *life,* which, on the whole, is no bad thing. Was it all
transcendentalism? magic-lantern pictures on mist? As you will.
Those, then, were just what we wanted. But it was not so. The delight and the benefit were that he put us in communication with a
larger style of thought, sharpened our wits with a more pungent
phrase, gave us ravishing glimpses of an ideal under the dry husk
of our New England; made us conscious of the supreme and everlasting originality of whatever bit of soul might be in any of us;
freed us, in short, from the stocks of prose in which we had sat so
long that we had grown wellnigh contented in our cramps. And who
that saw the audience will ever forget it, where every one still capable of fire, or longing to renew in them the half-forgotten sense of
it, was gathered? Those faces, young and old, agleam with pale intellectual light, eager with pleased attention, flash upon me once
more from the deep recesses of the years with an exquisite pathos.
Ah, beautiful young eyes, brimming with love and hope, wholly
vanished now in that other world we call the Past, or peering doubt-
fully through the pensive gloaming of memory, your light impover-
ishes these cheaper days! I hear again that rustle of sensation, as
they turned to exchange glances over some pithier thought, some
keener flash of that humor which always played about the horizon
of his mind like heat-lightning, and it seems now like the sad whis-

per of the autumn leaves that are whirling around me. But would my picture be complete if I forgot that ample and vegete countenance of Mr. R— of W—, — how, from its regular post at the corner of the front bench, it turned in ruddy triumph to the profaner audience as if he were the inexplicably appointed fugleman of appreciation? I was reminded of him by those hearty cherubs in Titian's Assumption that look at you as who should say, "Did you ever see a Madonna like *that?* Did you ever behold one hundred and fifty pounds of womanhood mount heavenward before like a rocket?"

To some of us that long-past experience remains as the most marvellous and fruitful we have ever had. Emerson awakened us, saved us from the body of this death. It is the sound of the trumpet that the young soul longs for, careless what breath may fill it. Sidney heard it in the ballad of "Chevy Chase," and we in Emerson. Nor did it blow retreat, but called to us with assurance of victory. Did they say he was disconnected? So were the stars, that seemed larger to our eyes, still keen with that excitement, as we walked homeward with prouder stride over the creaking snow. And were *they* not knit together by a higher logic than our mere sense could master? Were we enthusiasts? I hope and believe we were, and am thankful to the man who made us worth something for once in our lives. If asked what was left? what we carried home? we should not have been careful for an answer. It would have been enough if we had said that something beautiful had passed that way. Or we might have asked in return what one brought away from a symphony of Beethoven? Enough that he had set that ferment of wholesome discontent at work in us. . . .

I am unconsciously thinking, as I write, of the third lecture of the present course, in which Mr. Emerson gave some delightful reminiscences of the intellectual influences in whose movement he had shared. It was like hearing Goethe read some passages of the "Wahrheit aus seinem Leben." Not that there was not a little *Dichtung*, too, here and there, as the lecturer built up so lofty a pedestal under certain figures as to lift them into a prominence of obscurity, and seem to masthead them there. Everybody was asking his neighbor who this or that recondite great man was, in the faint hope that somebody might once have heard of him. There are those who call Mr. Emerson cold. Let them revise their judgment in presence of this loyalty of his that can keep warm for half a century, that never forgets a friendship, or fails to pay even a fancied obligation to the uttermost farthing. This substantiation of shadows was but incidental, and pleasantly characteristic of the man to those who know and love him. The greater part of the lecture was devoted to reminiscences of things substantial in themselves. He spoke of Everett, fresh from Greece and Germany; of Channing; of the translations of Margaret Fuller, Ripley, and Dwight; of the Dial and Brook Farm. To what he said of the latter an undertone of good-humored irony gave special zest. But what every one of his hearers felt was that the protagonist in the drama was left out. The lecturer was no Æneas to babble the *quorum magna pars fui*, and, as one of his listeners. I cannot help wishing to say how each of them was commenting the story as it went along, and filling up the necessary gaps in it from his own private store of memories. His younger hearers could not know how much they owed to the benign impersonality, the quiet scorn of everything ignoble, the never-sated hunger of self-culture, that were personified in the man before them. But the older knew how much the country's intellectual emancipation was due to the stimulus of his teaching and example, how constantly he had kept burning the beacon of an ideal life above our lower region of turmoil. To him more than to all other causes together did the young martyrs of our civil war owe the sustaining strength of thoughtful heroism that is so touching in every record of their lives. Those who are grateful to Mr. Emerson, as many of us are, for what they feel to be most valuable in their culture, or perhaps I should say their impulse, are grateful not so much for any direct teachings of his as for that inspiring lift which only genius can give, and without which all doctrine is chaff.

This was something like the *caret* which some of us older boys wished to fill up on the margin of the master's lecture. Few men have been so much to so many, and through so large a range of aptitudes and temperaments, and this simply because all of us value manhood beyond any or all other qualities of character. We may suspect in him, here and there, a certain thinness and vagueness of quality, but let the waters go over him as they list, this masculine fibre of his will keep its lively color and its toughness of texture. I have heard some great speakers and some accomplished orators, but never any that so moved and persuaded men as he. There is a kind of undertow in that rich baritone of his that sweeps our minds from their foothold into deeper waters with a drift we cannot and would not resist. And how artfully (for Emerson is a long-studied artist in these things) does the deliberate utterance, that seems waiting for the fit word, appear to admit us partners in the labor of thought and make us feel as if the glance of humor were a sudden suggestion, as if the perfect phrase lying written there on the desk were as unexpected to him as to us! In that closely-filled speech of his at the Burns centenary dinner every word seemed to have just dropped down to him from the clouds. He looked far away over the heads of his hearers, with a vague kind of expectation, as into some private heaven of invention, and the winged period came at last obedient to his spell. "My dainty Ariel!" he seemed murmuring to himself as he cast down his eyes as if in deprecation of the frenzy of approval and caught another sentence from the Sibylline leaves that lay before him ambushed behind a dish of fruit and seen only by nearest neighbors. Every sentence brought down the house, as I never saw one brought down before,—and it is not so easy to hit Scotsmen with a sentiment that has no hint of native brogue in it. I watched, for it was an interesting study, how the quick sympathy ran flashing from face to face down the long tables, like an electric spark thrilling as it went, and then exploded in a thunder of plaudits. I watched till tables and faces vanished, for I, too, found myself caught up in the common enthusiasm, and my excited fancy set me under the *bema* listening to him who fulmined over Greece. I can never help applying to him what Ben Jonson said of Bacon: "There happened in my time one noble speaker, who was full of gravity in his speaking. His language was nobly censorious. No man ever spake more neatly, more pressly, more weightily, or suffered less emptiness, less idleness, in what he uttered. No member of his speech but consisted of his own graces. His hearers could not cough, or look aside from him, without loss. He commanded where he spoke." Those who heard him while their natures were yet plastic, and their mental nerves trembled under the slightest breath of divine air, will never cease to feel and say:—

> "Was never eye did see that face,
>   Was never ear did hear that tongue,
> Was never mind did mind his grace,
>   That ever thought the travail long;
> But eyes, and ears, and every thought,
> Were with his sweet perfections caught."

OCTAVIUS BROOKS FROTHINGHAM (1822–1895), an unorthodox Unitarian, was influenced by Theodore Parker but was more radical and skeptical in his religious thought than Parker. For twenty years Frothingham was minister of the Independent Liberal Church in New York, which met in various large public halls. He was widely admired and respected; his weekly sermons were reprinted in newspapers and pamphlets. His *Transcendentalism in New England: a History* (1876) is his best-known work. The following is from chapter 9 of this book.

Emerson the Seer

OCTAVIUS BROOKS FROTHINGHAM

A discerning German writer, Herman Grimm, closes a volume of fifteen essays with one on Ralph Waldo Emerson, written in 1861, approved in 1874. The essay is interesting, apart from its literary merit, as giving the impression made by Mr. Emerson on a foreigner to whom his reputation was unknown, and a man of culture to whom books and opinions rarely brought surprise. He saw a volume of the "Essays" lying on the table of an American acquaintance, looked into it, and was surprised that, being tolerably well practised in reading English, he understood next to nothing of the contents. He asked about the author, and, learning that he was highly esteemed in his own country, he opened the book again, read further, and was so much struck by passages here and there, that he borrowed it, carried it home, took down Webster's dictionary, and began reading in earnest. The extraordinary construction of the sentences, the apparent absence of logical continuity, the unexpected turns of thought, the use of original words, embarrassed him at first; but soon he discovered the secret and felt the charm. The man had fresh thoughts, employed a living speech, was a genuine person. The book was bought, read and re-read, "and now everytime I take it up, I seem to take it up for the first time."

The power that the richest genius has in Shakspeare, Rafael, Goethe, Beethoven, to reconcile the soul to life, to give joy for heaviness, to dissipate fears, to transfigure care and toil, to convert lead into gold, and lift the veil that conceals the forms of hope, Grimm ascribes in the highest measure to Emerson.

"As I read, all seems old and familiar as if it was my own well-worn thought; all seems new as if it never occurred to me before. I found myself depending on the book and was pro-

voked with myself for it. How could I be so captured and en-
thralled; so fascinated and bewitched? The writer was but a
man like any other; yet, on taking up the volume again, the spell
was renewed—I felt the pure air; the old weather-beaten motives recovered their tone."

To him Emerson seemed to stand on the ground of simple fact,
which he accepted in all sincerity.

"He regards the world in its immediate aspect, with fresh
vision; the thing done or occurring before him opens the way
to serene heights. The living have precedence of the dead.
Even the living of to-day of the Greeks of yesterday, nobly as
the latter thought, moulded, chiselled, sang. For me was the
breath of life, for me the rapture of spring, for me love and
desire, for me the secret of wisdom and power." * * *
"Emerson fills me with courage and confidence. He has read
and observed, but he betrays no sign of toil. He presents familiar facts, but he places them in new lights and combinations.
From every object the lines run straight out, connecting it with
the central point of life. What I had hardly dared to think, it
was so bold, he brings forth as quietly as if it was the most
familiar commonplace. He is a perfect swimmer on the ocean
of modern existence. He dreads no tempest, for he is sure that
calm will follow it; he does not hate, contradict, or dispute,
for he understands men and loves them. I look on with wonder
to see how the hurly-burly of modern life subsides, and the
elements gently betake themselves to their allotted places. Had
I found but a single passage in his writings that was an exception to this rule, I should begin to suspect my judgment, and
should say no further word; but long acquaintance confirms
my opinion. As I think of this man, I have understood the devotion of pupils who would share any fate with their master, because his genius banished doubt and imparted life to all things."

Grimm tells us that one day he found Emerson's Essays in the
hands of a lady to whom he had recommended them without effect.
She had made a thousand excuses; had declared herself quite satisfied with Goethe, who had all that Emerson could possibly have,
and a great deal more; had expressed doubts whether, even if Emerson were all that his admirers represented, it was worth while to
make a study of him. Besides, she had read in the book, and found
only commonplace thoughts which had come to herself, and which

she considered not of sufficient importance to express. So Emerson was neglected.

> "On this occasion she made him the subject of conversation. She had felt that he was something remarkable. She had come upon sentences, many times, that opened the darkest recesses of thought. I listened quietly, but made no response. Not long afterwards she poured out to me her astonished admiration in such earnest and impassioned strain, that she made me feel as if I was the novice and she the apostle."

This experience was repeated again and again, and Grimm had the satisfaction of seeing the indifferent kindle, the adverse turn, the objectors yield. The praise was not universal indeed; there were stubborn dissentients who did not confess the charm, and declared that the enthusiasm was infatuation. Such remained unconverted. It was discovered that Emerson came to his own only, though his own were a large and increasing company.

The reasons of Grimm's admiration have been sufficiently indicated in the above extracts. They are good reasons, but they are not the best. They do not touch the deeper secret of power. The secret lies in the writer's pure and perfect idealism, in his absolute and perpetual faith in thoughts, his supreme confidence in the spiritual laws. He lives in the region of serene ideas; lives there all the day and all the year; not visiting the mount of vision occasionally, but setting up his tabernacle there, and passing the night among the stars that he may be up and dressed for the eternal sunrise. To such a spirit there is no night: "the darkness shineth as the day; the darkness and the light are both alike." There are no cloudy days. Tyndall's expression "in his case Poetry, with the joy of a bacchanal, takes her graver brother science by the hand, and cheers him with immortal laughter"—is singularly infelicitous in phrase, for it is as easy to associate night orgies with the dawn as the bacchanalian spirit with Emerson, who never riots and never laughs, but is radiant with a placid buoyancy that diffuses itself over his countenance and person. Mr. Emerson's characteristic trait is serenity. He is faithful to his own counsel, "Shun the negative side. Never wrong people with your contritions, nor with dismal views of politics or society. Never name sickness; even if you could trust yourself on that perilous topic, beware of unmuzzling a valetudinarian who will soon give you your fill of it." He seems to be perpetually saying "Good Morning."

This is not wholly a result of philosophy; it is rather a gift of nature. . . .

Idealism is native to this temperament, the proper expression of its feeling. Emerson was preordained an idealist; he is one of the eternal men, bearing about him the atmosphere of immortal youth. He is now seventy-three years old, having been born in Boston May 25th, 1803; but his last volume, "Letters and Social Aims," shows the freshness of his first essays. The opening chapter, "Poetry and Imagination," has the emphasis and soaring confidence of undimmed years; and the closing one, "Immortality," sustains an unwearied flight among the agitations of this most hotly-debated of beliefs. The address before the Phi Beta Kappa Society at Cambridge, in 1867, equals in moral grandeur and earnestness of appeal, in faithfulness to ideas and trust in principles, the addresses that made so famous the prime of his career. There is absolutely no abatement of heart or hope; if anything, the tone is richer and more assured than ever it was. During the season of his popularity as a lyceum lecturer, the necessity of making his discourse attractive and entertaining, brought into the foreground the play of his wit, and forced the graver qualities of his mind into partial concealment; but in later years, in the solitude of his study, the undertone of high purpose is heard again, in solemn reverberations, reminding us that the unseen realities are present still; that no opening into the eternal has ever been closed. . . .

Emerson has been called the prince of Transcendentalists. It is nearer the truth to call him the prince of idealists. A Transcendentalist, in the technical sense of the term, it cannot be clearly affirmed that he was. Certainly he cannot be reckoned a disciple of Kant, or Jacobi, or Fichte, or Schelling. He calls no man master; he receives no teaching on authority. It is not certain that he ever made a study of the Transcendental philosophy in the works of its chief exposition. . . .

Emerson does not claim for the soul a special faculty, like faith or intuition, by which truths of the spiritual order are perceived, as objects are perceived by the senses. He contends for no doctrines, whether of God or the hereafter, or the moral law, on the credit of such interior revelation. He neither dogmatizes nor defines. On the contrary, his chief anxiety seems to be to avoid committing himself to opinions; to keep all questions open; to close no avenue in any direction to the free ingress and egress of the mind. He gives no description of God that will class him as theist or pantheist; no definition of immortality that justifies his readers in imputing to him any form of the popular belief in regard to it. Does he believe in personal immortality? It is impertinent to ask. He will not be questioned; not because he doubts, but because his beliefs are so rich, various and many-sided, that he is unwilling, by laying emphasis on any one, to do an apparent injustice to others. He will be held to no definitions; he will be reduced to no final statements. The mind must have free range. Critics complain of the tantalizing fragmentariness of his writing; it is evidence of the shyness and modesty of his mind. He dwells in principles, and will not be cabined in beliefs. He needs the full expanse of the Eternal Reason.

It is thought worth while to dwell so long on this point, because it furnishes a perfect illustration of Emerson's intellectual attitude towards beliefs, its entire sincerity, disinterestedness and modesty. The serenity of his faith makes it impossible for him to be a controversialist. He never gave a sweeter or more convincing proof of this than in the sermon he preached on the Communion Supper, which terminated his connection with his Boston parish, and with it his relations to the Christian ministry, after a short service of less than four years. The rite in question was held sacred by his sect, as a personal memorial of Jesus perpetuated according to his own request. To neglect it was still regarded as a reproach; to dispute its authority was considered contumacious; to declare it obsolete and useless, an impediment to spiritual progress, a hindrance to Christian growth, was to excite violent animosities, and call down angry rebuke. Yet this is what Mr. Emerson deliberately did. That the question of retaining a minister who declined to bless and distribute the bread and wine, was debated at all, was proof of the extraordinary hold he had on his people. Through the crisis he remained unruffled, calm and gracious as in the sunniest days. On the evening when the church were considering his final proposition, with such result as he clearly foresaw, he sat with a brother clergyman talking pleasantly on literature and general topics, never letting fall a hint of the impending judgment, until, as he rose to leave, he said gently, "this is probably the last time we shall meet as brethren in the same calling," added a few words in explanation of the remark, and passed into the street.

Mr. Emerson's place is among poetic, not among philosophic minds. He belongs to the order of imaginative men. The imagination is his organ. His reading, which is very extensive in range, has covered this department more completely than any. He is at home with the seers, Swedenborg, Plotinus, Plato, the books of the Hindus, the Greek mythology, Plutarch, Chaucer, Shakspeare, Henry More, Hafiz; the books called sacred by the religious world; "books of natural science, especially those written by the ancients,—geography, botany, agriculture, explorations of the sea, of meteors, of astronomy;" he recommends "the deep books." Montaigne has been a favorite author on account of his sincerity. He thinks Hindu books the best gymnastics for the mind. . . .

By the poet, Emerson is careful to say that he means the potential or ideal man, not found now in any one person.

The upshot of it all is that soul is supreme. Not *the* soul, as if that term designated a constituent part of each man's nature.

> "All goes to show that the soul is not an organ, but animates and exercises all the organs; is not a function, like the power of memory, or calculation, of comparison, but uses these as hands and feet; is not a faculty, but a light; is not the intellect or the will, but the master of the intellect and the will; is the background of our being, in which they lie—an immensity not possessed, and that cannot be possessed. From within or from behind, a light shines through us upon things, and makes us aware that we are nothing, but the light is all. A man is the façade of a temple, wherein all wisdom and all good abide."

We stand now at the centre of Emerson's philosophy. His thoughts are few and pregnant; capable of infinite expansion, illustration and application. They crop out on almost every page of his characteristic writings; are iterated and reiterated in every form of speech; and put into gems of expression that may be worn on any part of the person. His prose and his poetry are aglow with them. They make his essays oracular, and his verse prophetic. By virtue of them his best books belong to the sacred literature of the race; by virtue of them, but for the lack of artistic finish of rhythm and rhyme, he would be the chief of American poets.

The first article in Mr. Emerson's faith is the primacy of Mind. That Mind is supreme, eternal, absolute, one, manifold, subtle, living, immanent in all things, permanent, flowing, self-manifesting; that the universe is the result of mind, that nature is the symbol of mind; that finite minds live and act through concurrence with infinite mind. This idea recurs with such frequency that, but for Emerson's wealth of observation, reading, wit, mental variety and buoyancy, his talent for illustration, gift at describing details, it would weary the reader. As it is, we delight to follow the guide through the labyrinth of his expositions, and gaze on the wonderful phantasmagoria that he exhibits.

His second article is the connection of the individual intellect with the primal mind, and its ability to draw thence wisdom, will, virtue, prudence, heroism, all active and passive qualities. This belief, as being the more practical, has even more exuberant expression than the other. . . .

Mr. Emerson is never concerned to defend himself against the charge of pantheism, or the warning to beware lest he unsettle the foundations of morality, annihilate the freedom of the will, abolish the distinction between right and wrong, and reduce personality to a mask. He makes no apology; he never explains; he trusts to affirmation, pure and simple. By dint of affirming all the facts that appear, he makes his contribution to the problem of solving all, and by laying incessant emphasis on the cardinal virtues of humility, fidelity, sincerity, obedience, aspiration, simple acquiescence in the will of the supreme power, he not only guards himself against vulgar misconception, but sustains the mind at an elevation that makes the highest hill-tops of the accepted morality disappear in the dead level of the plain.

The primary thoughts of his philosophy, if such it may be termed, Emerson takes with him wherever he goes. Does he study history, history is the autobiography of the Eternal Mind. . . .

In the appreciation of scientific facts the same method avails. Tyndall commends Emerson as "a poet and a profoundly religious man, who is really and entirely undaunted by the discoveries of science, past, present, or prospective." The praise seems to imply some misconception of Emerson's position. Tyndall intimates that Emerson is undaunted where others fear. But this is not so. No man deserves commendation for not dreading precisely what he desires. Emerson, by his principle, is delivered from the alarm of the religious man who has a creed to defend, and from the defiance of the scientific man who has creeds to assail. To him Nature is but the symbol of spirit; this the scientific men, by their discoveries, are continually proving. The faster they disclose facts, and the more accurately, the more brilliantly do they illustrate the lessons of the perfect wisdom. For the scientific *method* he professes no deep respect; for the scientific *assumptions* none whatever. He begins at the opposite end. They start with matter, he starts with mind. They feel their way up, he feels his way down. They observe phenomena, he watches thoughts. They fancy themselves to be gradually pushing away as illusions the so-called entities of the soul; he dwells serenely with those entities, rejoicing to see men paying jubilant honor to what they mean to overturn. The facts they bring in, chemical, physiological, biological, Huxley's facts, Helmholtz's, Darwin's, Tyndall's, Spencer's, the ugly facts which the theologians dispute, he accepts with eager hands, and uses to demonstrate the force and harmony of the spiritual laws. . . .

Emerson is faithful in applying his principle to social institutions and laws. His faith in ideal justice and love never blenches. In every emergency, political, civil, national, he has been true to his regenerating idea; true as a recreator from the inside, rather than as a reformer of the outside world. A profounder, more consistent, more uncompromising radical does not exist; a less heated, ruffled or anxious one cannot be thought of. He scarcely ever suggested measures, rarely joined in public assemblies, did not feel at home among politicians or agitators. But his thought never swerved from the line of perfect rectitude, his sympathies were always human. His heart was in the anti-slavery movement from the beginning. He was abroad in its stormy days, his steadfast bearing and cheerful countenance carrying hope whenever he appeared. His name stood with that of his wife in the list of signers to the call for the first National Woman's Rights Convention, in 1850. The Massachusetts Historical Society, the American Society of Arts and Sciences have honored themselves by electing him a member; the Alumni of Harvard University joyfully made him an overseer; he was proposed as rector of the University of Glasgow. Such confidence did the great idealist inspire, that he has been even called to the duty of Examiner at West Point Military Academy. His name is spoken in no company with other than respect, and his influence is felt in places where it is not acknowledged, and would be officially disavowed.

Mr. A. B. Alcott, a townsman of Mr. Emerson, and a close acquaintance, in his "Concord Days" says pleasant things of his friend, just and discerning things, as well as pleasant.

"Consider," he says, "how largely our letters have been enriched by his contributions. Consider, too, the change his views have wrought in our methods of thinking; how he has won over the bigot, the unbeliever, at least to tolerance and moderation, if not acknowledgment, by his circumspection and candor of statement." "A poet, speaking to individuals as few others can speak, and to persons in their privileged moments, he is heard as none others are. 'Tis every thing to have a true believer in the world, dealing with men and matters as if they were divine in idea and real in fact, meeting persons and events at a glance, directly, not at a millionth remove, and so passing fair and fresh into life and literature." "His compositions affect us, not as logic linked in syllogisms, but as voluntaries rather, as preludes, in which one is not tied to any design of air, but may vary his key or not at pleasure, as if improvised without any particular scope of argument; each period, paragraph, being a perfect note in itself, however it may chance chime with its accompaniments in the piece, as a waltz of wandering stars, a dance of Hesperus with Orion."

After this, one is surprised to hear Mr. Alcott say, "I know of but one subtraction from the pleasure the reading of his books— shall I say his conversation?—gives me; his pains to be impersonal or discreet, as if he feared any the least intrusion of himself were an offense offered to self-respect, the courtesy due to intercourse and authorship." To others this exquisite reserve, this delicate withdrawal behind his thought, has seemed not only one of Emerson's peculiar charms, but one of his most subtle powers. Personal magnetism is very delightful for the moment. The exhibition of attractive personal traits is interesting in the lecture room; sometimes in the parlor. The public, large or small, enjoy confidences. But in an age of personalities, voluntary and involuntary, the man who keeps his individual affairs in the background, tells nothing of his private history, holds in his own breast his petty concerns and opinions, and lets thoughts flow through him, as light streams through plate glass, is more than attractive—is noble, is venerable. To his impersonality in his books and addresses, Emerson owes perhaps a large measure of his extraordinary influence. You may search his volumes in vain for a trace of egotism. In the lecture room, he seems to be so completely under the spell of his idea, so wholly abstracted from his audience, that he is as one who waits for the thoughts to come, and drops them out one by one, in a species of soliloquy or trance. He is a bodiless idea. When he speaks or writes, the power is that of pure mind. The incidental, accidental, occasional, does not intrude. No abatement on the score of personal antipathy needs to be made. The thought is allowed to present and commend itself. Hence, when so many thoughts are forgotten, buried beneath affectation and verbiage, his gain in brilliancy and value as time goes on; and in an age of ephemeral literature his books find new readers, his mind exerts wider sway. That his philosophy can be recommended as a sound rule to live by for ordinary practitioners may be questioned. It is better as inspiration than as prescription. For maxims it were wiser to go to Bentham, Mill or Bain. The plodders had best keep to the beaten road. But for them who need an atmosphere for wings, who require the impulse of great motives, the lift of upbearing aspirations—for the imaginative, the passionate, the susceptible, who can achieve nothing unless they attempt the impossible—Emerson is the master. A single thrill sent from his heart to ours is worth more to the heart that feels it, than all the schedules of motive the utilitarian can offer.

1883-1900

WALT WHITMAN (1819–1892). When *Leaves of Grass* was first published in 1855, the book contained only twelve poems. The affinity between those poems and Emerson is too obvious to be a mere coincidence. Whitman sent a copy of the book to Emerson, who acknowledged the gift with words that have become famous in literary history:

> I am not blind to the worth of the wonderful gift of *Leaves of Grass*. I find it the most extraordinary piece of wit and wisdom that America has yet contributed. . . . I greet you at the beginning of a great career. . . .

The second edition (1856) contained twenty-one new poems, and on the back of the book appeared, stamped in gold, the following legend: "I greet you at the beginning of a great career, R. W. Emerson." An appendix included a long letter from Whitman to Emerson addressed: "Dear friend and Master."

In 1881, when Whitman visited in Concord, Emerson drove over to Frank Sanborn's to visit with Whitman, and the next day the Emersons gave a dinner for Whitman in their home.

At one time Whitman acknowledged that he had learned much from Emerson before 1855, but in 1887 he wrote in a letter that he had not read Emerson before writing the first edition of his *Leaves of Grass*.

The following is from *Specimen Days and Collect* (1882–1883) in which Whitman attempts a critical, impersonal estimate of Emerson.

Emerson

WALT WHITMAN

In the regions we call Nature, towering beyond all measurement, with infinite spread, infinite depth and height—in those regions, including Man, socially and historically, with his moral-emotional influences—how small a part (it came in my mind to-day) has literature really depicted—even summing up all of it, all ages. Seems at its best some little fleet of boats, hugging the shores of a boundless sea, and never venturing, exploring the unmapp'd—never, Columbus-like, sailing out for New Worlds, and to complete the orb's rondure. Emerson writes frequently in the atmosphere of this thought, and his books report one or two things from that very ocean and air, and more legibly address'd to our age and American polity than by any man yet. But I will begin by scarifying him—thus proving that I am not insensible to his deepest lessons. I will consider his books from a democratic and Western point of view. I will specify the shadows on these sunny expanses. Somebody has said of heroic character that "wherever the tallest peaks are present, must inevitably be deep chasms and valleys." Mine be the ungracious task (for reasons) of leaving unmention'd both sunny expanses and sky-reaching heights, to dwell on the bare spots and darkness. I have a theory that no artist or work of the very first class may be or can be without them.

First, then, these pages are perhaps too perfect, too concentrated. (How good, for instance, is good butter, good sugar. But to be eating nothing but sugar and butter all the time! even if ever so good.) And though the author has much to say of freedom and wildness and simplicity and spontaneity, no performance was ever more based on artificial scholarships and decorums at third or fourth removes (he calls it culture), and built up from them. It is always a *make*, never an unconscious *growth*. It is the porcelain figure or statuette of lion, or stag, or Indian hunter—and a very choice statuette, too—appropriate for the rosewood or marble bracket of parlor or library; never the animal itself, or the hunter himself. Indeed, who wants the real animal or hunter? What would that do amid astral and bric-a-brac and tapestry, and ladies and gentlemen talking in subdued tones of Browning and Longfellow and art? The least suspicion of such actual bull, or Indian, or of Nature carrying out itself, would put all those good people to instant terror and flight.

Emerson, in my opinion, is not most eminent as poet or artist or teacher, though valuable in all those. He is best as critic, or diagnoser. Not passion or imagination or warp or weakness, or any pronounced cause or speciality, dominates him. Cold and bloodless intellectuality dominates him. (I know the fires, emotions, love, egotisms, glow deep, perennial, as in all New Englanders—but the façade hides them well—they give no sign.) He does not see or take one side, one presentation only or mainly (as all the poets, or most of the fine writers anyhow)—he sees all sides. His final influence is to make his students cease to worship anything—almost cease to believe in anything, outside of themselves. These books will fill, and well fill, certain stretches of life, certain stages of development—are, (like the tenets or theology the author of them preach'd when a young man,) unspeakably serviceable and precious as a stage. But in old or nervous or solemnest or dying hours, when one needs the impalpably soothing and vitalizing influences of abysmic Nature, or its affinities in literature or human society, and the soul resents the keenest mere intellection, they will not be sought for.

At times it has been doubtful to me if Emerson really knows or feels what Poetry is at its highest, as in the Bible, for instance, or Homer or Shakspere. I see he covertly or plainly likes best superb verbal polish, or something old or odd—Waller's *Go, Lovely Rose,* or

Lovelace's lines *To Lucasta*—the quaint conceits of the old French bards, and the like. Of *power* he seems to have a gentleman's admiration—but in his inmost heart the grandest attribute of God and Poets is always subordinate to the octaves, conceits, polite kinks, and verbs.

The reminiscence that years ago I began like most youngsters to have a touch (though it came late, and was only on the surface) of Emerson-on-the-brain—that I read his writings reverently, and address'd him in print as "Master," and for a month or so thought of him as such—I retain not only with composure, but positive satisfaction. I have noticed that most young people of eager minds pass through this stage of exercise.

The best part of Emersonianism is, it breeds the giant that destroys itself. Who wants to be any man's mere follower? lurks behind every page. No teacher ever taught, that has so provided for his pupil's setting up independently—no truer evolutionist.

MATTHEW ARNOLD (1822–1888), poet and literary and social critic, was among the most influential writers of England in the nineteenth century. In 1883 he came to the United States on a lecture tour, which resulted in his *Discourses in America* (1885), followed by *Civilization in the United States* (1888). The following is from his lecture on Emerson as it was published in the former volume. His characterization of Emerson as "the friend and aider of those who would live in the spirit" has become famous.

Emerson

MATTHEW ARNOLD

And besides those voices, there came to us in that old Oxford time a voice also from this side of the Atlantic—a clear and pure voice, which for my ear, at any rate, brought a strain as new, and moving, and unforgettable, as the strain of Newman, or Carlyle, or Goethe. Mr. Lowell has well described the apparition of Emerson to your young generation here, in that distant time of which I am speaking, and of his workings upon them. He was your Newman, your man of soul and genius visible to you in the flesh, speaking to your bodily ears, a present object for your heart and imagination. That is surely the most potent of all influences! nothing can come up to it. To us at Oxford Emerson was but a voice speaking from three thousand miles away. But so well he spoke, that from that time forth Boston Bay and Concord were names invested to my ear with a sentiment akin to that which invests for me the names of Oxford and of Weimar; and snatches of Emerson's strain fixed themselves in my mind as imperishably as any of the eloquent words which I have been just now quoting. "Then dies the man in you; then once more perish the buds of art, poetry, and science, as they have died already in a thousand thousand men." "What Plato has thought, he may think; what a saint has felt, he may feel; what at any time has befallen any man, he can understand." "Trust thyself! every heart vibrates to that iron string. Accept the place the Divine Providence has found for you, the society of your contemporaries, the connexion of events. Great men have always done so, and confided themselves childlike to the genius of their age; betraying their perception that the Eternal was stirring at their heart, working through their hands, predominating in all their being. And we are now men, and must accept in the highest spirit the same transcendent destiny; and not pinched in a corner, not cowards fleeing before a revolution, but redeemers and benefactors, pious aspirants to be noble clay plastic

66

under the Almighty effort, let us advance and advance on chaos and the dark!" These lofty sentences of Emerson, and a hundred others of like strain, I never have lost out of my memory; I never *can* lose them.

At last I find myself in Emerson's own country, and looking upon Boston Bay. Naturally I revert to the friend of my youth. It is not always pleasant to ask oneself questions about the friends of one's youth; they cannot always well support it. Carlyle, for instance, in my judgment, cannot well support such a return upon him. Yet we should make the return; we should part with our illusions, we should know the truth. When I come to this country, where Emerson now counts for so much, and where such high claims are made for him, I pull myself together, and ask myself what the truth about this object of my youthful admiration really is. Improper elements often come into our estimate of men. We have lately seen a German critic make Goethe the greatest of all poets, because Germany is now the greatest of military powers, and wants a poet to match. Then, too, America is a young country; and young countries, like young persons, are apt sometimes to evince in their literary judgments a want of scale and measure. I set myself, therefore, resolutely to come at a real estimate of Emerson, and with a leaning even to strictness rather than to indulgence. That is the safer course. Time has no indulgence; any veils of illusion which we may have left around an object because we loved it, Time is sure to strip away.

I was reading the other day a notice of Emerson by a serious and interesting American critic. Fifty or sixty passages in Emerson's poems, says this critic—who had doubtless himself been nourished on Emerson's writings, and held them justly dear—fifty or sixty passages from Emerson's poems have already entered into English speech as a matter of familiar and universally current quotation. Here is a specimen of that personal sort of estimate which, for my part, even in speaking of authors dear to me, I would try to avoid. What is the kind of phrase of which we may fairly say that it has entered into English speech as matter of familiar quotation? Such a phrase, surely, as the "Patience on a monument" of Shakespeare; as the "Darkness visible" of Milton; as the "Where ignorance is bliss" of Gray. Of not one single passage in Emerson's poetry can it be truly said that it has become a familiar quotation like phrases of this kind. It is not enough that it should be familiar to his admirers, familiar in New England, familiar even throughout the United States; it must be familiar to all readers and lovers of English poetry. Of not more than one or two passages in Emerson's poetry can it,

I think, be truly said, that they stand ever-present in the memory of even many lovers of English poetry. A great number of passages from his poetry are no doubt perfectly familiar to the mind and lips of the critic whom I have mentioned, and perhaps a wide circle of American readers. But this is a very different thing from being matter of universal quotation, like the phrases of the legitimate poets.

And, in truth, one of the legitimate poets, Emerson, in my opinion, is not. His poetry is interesting, it makes one think; but it is not the poetry of one of the born poets. I say it of him with reluctance, although I am sure that he would have said it of himself; but I say it with reluctance, because I dislike giving pain to his admirers, and because all my own wish, too, is to say of him what is favorable. But I regard myself, not as speaking to please Emerson's admirers, not as speaking to please myself; but rather, I repeat, as communing with Time and Nature concerning the productions of this beautiful and rare spirit, and as resigning what of him is by their unalterable decree touched with caducity, in order the better to mark and secure that in him which is immortal.

Milton says that poetry ought to be simple, sensuous, impassioned. Well, Emerson's poetry is seldom either simple, or sensuous, or impassioned. In general it lacks directness; it lacks concreteness; it lacks energy. His grammar is often embarrassed; in particular, the want of clearly-marked distinction between the subject and the object of his sentence is a frequent cause of obscurity in him. A poem which shall be a plain, forcible, inevitable whole he hardly ever produces. Such good work as the noble lines graven on the Concord Monument is the exception with him; such ineffective work as the "Fourth of July Ode" or the "Boston Hymn" is the rule. Even passages and single lines of thorough plainness and commanding force are rare in his poetry. They exist, of course; but when we meet with them they give us a slight shock of surprise, so little has Emerson accustomed us to them. Let me have the pleasure of quoting one or two of these exceptional passages:

> So nigh is grandeur to our dust,
>   So near is God to man,
> When Duty whispers low, *Thou must*,
>   The youth replies, *I can.*

Or again this:

> Though love repine and season chafe,
> There came a voice without reply:

" 'Tis man's perdition to be safe,
When for the truth he ought to die."

Excellent! but how seldom do we get from him a strain blown so clearly and firmly! Take another passage where his strain has not only clearness, it has also grace and beauty:

And ever, when the happy child
In May beholds the blooming wild,
And hears in heaven the bluebird sing,
"Onward," he cries, "your baskets bring!
In the next field is air more mild,
And in yon hazy west is Eden's balmier
    spring."

In the style and cadence here there is a reminiscence, I think, of Gray; at any rate the pureness, grace, and beauty of these lines are worthy even of Gray. But Gray holds his high rank as a poet, not merely by the beauty and grace of passages in his poems; not merely by a diction generally pure in an age of impure diction: he holds it, above all, by the power and skill with which the evolution of his poems is conducted. Here is his grand superiority to Collins, whose diction in his best poem, the "Ode to Evening," is purer than Gray's; but then the "Ode to Evening" is like a river which loses itself in the sand, whereas Gray's best poems have an evolution sure and satisfying. Emerson's "Mayday," from which I just now quoted, has no real evolution at all; it is a series of observations. And, in general, his poems have no evolution. Take, for example, his "Titmouse." Here he has an excellent subject; and his observation of Nature, moreover, is always marvellously close and fine. But compare what he makes of his meeting with his titmouse with what Cowper or Burns makes of the like kind of incident! One never quite arrives at learning what the titmouse actually did for him at all, though one feels a strong interest and desire to learn it; but one is reduced to guessing, and cannot be quite sure that after all one has guessed right. He is not plain and concrete enough—in other words, not poet enough—to be able to tell us. And a failure of this kind goes through almost all his verse, keeps him amid symbolism and allusion and the fringes of things, and, in spite of his spiritual power, deeply impairs his poetic value. Through the inestimable virtue of concreteness, a simple poem like "The Bridge" of Longfellow, or the "School Days" of Mr. Whittier, is of more poetic worth, perhaps, than all the verse of Emerson.

I do not, then, place Emerson among the great poets. But I go further, and say that I do not place him among the great writers, the great men of letters. Who are the great men of letters? They are men like Cicero, Plato, Bacon, Pascal, Swift, Voltaire—writers with, in the first place, a genius and instinct for style; writers whose prose is by a kind of native necessity true and sound. Now the style of Emerson, like the style of his transcendentalist friends and of the *Dial* so continually—the style of Emerson is capable of falling into a strain like this, which I take from the beginning of his "Essay on Love": "Every soul is a celestial being to every other soul. The heart has its sabbaths and jubilees, in which the world appears as a hymeneal feast, and all natural sounds and the circle of the seasons are erotic odes and dances." Emerson altered this sentence in the later editions. Like Wordsworth, he was in later life fond of altering; and in general his later alterations, like those of Wordsworth, are not improvements. He softened the passage in question, however, though without really mending it. I quote it in its original and strongly-marked form. Arthur Stanley used to relate that about the year 1840, being in conversation with some Americans in quarantine at Malta, and thinking to please them, he declared his warm admiration for Emerson's "Essays," then recently published. However, the Americans shook their heads, and told him that for home taste Emerson was decidedly too *greeny*. We will hope, for their sakes, that the sort of thing they had in their heads was such writing as I have just quoted. Unsound it is, indeed, and in a style almost impossible to a born man of letters.

It is a curious thing, that quality of style which marks the great writer, the born man of letters. It resides in the whole tissue of his work, and of his work regarded as a composition for literary purposes. Brilliant and powerful passages in a man's writings do not prove his possesssion of it; it lies in their whole tissue. Emerson has passages of noble and pathetic eloquence, such as those which I quoted at the beginning; he has passages of shrewd and felicitous wit; he has crisp epigram; he has passages of exquisitely touched observation of nature. Yet he is not a great writer; his style has not the requisite wholeness of good tissue. Even Carlyle is not, in my judgment, a great writer. . . .

You will think I deal in nothing but negatives. I have been saying that Emerson is not one of the great poets, the great writers. He has not their quality of style. He is, however, the propounder of a philosophy. The Platonic dialogues afford us the example of exquisite literary form and treatment given to philosophical ideas.

Plato is at once a great literary man and a great philosopher. If we speak carefully, we cannot call Aristotle or Spinoza or Kant great literary men, or their productions great literary works. But their work is arranged with such constructive power that they build a philosophy and are justly called great philosophical writers. Emerson cannot, I think, be called with justice a great philosophical writer. He cannot build; his arrangement of philosophical ideas has no progress in it, no evolution; he does not construct a philosophy. Emerson himself knew the defects of his method, or rather want of method, very well; indeed, he and Carlyle criticize themselves and one another in a way which leaves little for any one else to do in the way of formulating their defects. . . .

Some people will tell you that Emerson's poetry, indeed, is too abstract, and his philosophy too vague, but that his best work is his "English Traits." The "English Traits" are beyond question very pleasant reading. It is easy to praise them, easy to commend the author of them. But I insist on always trying Emerson's work by the highest standards. I esteem him too much to try his work by any other. Tried by the highest standards, and compared with the work of the excellent markers and recorders of the traits of human life—of writers like Montaigne, La Bruyère, Addison—the "English Traits" will not stand the comparison. Emerson's observation has not the disinterested quality of the observation of these masters. It is the observation of a man systematically benevolent, as Hawthorne's observation in "Our Old Home" is the work of a man chagrined. Hawthorne's literary talent is of the first order. His subjects are generally not to me subjects of the highest interest; but his literary talent is of the first order, the finest, I think, which America has yet produced—finer, by much, than Emerson's. Yet "Our Old Home" is not a masterpiece any more than "English Traits." In neither of them is the observer disinterested enough. The author's attitude in each of these cases can easily be understood and defended. Hawthorne was a sensitive man, so situated in England that he was perpetually in contact with the British Philistine; and the British Philistine is a trying personage. Emerson's systematic benevolence comes from what he himself calls somewhere his "persistent optimism"; and his persistent optimism is the root of his greatness and the source of his charm. But still let us keep our literary conscience true, and judge every kind of literary work by the laws really proper to it. The kind of work attempted in the "English Traits" and in "Our Old Home" is work which cannot be done perfectly with a bias such as that given by Emerson's optimism or by Hawthorne's chagrin. Consequently, neither "English Traits" nor "Our Old Home" is a work of perfection in its kind.

Not with the Miltons and Grays, not with the Platos and Spinozas, not with the Swifts and Voltaires, not with the Montaignes and Addisons, can we rank Emerson. His work of various kinds, when one compares it with the work done in a corresponding kind by these masters, fails to stand the comparison. No man could see this clearer than Emerson himself. It is hard not to feel despondency when we contemplate our failures and shortcomings: and Emerson, the least self-flattering and the most modest of men, saw so plainly what was lacking to him that he had his moments of despondency. . . .

And now I think I have cleared the ground. I have given up to envious Time as much of Emerson as Time can fairly expect ever to obtain. We have not in Emerson a great poet, a great writer, a great philosophy-maker. His relation to us is not that of one of those personages; yet it is a relation of, I think, even superior importance. His relation to us is more like that of the Roman Emperor Marcus Aurelius. Marcus Aurelius is not a great writer, a great philosophy-maker; he is the friend and aider of those who would live in the spirit. Emerson is the same. He is the friend and aider of those who would live in the spirit. All the points in thinking which are necessary for this purpose he takes; but he does not combine them into a system, or present them as a regular philosophy. Combined in a system by a man with the requisite talent for this kind of thing, they would be less useful than as Emerson gives them to us; and the man with the talent so to systematize them would be less impressive than Emerson. They do very well as they now stand—like "boulders," as he says— in "paragraphs incompressible, each sentence an infinitely repellent particle." In such sentences his main points recur again and again, and become fixed in the memory. . . .

Yes, truly, his insight is admirable; his truth is precious. Yet the secret of his effect is not even in these; it is in his temper. It is in the hopeful, serene, beautiful temper wherewith these, in Emerson, are indissolubly joined; in which they work, and have their being. He says himself: "We judge of a man's wisdom by his hope, knowing that the perception of the inexhaustibleness of nature is an immortal youth." If this be so, how wise is Emerson! for never had man such a sense of the inexhaustibleness of nature, and such hope. It was the ground of his being; it never failed him. Even when he is sadly avowing the imperfection of his literary power and resources, lamenting his fumbling fingers and stammering tongue, he adds: "Yet, as I tell you, I am very easy in my mind and never dream of suicide. My whole philosophy, which is very real, teaches acquiescence and optimism. Sure I am that the right word will be spoken, though I cut out my tongue." In his old age, with friends dying and life failing, his tone of cheerful, forward-looking hope is still the same. "A multitude of young men are growing up here of high promise, and I compare gladly the social poverty of my youth with the power on which these draw." His abiding word for us, the word by which being dead he yet speaks to us, is this: "That which befits us, embosomed in beauty and wonder as we are, is cheerfulness and courage, and the endeavour to realise our aspirations. Shall not the heart, which has received so much, trust the Power by which it lives?"

One can scarcely overrate the importance of thus holding fast to happiness and hope. It gives to Emerson's work an invaluable virtue. As Wordsworth's poetry is, in my judgment, the most important work done in verse, in our language, during the present century, so Emerson's "Essays" are, I think, the most important work done in prose. His work is more important than Carlyle's. . . .

Happiness in labor, righteousness, and veracity; in all the life of the spirit; happiness and eternal hope—that was Emerson's gospel. I hear it said that Emerson was too sanguine; that the actual generation in America is not turning out so well as he expected. Very likely he was too sanguine as to the near future; in this country it is difficult not to be too sanguine. Very possibly the present generation may prove unworthy of his high hopes; even several generations succeeding this may prove unworthy of them. But by his conviction that in the life of the spirit is happiness, and by his hope that this life of the spirit will come more and more to be sanely understood, and to prevail, and to work for happiness—by this conviction and hope Emerson was great, and he will surely prove in the end to have been right in them. In this country it is difficult, as I said, not to be sanguine. Very many of your writers are over-sanguine, and on the wrong grounds. But you have two men who in what they have written show their sanguineness in a line where courage and hope are just, where they are also infinitely important, but where they are not easy. The two men are Franklin and Emerson. These two are, I think, the most distinctively and honorably American of your writers; they are the most original and the most valuable. Wise men everywhere know that we must keep up our courage and hope; they know that hope is, as Wordsworth well says—

> The paramount *duty* which Heaven lays,
> For its own honour, on man's suffering heart.

But the very word *duty* points to an effort and a struggle to maintain our hope unbroken. Franklin and Emerson maintained theirs with a convincing ease, an inspiring joy. Franklin's confidence in the happiness with which industry, honesty, and economy will crown the life of this work-day world, is such that he runs over with felicity. With a like felicity does Emerson run over, when he contemplates the happiness eternally attached to the true life in the spirit. You cannot prize him too much, nor heed him too diligently. He has lessons for both the branches of our race. I figure him to my mind as visible upon earth still, as still standing here by Boston Bay, or at his own Concord, in his habit as he lived, but of heightened stature and shining feature, with one hand stretched out towards the East, to our laden and laboring England; the other towards the ever-growing West, to his own dearly loved America—"great, intelligent, sensual, avaricious America." To us he shows for guidance his lucid freedom, his cheerfulness and hope; to you his dignity, delicacy, serenity, elevation.

JOHN MORLEY (1838–1923), English man of letters and statesman, was for fifteen years (1867–1882) editor of the influential *Fortnightly Review*. Some of his own long studies that later appeared in book form were first published in the magazine. In 1867 he visited the United States and met Emerson. Morley edited the *English Men of Letters* series. His *Life of Cobden* (1881) is still rated as a classic political biography. An edition of his works in fifteen volumes was published in 1921. His essay on Emerson, which first was published in 1881, is in Volume I of his *Critical Miscellanies* (1888).

Emerson

JOHN MORLEY

A great interpreter of life ought not himself to need interpretation, least of all can he need it for contemporaries. When time has wrought changes of fashion, mental and social, the critic serves a useful turn in giving to a poet or a teacher his true place, and in recovering ideas and points of view that are worth preserving. Interpretation of this kind Emerson cannot require. His books are no palimpsest, 'the prophet's holograph, defiled, erased, and covered by a monk's.' What he has written is fresh, legible, and in full conformity with the manners and the diction of the day, and those who are unable to understand him without gloss and comment are in fact not prepared to understand what it is that the original has to say. Scarcely any literature is so entirely unprofitable as the so-called criticism that overlays a pithy text with a windy sermon. For our time at least Emerson may best be left to be his own expositor.

Nor is Emerson, either, in the case of those whom the world has failed to recognise, and whom therefore it is the business of the critic to make known and to define. It is too soon to say in what particular niche among the teachers of the race posterity will place him; enough that in our own generation he has already been accepted as one of the wise masters, who, being called to high thinking for generous ends, did not fall below his vocation, but, steadfastly pursuing the pure search for truth, without propounding a system or founding a school or cumbering himself overmuch about applications, lived the life of the spirit, and breathed into other men a strong desire after the right governance of the soul. All this is generally realised and understood, and men may now be left to find their way to the Emersonian doctrine without the critic's prompting. Though it is only the other day that Emerson walked the earth and was alive and among us, he is already one of the privileged few whom the reader approaches in the mood of settled respect, and whose names have surrounded themselves with an atmosphere of religion.

It is not particularly profitable, again, to seek for Emerson one of the labels out of the philosophic handbooks. Was he the prince of Transcendentalists, or the prince of Idealists? Are we to look for the sources of his thought in Kant or Jacobi, in Fichte or Schelling? How does he stand towards Parmenides and Zeno, the Egotheism of the Sufis, or the position of the Megareans? Shall we put him on the shelf with the Stoics or the Mystics, with Quietist, Pantheist, Determinist? If life were long, it might be worth while to trace Emerson's affinities with the philosophic schools; to collect and infer his answers to the everlasting problems of psychology and metaphysics; to extract a set of coherent and reasoned opinions about knowledge and faculty, experience and consciousness, truth and necessity, the absolute and the relative. But such inquiries would only take us the further away from the essence and vitality of Emerson's mind and teaching. In philosophy proper Emerson made no contribution of his own, but accepted, apparently without much examination of the other side, from Coleridge after Kant, the intuitive, *à priori* and realist theory respecting the sources of human knowledge, and the objects that are within the cognisance of the human faculties. This was his starting-point, and within its own sphere of thought he cannot be said to have carried it any further. What he did was to light up these doctrines with the rays of ethical and poetic imagination. As it has been justly put, though Emersonian transcendentalism is usually spoken of as a philosophy, it is more justly regarded as a gospel. But before dwelling more on this, let us look into the record of his life, of which we may say in all truth that no purer, simpler, and more harmonious story can be found in the annals of far-shining men. . . .

It cannot be truly said that Emerson is one of the writers who make their way more easily into our minds by virtue of style. That his writing has quality and flavour none but a pure pedant would deny. His more fervent votaries, however, provoke us with a challenge that goes far beyond this. They declare that the finish, charm, and beauty of the writing are as worthy of remark as the truth and depth of the thought. It is even 'unmatchable and radiant,' says one. Such exaggerations can have no reference to any accepted standard. It would in truth, have been a marvel if Emerson had excelled in the virtues of the written page, for most of his published work was originally composed and used for the platform. Everybody knows how different are the speaker's devices for gaining possession of his audience, from the writer's means of winning, persuading, and impressing the attention of his reader. The key to the difference may be that in the speech the personality of the orator before our eyes gives of itself that oneness and continuity of communication, which the writer has to seek in the orderly sequence and array of marshalled sentence and well-sustained period. One of the traits that every critic notes in Emerson's writing, is that it is so abrupt, so sudden in its transistions, so discontinuous, so inconsecutive. Dislike of a sentence that drags made him unconscious of the quality, that French critics name *coulant*. Everything is thrown in just as it comes, and sometimes the pell-mell is enough to persuade us that Pope did not exaggerate when he said that no qualification is so likely to make a good writer, as the power of rejecting his own thoughts.

His manner as a lecturer, says Dr. Holmes, was an illustration of his way of thinking. 'He would lose his place just as his mind would drop its thought and pick up another, twentieth cousin or no relation at all to it.' The same manner, whether we liken it to mosaic or to kaleidoscope, marks his writing. It makes him hard to follow, oracular, and enigmatical. 'Can you tell me,' asked one of his neighbour, while Emerson was lecturing, 'what connection there is between that last sentence and the one that went before, and what connection it all has with Plato?' 'None, my friend, save in God!' This is excellent in a seer, but less so in the writer.

Apart from his difficult staccato, Emerson is not free from secondary faults. He uses words that are not only odd, but vicious in construction; he is not always grammatically correct; he is sometimes oblique, and he is often clumsy; and there is a visible feeling after epigrams that do not always come. When people say that Emerson's style must be good and admirable because it fits his thought, they forget that though it is well that a robe should fit, there is still something to be said about its cut and fashion.

No doubt, to borrow Carlyle's expression, 'the talent is not the chief question here: the idea—that is the chief question.' We do not profess to be of those to whom mere style is as dear as it was to Plutarch; of him it was said that he would have made Pompey win the battle of Pharsalia, if it could have given a better turn to a phrase. It would not be worth while to speak of form in a thinker to whom our debt is so large for his matter, if there were not so much bad literary imitation of Emerson. Dr. Holmes mournfully admits that 'one who talks like Emerson or like Carlyle soon finds himself surrounded by a crowd of walking phonographs, who mechanically reproduce his mental and oral accents. Emerson was before long talking in the midst of a babbling Simonetta of echoes.' Inferior writers have copied the tones of the oracle without first making sure of the inspiration. They forget that a platitude is not turned into a profundity by being dressed up as a conundrum. Pithiness in him dwindles into tenuity in them; honest discontinuity in the master is made an excuse for finical incoherencies in the disciples; the quaint, ingenious, and unexpected collocations of the original degenerate in the imitators into a trick of unmeaning surprise and vapid antithesis; and his pregnant sententiousness set the fashion of a sententiousness that is not fertility but only hydropsy. This curious infection, which has spread into divers forms of American literature that are far removed from philosophy, would have been impossible if the teacher had been as perfect in expression as he was pure, diligent, and harmonious in his thinking.

Yet, as happens to all fine minds, there came to Emerson ways of expression deeply marked with character. On every page there is set the strong stamp of sincerity, and the attraction of a certain artlessness; the most awkward sentence rings true; and there is often a pure and simple note that touches us more than if it were the perfection of elaborated melody. The uncouth procession of the periods discloses the travail of the thought, and that too is a kind of eloquence. An honest reader easily forgives the rude jolt or unexpected start when it shows a thinker faithfully working his way along arduous and unworn tracks. Even at the roughest, Emerson often interjects a delightful cadence. As he says of Landor, his sentences are cubes which will stand firm, place them how or where you will. He criticised Swedenborg for being superfluously explanatory, and having an exaggerated feeling of the ignorance of men. 'Men take truths of this nature,' said Emerson, 'very fast;' and his own style does no doubt very boldly take this capacity for granted in us. In 'choice and pith of diction,' again, of which Mr. Lowell speaks, he hits the mark with a felicity that is almost his own in this generation. He is terse, concentrated, and free from the important blunder of mistaking intellectual dawdling for meditation. Nor in fine does his abruptness ever impede a true urbanity. The accent is homely and the apparel plain, but his bearing has a friendliness, a courtesy, a hospitable humanity, which goes nearer to our hearts than either literary decoration or rhetorical unction. That modest and lenient fellow-feeling which gave such charm to his companionship breathes in his gravest writing, and prevents us from finding any page of it cold or hard or dry.

Though Emerson was always urgent for 'the soul of the world, clean from all vestige of tradition,' yet his work is full of literature. He at least lends no support to the comforting fallacy of the indolent, that originating power does not go with assimilating power. Few thinkers on his level display such breadth of literary reference. Unlike Wordsworth, who was content with a few tattered volumes on a kitchen shelf, Emerson worked among books. When he was a boy he found a volume of Montaigne, and he never forgot the delight and wonder in which he lived with it. His library is described as filled with well-selected authors, with curious works from the eastern world, with many editions in both Greek and English of his favourite Plato; while portraits of Shakespeare, Montaigne, Goethe, Dante, looked down upon him from the walls. Produce a volume of Plato or Shakespeare, he says somewhere, or *only remind us of their names,* and instantly we come into a feeling of longevity. That is the scholar's speech. Opening a single essay at random, we find in it citations from Montesquieu, Schiller, Milton, Herodotus, Shelley, Plutarch, Franklin, Bacon, Van Helmont, Goethe. So little does Emerson lend himself to the idle vanity of seeking all the treasures of wisdom in his own head, or neglecting the hoarded authority of the ages. It is true that he held the unholy opinion that a translation is as good as the original, or better. Nor need we suppose that he knew that pious sensation of the book-lover, the feel of a library; that he had any of the collector's amiable foolishness about rare editions; or that he nourished festive thoughts of 'that company of honest old fellows in their leathern jackets in his study,' as comrades in a sober old-world conviviality. His books were for spiritual use, like maps and charts of the mind of man, and not much for 'excellence of divertisement.' He had the gift of bringing his reading to bear easily upon the tenor of his musings, and knew how to use books as an aid to thinking, instead of letting them take the edge off thought. There was assuredly nothing of the compiler or the erudite collegian in him. It is a graver defect that he introduces the great names of literature without regard for true historical perspective in their place, either in relation to one another, or to the special phases of social change and shifting time. Still let his admirers not forget that Emerson was in his own way Scholar no less than Sage.

A word or two must be said of Emerson's verses. He disclaimed, for his own part, any belief that they were poems. Enthusiasts, however, have been found to declare that Emerson 'moves more constantly than any recent poet in the atmosphere of poesy. Since Milton and Spenser no man—not even Goethe—has equalled Emerson in this trait.' *The Problem,* according to another, 'is wholly unique, and transcends all contemporary verse in grandeur of style.' Such poetry, they say, is like Westminster Abbey, 'though the Abbey is inferior in boldness.' Yet, strangely enough, while Emerson's poetic form is symbolised by the flowing lines of Gothic architecture, it is also 'akin to Doric severity.' With all the good will in the world, I do not find myself able to rise to these heights; in fact, they rather seem to deserve Wordsworth's description, as mere obliquities of admiration.

Taken as a whole, Emerson's poetry is of that kind which springs, not from excitement of passion or feeling, but from an intellectual demand for intense and sublimated expression. We see the step that lifts him straight from prose to verse, and that step is the shortest possible. The flight is awkward and even uncouth, as if nature had intended feet rather than wings. It is hard to feel of Emerson, any more than Wordsworth could feel of Goethe, that his poetry is inevitable. The measure, the colour, the imaginative figures, are the product of search, not of spontaneous movements of sensation and reflection combining in a harmony that is delightful to the ear. They are the outcome of discontent with prose, not of that highstrung sensibility which compels the true poet into verse. This must not be said without exception. *The Threnody,* written after the death of a deeply loved child, is a beautiful and impressive lament. Pieces like *Musquetaquid,* the *Adirondacs,* the *Snowstorm, The Humble-Bee,* are pretty and pleasant bits of pastoral. In all we feel the pure breath of nature, and

> The primal mind,
> That flows in streams, that breathes in wind.

There is a certain charm of *naiveté,* that recalls the unvarnished simplicity of the Italian painters before Raphael. But who shall say that he discovers that 'spontaneous overflow of powerful feeling,' which a great poet has made the fundamental element of poetry? There are too few melodious progressions; the melting of the thought with natural images and with human feeling is incomplete; we miss the charm of perfect assimilation, fusion, and incorporation; and in the midst of all the vigour and courage of his work, Emerson has almost forgotten that it is part of the poet's business to give pleasure. It is true that pleasure is sometimes undoubtedly to be had from verse that is not above mediocrity, and Wordsworth once deigned to write an essay examining why bad poetry pleases. Poetry that pleases may be bad, but it is equally true that no poetry which fails to please can be really good. Some one says that gems of expression make Emerson's essays oracular and his verse prophetic. But, to borrow Horace's well-known phrase, 'tis not enough that poems should be sublime; *dulcia sunto,*—they must be touching and sympathetic. Only a bold critic will say that this is a mark of Emerson's poems. They are too naked, unrelated, and cosmic; too little clad with the vesture of human associations. Light and shade do not alternate in winning and rich relief, and as Carlyle found it, the radiance is 'thin piercing,' leaving none of the sweet and dim recesses so dear to the lover of nature. We may, however, well be content to leave a man of Emerson's calibre to choose his own exercises. It is best to suppose that he knew what he was about when he wandered into the fairyland of verse, and that in such moments he found nothing better to his hand. Yet if we are bidden to place him among the poets, it is enough to open Keats at the *Ode to a Nightingale,* or Shelley at *The Cloud,* the *Skylark,* or the *Sensitive Plant,* or Wordsworth at *Tintern Abbey,* or Goethe at *Das Göttliche,* or Victor Hugo in the *Contemplations.* Then in spite of occasional formality of rhythm and artifice in ornament, we cannot choose but perceive how tuneful is their music, how opulent the resources of their imagination, how various, subtle, and penetrating their affinity for the fortunes and sympathies of men, and next how modest a portion of all these rare and exquisite qualifications reveals itself in the verse of Emerson.

Few minds of the first order that have busied themselves in contemplating the march of human fortunes, have marched forward in a straight line of philosophic speculation unbroken to the end. Like Burke, like Coleridge, like Wordsworth, at a given point they have a return upon themselves. Having mastered the truths of one side, their eyes open to what is true on the other; the work of revolution finished or begun, they experience fatigue and reaction. In Hawthorne's romance, after Miles Coverdale had passed his spring and summer among the Utopians of Blithedale, he felt that the time had come when he must for sheer sanity's sake go and hold a little talk with the Conservatives, the merchants, the politicians, 'and all those respectable old blockheads, who still in this intangibility and mistiness of affairs kept a death-grip on one or two ideas which had not come into vogue since yesterday morning.' 'No sagacious man,' says Hawthorne, 'will long retain his sagacity if he lives exclusively among reformers and progressive people, without periodically returning into the settled system of things, to correct himself by a new observation from that old stand-point.' Yet good men rightly hoped that 'out of the very thoughts that were wildest and most destructive might grow a wisdom, holy, calm, and pure, and that should incarnate itself with the substance of a noble and happy life.' Now that we are able to look back on the crisis of the times that Hawthorne describes, we perceive that it was as he expected, and that in the person of Emerson the ferment and dissolvency of thought worked itself out in a strain of wisdom of the highest and purest.

In 1842 Emerson told Carlyle, in vindication of the *Dial* and its transcendentalisms, that if the direction of their speculations was as deplorable as Carlyle declared, it was yet a remarkable fact for history that all the bright young men and young women in New England, 'quite ignorant of each other, take the world so, and come and make confession to fathers and mothers—the boys, that they do not wish to go into trade; the girls, that they do not like morning calls and evening parties. They are all religious, but hate the churches; they reject all the ways of living of other men, but have none to offer in their stead.'

It is worth while to transcribe from the *Dial* itself the scene at one of the many Bostonian Conventions of that date—the Friends of Universal Progress, in 1840:—'The composition of the Assembly was rich and various. The singularity and latitude of the summons drew together, from all parts of New England, and also from the Middle States, men of every shade of opinion, from the straightest orthodoxy to the wildest heresy, and many persons whose church was a church of one member only. A great variety of dialect and of costume was noticed; a great deal of confusion, eccentricity, and freak appeared, as well as of zeal and enthusiasm. If the Assembly was disorderly, it was picturesque. Madmen, madwomen, men with beards, Dunkers, Muggletonians, Come-outers, Groaners, Agrarians, Seventh-day Baptists, Quakers, Abolitionists, Calvinists, Unitarians, and philosophers, all came successively to the top, and seized their moment, if not their *hour,* wherein to chide or pray or preach or protest. The faces were a study. The most daring innovators, and the champions-until-death of the old cause, sat side by side. The still living merit of the oldest New England families, glowing yet after several generations, encountered the founders of families, fresh merit emerging and expanding the brows to a new breadth, and lighting a clownish face with sacred fire. The Assembly was characterised by the predominance of a certain plain sylvan strength and earnestness' (*Dial,* iii. 101).

If the shade of Bossuet could have looked down upon the scene, he would have found fresh material for the sarcasms which a hundred and fifty years before he had lavished on the Variations of the Protestant Churches. Yet this curious movement, bleak and squalid as it may seem to men nurtured in the venerable decorum of ecclesiastical tradition, was at bottom identical with the yearning for stronger spiritual emotions, and the cravings of religious zeal, that had in older times filled monasteries, manned the great orders, and sent wave upon wave of pilgrims and crusaders to holy places. 'It is really amazing,' as was said by Franklin or somebody else of his fashion of utilitarianism, 'that one of the passions which it is hardest to develop in man is the passion for his own material comfort and temporal well-being.'

Emerson has put on record this mental intoxication of the progressive people around him, with a pungency that might satisfy the Philistines themselves. From 1820 to 1844, he said, New England witnessed a general criticism and attack on institutions, and in all practical activities a gradual withdrawal of tender consciences from the social organisations. Calvinists and Quakers began to split into old school and new school. Goethe and the Germans became known. Swedenborg, in spite of his taint of craziness, by the mere prodigy of his speculations, began 'to spread himself into the minds of thousands'—including in no unimportant degree the mind of Emerson himself. Literary criticism counted for something in the universal thaw, and even the genial humanity of Dickens helped to break up the indurations of old theology. Most powerful of all was the indirect influence of science. Geology disclosed law in an unsuspected region, and astronomy caused men to apprehend that 'as the earth is not the centre of the Universe, so it is not the special scene or stage on which the drama of divine justice is played before the assembled angels of heaven.'

A temper of scrutiny and dissent broke out in every direction. In almost every relation men and women asked themselves by what right Conformity levied its tax, and whether they were not false to their own consciences in paying it. 'What a fertility of projects for the salvation of the world! One apostle thought that all men should go to farming; and another thought that no man should buy or sell—that use of money was the cardinal evil; another thought the mischief was in our diet—that we eat and drink damnation. These made unleavened bread, and were foes to the death to fermentation. Others attacked the system of agriculture, the use of animal manures in farming, and the tyranny of man over brute instinct. These abuses polluted his food. The ox must be taken from the plough, and the horse from the cart, the hundred acres of the farm must be spaded, and the man must walk wherever boats and locomotives will not carry him. . . . Others assailed particular vocations. . . . Others attacked the institution of marriage as the fountain of social evils. . . . Who gave me the money with which I bought my coat? Why should professional labour and that of the counting-house be paid so disproportionately to the labour of the porter and the woodsawer? Am I not too protected a person? Is there not a wide disparity between the lot of me and the lot of thee, my poor brother, my poor sister?'

One of Emerson's glories is, that while wise enough to discern the peril and folly of these excesses, he was under no temptation to fall back. It was giddy work, but he kept his eye on the fixed stars. Certainly Emerson was not assailed by the stress of mighty and violent events, as Burke and Wordsworth were in some sense turned into reactionaries by the calamities of revolution in France. The 'distemper of enthusiasm,' as Shaftesbury would have called it, took a mild and harmless form in New England: there the work in hand was not the break-up of a social system, but only the mental evolution of new ideals, the struggle of an ethical revival, and the satisfaction of a livelier spirit of scruple. In face of all delirations, Emerson kept on his way of radiant sanity and perfect poise. Do not, he warned his enthusiasts, expend all energy on some accidental evil, and so lose sanity and power of benefit. *'It is of little moment that one or two or twenty errors of our social system be corrected, but of much that the man be in his senses.* Society gains nothing whilst a man, not himself renovated, attempts to renovate things around him; he has become tediously good in some particular, but negligent or narrow in the rest, and hypocrisy and vanity are often the disgusting result. It is handsomer to remain in the establishment, better than the establishment, and conduct that in the best manner, than to make a sally against evil by some single improvement, without supporting it by a total regeneration.'

Emerson, then, is one of the few moral reformers whose mission lay in calming men rather than in rousing them, and in the inculcation of serenity rather than in the spread of excitement. Though he had been ardent in protest against the life conventional, as soon as the protest ran off its extravagance, instead of either following or withstanding it with rueful petulancies, he delicately and successfully turned a passing agitation into an enduring revival. The last password given by the dying Antonine to the officer of the watch was *Æquanimitas*. In a brighter, wider, and more living sense than was possible even to the noblest in the middle of the second century, this, too, was the watchword of the Emersonian teaching. Instead of cultivating the tormenting and enfeebling spirit of scruple, instead of multiplying precepts, he bade men not to crush their souls out under the burden of Duty; they are to remember that a wise life is not wholly filled up by commandments to do and to abstain from doing. Hence, we have in Emerson the teaching of a vigorous morality without the formality of dogma and the deadly tedium of didactics. If not laughter, of which only Shakespeare among the immortals has a copious and unfailing spring, there is at least gaiety in every piece, and a cordial injunction to men to find joy in their existence to the full. Happiness is with him an aim that we are at liberty to seek directly and without periphrasis. Provided men do not lose their balance by immersing themselves in their pleasures, they are right, according to Emerson, in pursuing them. But joy is no neighbour to artificial ecstasy. What Emerson counsels the poet, he intended in its own way and degree for all men. The poet's habit of living, he says beautifully, should be set on a key so low that the commonest influence should delight him. 'That spirit which suffices quiet hearts, which seems to come forth to such from every dry knoll of sere grass, from every pine-stump and half-embedded stone on which the dull March sun shines, comes forth to the poor and hungry, and such as are of simple taste. If thou fill thy brain with Boston and New York, with fashion and covetousness, and wilt stimulate thy jaded senses with wine and French coffee, thou shalt find no radiance of wisdom in the lonely waste of the pinewoods.'

It was perhaps the same necessity of having to guide men away from the danger of transcendental aberrations, while yet holding up lofty ideals of conduct, that made Emerson say something about many traits of conduct to which the ordinary high-flying moralist of the treatise or the pulpit seldom deigns to stoop. The essays on Domestic Life, on Behaviour, on Manners, are examples of the attention that Emerson paid to the right handling of the outer conditions of a wise and brave life. With him small circumstances are the occasions of great qualities. The parlour and the counting-house are as fit scenes for fortitude, self-control, considerateness, and vision, as the senate or the battlefield. He re-classifies the virtues.

No modern, for example, has given so remarkable a place to Friend-ship among the sacred necessities of well-endowed character. Neither Plato nor Cicero, least of all Bacon, has risen to so noble and profound a conception of this most strangely commingled of all human affections. There is no modern thinker, again, who makes Beauty—all that is gracious, seemly, and becoming—so conspicuous and essential a part of life. It would be inexact to say that Emerson blended the beautiful with the precepts of duty or of prudence into one complex sentiment, as the Greeks did, but his theory of ex-cellence might be better described than any other of modern times by the . . . virtue of the true gentleman, as set down in Plato and Aristotle.

So untrue is it that in his quality of Sage Emerson always haunted the perilous altitudes of Transcendentalism, 'seeing nothing under him but the everlasting snows of Himalaya, the Earth shrink-ing to a Planet, and the indigo Firmament sowing itself with day-light stars.' He never thinks it beneath his dignity to touch a point of minor morals, or to say a good word for what he somewhere calls subterranean prudence. Emerson values mundane circumspection as highly as Franklin, and gives to manners and rules of daily be-haviour an importance that might have satisfied Chesterfield. In fact, the worldly and the selfish are mistaken when they assume that Common Sense is their special and exclusive portion. The small Transcendentalist goes in search of truth with the meshes of his net so large that he takes no fish. His landscapes are all horizon. It is only the great idealists, like Emerson, who take care not to miss the real.

The remedy for the break-down of the old churches would, in the mind of the egotist, have been to found a new one. But Emerson knew well before Carlyle told him, that 'no truly great man, from Jesus Christ downwards, ever founded a sect—I mean wilfully in-tended founding one.' Not only did he establish no sect, but he preached a doctrine that was positively incompatible with the erec-tion of any sect upon its base. His whole hope for the world lies in the internal and independent resources of the individual. If mankind is to be raised to a higher plane of happiness and worth, it can only be by the resolution of each to live his own life with fidelity and courage. The spectacle of one liberated from the malign obstructions to free human character, is a stronger incentive to others than ex-hortation, admonition, or any sum of philanthropical association. If I, in my own person and daily walk, quietly resist heaviness of custom, coldness of hope, timidity of faith, then without wishing, contriving, or even knowing it, I am a light silently drawing as many as have vision and are fit to walk in the same path. Whether I do that or not, I am at least obeying the highest law of my own being.

In the appeal to the individual to be true to himself, Emerson does not stand apart from other great moral reformers. His distinction lies in the peculiar direction that he gives to his appeal. All those regenerators of the individual, from Rousseau down to J. S. Mill, who derived their first principles, whether directly or indirectly, from Locke and the philosophy of sensation, experience, and acquisition, began operations with the will. They laid all their stress on the shaping of motives by education, institutions, and action, and placed virtue in deliberateness and in exercise. Emerson, on the contrary, coming from the intuitional camp, holds that our moral nature is vitiated by any interference of our will. Translated into the language of theology, his doctrine makes regeneration to be a result of grace, and the guide of conscience to be the indwelling light; though, unlike the theologians, he does not trace either of these mysterious gifts to the special choice and intervention of a personal Deity. Impulsive and spontaneous innocence is higher than the strength to conquer temptation. The natural motions of the soul are so much better than the voluntary ones. 'There is no such thing as manufacturing a strong will,' for all great force is real and elemental. In all this Emerson suffers from the limitations that are inseparable from pure spiritualism in all its forms. As if the spiritual constitution were ever independent of the material organisation bestowed upon the individual at the moment when he is conceived, or of the social conditions that close about him from the instant of his birth. The reaction, however, against what was superficial in the school of the eighteenth century went to its extreme length in Emerson, and blinded his eyes to the wisdom, the profundity, and the fruitfulness of their leading speculations. It is enough for us to note the fact in passing, without plunging into contention on the merits. All thoughts are always ready, potentially if not actually. Each age selects and assimilates the philosophy that is most apt for its wants. Institutions needed regeneration in France, and so those thinkers came into vogue and power who laid most stress on the efficacy of good institutions. In Emerson's America, the fortunes of the country made external circumstances safe for a man, and his chance was assured; so a philosophy was welcomed which turned the individual inwards upon himself, and taught him to consider his own character and spiritual faculty as something higher than anything external could ever be.

Again to make a use which is not uninstructive of the old tongue, Emerson is for faith before works. Nature, he says, will not have us fret and fume. She does not like our benevolences, our churches, our pauper-societies, much better than she likes our frauds and wars. They are but so many yokes to the neck. Our painful labours are unnecessary and fruitless. A higher law than that of our will regulates events. If we look wider, things are all alike: laws and creeds and modes of living are a travesty of truth. Only in our easy, simple, spontaneous action are we strong, and by contenting ourselves with obedience we become strong. Our real action is in our silent moments. Why should we be awed by the name of Action? 'Tis a trick of the senses.

Justification by faith has had a savour of antinomianism and indifferency ever since the day when Saint Paul so emphatically denied that he made void the law through faith, and said of certain calumniators that their damnation was just. Emerson was open to the same charge, and he knew it. In a passage already quoted, Emerson says good-humouredly that his wife keeps his philosophy from running to antinomianism. He could not mistake the tendency of saying that, if you look wider, things are all alike, and that we are in the grasp of a higher law than our own will. On that side he only paints over in rainbow colours the grim doctrine which the High Calvinist and the Materialistic Necessarian hold in common.

All great minds perceive all things; the only difference lies in the order in which they shall choose to place them. Emerson, for good reason of his own, dwelt most on fate, character, and the unconscious and hidden sources, but he writes many a page of vigorous corrective. It is wholesome, he says, to man to look not at Fate, but the other way; the practical view is the other. As Mill says of his wish to disbelieve the doctrine of the formation of character by circumstances—'Remembering the wish of Fox respecting the doctrine of resistance to governments, that it might never be forgotten by Kings nor remembered by subjects, I said that it would be a blessing if the doctrine of necessity could be believed by all *quoad* the characters of others, and disbelieved in regard to their own.' So Emerson knew well enough that man's consciousness of freedom, action, and power over outer circumstances might be left to take care of itself, as the practical view generally can. The world did not need him to tell it that a man's fortunes are a part of his character. His task was the more far-reaching one of drawing them to recognise that love is the important thing, not benevolent works; that only impure men consider life as it is reflected in events, opinions, and persons; that they fail to see the action until it is done, whereas what is far better worth considering is that its moral element pre-existed in the actor.

It would be easy to show that Emerson has not worked out his answers to these eternal enigmas, for ever reproducing themselves in all ages, in such a form as to defy the logician's challenge. He never shrinks from inconsistent propositions. He was unsystematic on principle. 'He thought that truth has so many facets that the best we can do is to notice each in turn, without troubling ourselves whether they agree.' When we remember the inadequateness of human language, the infirmities of our vision, and all the imperfections of mental apparatus, the wise men will not disdain even partial glimpses of a scene too vast and intricate to be comprehended in a single map. To complain that Emerson is no systematic reasoner is to miss the secret of most of those who have given powerful impulses to the spiritual ethics of an age. It is not a syllogism that turns the heart toward purification of life and aim. it is not the logically enchained propositions of a *sorites*, but the flash of illumination, the indefinable accent, that attracts masses of men to a new teacher and a high doctrine. The teasing *ergoteur* is always right, but he never leads nor improves nor inspires.

Any one can see how this side of the Emersonian gospel harmonised with the prepossessions of a new democracy. Trust, he said, to leading instincts, not to traditional institutions, nor social ordering, nor the formulæ of books and schools for the formation of character; the great force is real and elemental. In art, Mr. Ruskin has explained the palpable truth that semi-civilised nations can colour better than we do, and that an Indian shawl and China vase are inimitable by us. 'It is their glorious ignorance of all rules that does it; the pure and true instincts have play, and do their work; and the moment we begin teaching people any rules about colour, and make them do this or that, we crush the instinct, generally for ever' (*Modern Painters,* iii. 91). Emerson said what comes to the same thing about morals. The philosophy of democracy, or the government of a great mixed community by itself, rests on a similar assumption in politics. The foundations of a self-governed society on a great scale are laid in leading instincts. Emerson was never tired of saying that we are wiser than we know. The path of science and of letters is not the way to nature. What was done in a remote age by men whose names have resounded far, has no deeper sense than what you and I do to-day. What food, or experience, or succour have Olympiads and Consulates for the Esquimaux seal-hunter, for the Kanáka in his canoe, for the fisherman, the stevedore, the porter? When he is in this vein Emerson often approaches curiously near to Rousseau's memorable and most potent paradox of 1750, that the sciences corrupt manners.

Most men will now agree that when the great fiery trial came, the Emersonian faith and the democratic assumption abundantly justified themselves. Even Carlyle wrote to Emerson at last (June 4, 1871): 'In my occasional explosions against Anarchy, and my inextinguishable hatred of *it*, I privately whisper to myself, "Could any Friedrich Wilhelm now, or Friedrich, or most perfect Governor you could hope to realise, guide forward what is America's essential task at present, faster or more completely than 'Anarchic America' is now doing?" Such "Anarchy" has a great deal to say for itself.'

The traits of comparison between Carlyle and Emerson may be regarded as having been pretty nearly exhausted for the present, until time has changed the point of view. In wit, humour, pathos, penetration, poetic grandeur, and fervid sublimity of imagination, Carlyle is the superior beyond measure. But Emerson is as much his superior in that high and transparent sanity, which is not further removed from midsummer madness than it is from a terrene and grovelling mediocrity. This sanity, among other things, kept Emerson in line with the ruling tendencies of his age, and his teaching brings all the aid that abstract teaching can, towards the solution of the moral problems of modern societies. Carlyle chose to fling himself headlong and blindfold athwart the great currents of things, against all the forces and elements that are pushing modern societies forward. Beginning in his earlier work with the same faith as Emerson in leading instincts, he came to dream that the only leading instinct worth thinking about is that of self-will, mastery, force, and violent strength. Emerson was for basing the health of a modern commonwealth on the only real strength, and the only kind of force that can be relied upon, namely, the honest, manly, simple, and emancipated character of the citizen. This gives to his doctrine a hold and a prize on the work of the day, and makes him our helper. Carlyle's perverse reaction had wrecked and stranded him when the world came to ask him for direction. In spite of his resplendent genius, he had no direction to give, and was only able in vague and turbid torrents of words to hide a shallow and obsolete lesson. His confession to Emerson, quoted above, looks as if at last he had found this out for himself.

If Emerson stood thus well towards the social and political drift of events, his teaching was no less harmoniously related to the new and most memorable drift of science which set in by his side. It is a misconception to pretend that he was a precursor of the Darwinian theory. Evolution, as a possible explanation of the ordering of the universe, is a great deal older than either Emerson or Darwin. What Darwin did was to work out in detail and with masses of minute evidence a definite hypothesis of the specific conditions under which new forms are evolved. Emerson, of course, had no definite hypothesis of this sort, nor did he possess any of the knowledge necessary to give it value. But it was his good fortune that some of his strongest propositions harmonise with the scientific theory of the survival of the fittest in the struggle for material existence. He connects his exhortation to self-reliance with the law working in nature for conservation and growth,—to wit, that 'Power is in nature the essential measure of right,' and that 'Nature suffers nothing to remain in her kingdom which cannot help itself.' The same strain is constantly audible. Nature on every side, within us and without, is for ever throwing out new forms and fresh varieties of living and thinking. To her experiments in every region there is no end. Those succeed which prove to have the best adaptation to the conditions. Let, therefore, neither society nor the individual check experiment, originality, and infinite variation. Such language, we may see, fits in equally well with democracy in politics and with evolution in science. If, moreover, modern science gives more prominence to one conception than another, it is to that of the natural universe of force and energy, as One and a Whole. This too is the great central idea with Emerson, repeated a thousand times in prose and in verse, and lying at the very heart of his philosophy. Newton's saying that 'the world was made at one cast' delights him. 'The secret of the world is that its energies are *solidaires.*' Nature 'publishes itself in creatures, reaching from particles and spicula, through transformation on transformation to the highest symmetries. A little heat, that is, a little motion, is all that differences the bald dazzling white and deadly cold poles of the earth from the prolific tropical climates.' Not only, as Professor Tyndall says, is Emerson's religious sense entirely undaunted by the discoveries of science; all such discoveries he comprehends and assimilates. 'By Emerson scientific conceptions are continually transmuted into the finer forms and warmer lines of an ideal world.'

That these transmutations are often carried by Emerson to the extent of vain and empty self-mystifications is hard to deny, even for those who have most sympathy with the general scope of his teaching. There are pages that to the present writer, at least, after reasonably diligent meditation, remain mere abracadabra, incomprehensible and worthless. For much of this in Emerson, the influence of Plato is mainly responsible, and it may be noted in passing that his account of Plato (*Representative Men*) is one of his most unsatisfactory performances. 'The title of Platonist,' says Mill, 'belongs by far better right to those who have been nourished in, and have endeavoured to practise Plato's mode of investigation, than to those who are distinguished only by the adoption of certain dogmatical conclusions, drawn mostly from the least intelligible of his works.' Nothing is gained by concealing that not every part of Emerson's work will stand the test of the Elenchus, nor bear reduction into honest and intelligible English.

One remarkable result of Emerson's idealism ought not to be passed over. 'The visible becomes the Bestial,' said Carlyle, 'when it rests not on the invisible.' To Emerson all rested on the invisible, and was summed up in terms of the invisible, and hence the Bestial was almost unknown in his philosophic scheme. Nay, we may say that some mighty phenomena in our universe were kept studiously absent from his mind. Here is one of the profoundest differences between Emerson and most of those who, on as high an altitude, have pondered the same great themes. A small trait will serve for illustration. It was well known in his household that he could not bear to hear of ailments. 'There is one topic,' he writes, 'peremptorily forbidden to all well-bred, to all rational mortals, namely, their distempers. If you have not slept, or if you have slept, or if you have headache, sciatica, or leprosy, or thunder-stroke, I beseech you by all angels to hold your peace, and not pollute the morning, to which all the housemates bring serene and pleasant thoughts, by corruption and groans. Come out of the azure. Love the day'—(*Conduct of Life*, 159).

If he could not endure these minor perturbations of the fair and smiling face of daily life, far less did he willingly think of Death. Of nothing in all the wide range of universal topics does Emerson say so little as of that which has lain in sombre mystery at the very core of most meditations on life, from Job and Solon down to Bacon and Montaigne. Except in two beautiful poems, already mentioned, Death is almost banished from his page. It is not the title or the subject of one of his essays, only secondarily even of that on Immortality. Love, Friendship, Prudence, Heroism, Experience, Manners, Nature, Greatness, and a score of other matters—but none to show that he ever sat down to gather into separate and concentrated shape his reflections on the terrifying phantom that has haunted the mind of man from the very birth of time.

Pascal bade us imagine a number of men in chains and doomed to death; some of them each day butchered in sight of the others; those who remained watching their own lot in that of their fellows, and awaiting their turn in anguish and helplessness. Such, he cried, is the pitiful and desperate condition of man. But nature has other cruelties more stinging than death. Mill, himself an optimist, yet declares the course of natural phenomena to be replete with everything which, when committed by human beings is most worthy of abhorrence, so that 'one who endeavoured in his actions to imitate the natural course of things would be universally seen and acknowledged to be the wickedest of men.' To man himself, moreover, 'the most criminal actions are not more unnatural than most of the virtues.' We need not multiply from poets and divines, from moralists and sages, these grim pictures. The sombre melancholy, the savage moral indignation, the passionate intellectual scorn, with which life and the universe have filled strong souls, some with one emotion and some with another, were all to Emerson in his habitual thinking unintelligible and remote. He admits, indeed, that 'the disease and deformity around us certify that infraction of natural, intellectual, and moral laws, and often violation on violation to breed such compound misery.' The way of Providence, he says in another place, is a little rude, through earthquakes, fever, the sword of climate, and a thousand other hints of ferocity in the interiors of nature. Providence has a wild rough incalculable road to its end, and 'it is of no use to try to whitewash its huge mixed instrumentalities, or to dress up that terrific benefactor in a clean shirt and white neckcloth of a student of divinity.' But he only drew from the thought of these cruelties of the universe the practical moral that 'our culture must not omit the arming of the man.' He is born into the state of war, and will therefore do well to acquire a military attitude of soul. There is perhaps no better moral than this of the Stoic, but greater impressiveness might have marked the lesson, if our teacher had been more indulgent to the man's sense of tragedy in that vast drama in which he plays his piteous part.

In like manner, Emerson has little to say of that horrid burden and impediment on the soul, which the churches call Sin, and which, by whatever name we call it, is a very real catastrophe in the moral nature of man. He had no eye, like Dante's, for the vileness, the cruelty, the utter despicableness to which humanity may be moulded. If he saw them at all, it was through the softening and illusive medium of generalised phrases. Nor was he ever shocked and driven into himself by 'the immoral thoughtlessness' of men. The courses of nature, and the prodigious injustices of man in society, affect him with neither horror nor awe. He will see no monster if he can help it. For the fatal Nemesis or terrible Erinnyes, daughters of Erebus and Night, Emerson substitutes a fair-weather abstraction named Compensation. One radical tragedy in nature he admits—'the distinction of More and Less.' If I am poor in faculty, dim in vision, shut out from opportunity, in every sense an outcast from the inheritance of the earth, that seems indeed to be a tragedy. 'But see the facts clearly and these mountainous inequalities vanish. Love reduces them, as the sun melts the iceberg in the sea. The heart and soul of all men being one, this bitterness of His and Mine ceases. His is mine.' Surely words, words, words! What can be more idle, when one of the world's bitter puzzles is pressed on the teacher, than that he should betake himself to an altitude whence it is not visible, and then assure us that it is not only invisible, but non-existent? This is not to see the facts clearly, but to pour the fumes of obscuration round them. When he comforts us by saying 'Love, and you shall be loved,' who does not recall cases which make the Jean Valjean of Victor Hugo's noble romance not a figment of the theatre, but an all too actual type? The believer who looks to another world to redress the wrongs and horrors of this; the sage who warns us that the law of life is resignation, renunciation, and doing-without (*entbehren sollst du*)—each of these has a foothold in common language. But to say that all infractions of love and equity are speedily punished—punished by fear—and then to talk of the perfect compensation of the universe, is mere playing with words, for it does not solve the problem in the terms in which men propound it. Emerson, as we have said, held the spirit of System in aversion as fettering the liberal play of thought, just as in morals, with greater boldness, he rebelled against a minute and cramping interpretation of Duty. We are not sure that his own optimistic doctrine did not play him the same tyrannical trick, by sealing his eyes to at least one half of the actualities of nature and the gruesome possibilities of things. It had no unimportant effect on Emerson's thought that he was born in a new world that had cut itself loose from old history. The black and devious ways through which the race has marched are not real in North America, as they are to us in old Europe, who live on the very site of secular iniquities, are surrounded by monuments of historic crime, and find present and future entangled, embittered, inextricably loaded both in blood and in institutions with desperate inheritances from the past.

There are many topics, and those no mean topics, on which the best authority is not the moralist by profession, as Emerson was, but the man of the world. The world hardens, narrows, desiccates common natures, but nothing so enriches generous ones. For knowledge of the heart of man, we must go to those who were closer to the passions and interests of actual and varied life than Emerson ever could have been—to Horace, Montaigne, La Bruyère, Swift, Molière, even to Pope. If a hostile critic were to say that Emerson looked at life too much from the outside, as the clergyman is apt to do, we should condemn such a remark as a disparagement, but we should understand what it is in Emerson that the critic means. He has not the temperament of the great humorists, under whatever planet they may have been born, jovial, mercurial, or saturnine. Even his revolt against formalism is only a new fashion of composure, and sometimes comes dangerously near to moral dilettantism. The persistent identification of everything in nature with everything else sometimes bewilders, fatigues, and almost afflicts us. Though he warns us that our civilisation is not near its meridian, but as yet only in the cock-crowing and the morning star, still all ages are much alike with him: man is always man, 'society never advances,' and he does almost as little as Carlyle himself to fire men with faith in social progress as the crown of wise endeavour. But when all these deductions have been made and amply allowed for, Emerson remains among the most persuasive and inspiring of those who by word and example rebuke our despondency, purify our sight, awaken us from the deadening slumbers of convention and conformity, exorcise the pestering imps of vanity, and lift men up from low thoughts and sullen moods of helplessness and impiety.

HENRY JAMES (1843–1916) knew Emerson as a friend of the James family, but he also knew him as a thinker. The following essay is from *Partial Portraits* (1888). He took his point of departure from the publication, in 1887, of James Elliot Cabot's memorial biography of Emerson, *A Memoir of Ralph Waldo Emerson.*

Emerson

H E N R Y   J A M E S

Mr. Elliot Cabot has made a very interesting contribution to a class of books of which our literature, more than any other, offers admirable examples: he has given us a biography intelligently and carefully composed. These two volumes are a model of responsible editing—I use that term because they consist largely of letters and extracts from letters: nothing could resemble less the manner in which the mere bookmaker strings together his frequently questionable pearls and shovels the heap into the presence of the public. Mr. Cabot has selected, compared, discriminated, steered an even course between meagerness and redundancy, and managed to be constantly and happily illustrative. And his work, moreover, strikes us as the better done from the fact that it stands for one of the two things that make an absorbing memoir a good deal more than for the other. If these two things be the conscience of the writer and the career of his hero, it is not difficult to see on which side the biographer of Emerson has found himself strongest. Ralph Waldo Emerson was a man of genius, but he led for nearly eighty years a life in which the sequence of events had little of the rapidity, or the complexity, that a spectator loves. There is something we miss very much as we turn these pages—something that has a kind of accidental, inevitable presence in almost any personal record—something that may be most definitely indicated under the name of color. We lay down the book with a singular impression of paleness—an impression that comes partly from the tone of the biographer and partly from the moral complexion of his subject, but mainly from the vacancy of the page itself. That of Emerson's personal history is condensed into the single word Concord, and all the condensation in the world will not make it look rich. It presents a most continuous surface. Mr. Matthew Arnold, in his *Discourses in America,* contests Emerson's complete right to the title of a man of letters; yet letters surely were the very texture of his history. Passions, alternations, affairs, adventures had absolutely no part in it. It stretched itself out in enviable quiet—a quiet in which we hear the jotting of the pencil in the notebook. It is the very life for literature (I mean for one's own, not that of another): fifty years of residence in the home of one's forefathers, pervaded by reading, by walking in the woods, and the daily addition of sentence to sentence.

If the interest of Mr. Cabot's penciled portrait is incontestable and yet does not spring from variety, it owes nothing either to a source from which it might have borrowed much and which it is impossible not to regret a little that he has so completely neglected: I mean a greater reference to the social conditions in which Emerson moved, the company he lived in, the moral air he breathed. If his biographer had allowed himself a little more of the ironic touch, had put himself once in a way under the protection of Sainte-Beuve and had attempted something of a general picture, we should have felt that he only went with the occasion. I may overestimate the latent treasures of the field, but it seems to me there was distinctly an opportunity—an opportunity to make up moreover in some degree for the white tint of Emerson's career considered simply in itself. We know a man imperfectly until we know his society, and we but half know a society until we know its manners. This is especially true of a man of letters, for manners lie very close to literature. From those of the New England world in which Emerson's character formed itself Mr. Cabot almost averts his lantern, though we feel sure that there would have been delightful glimpses to be had and that he would have been in a position—that is, that he has all the knowledge that would enable him—to help us to them. It is as if he could not trust himself, knowing the subject only too well. This adds to the effect of extreme discretion that we find in his volumes, but it is the cause of our not finding certain things, certain figures and scenes, evoked. What is evoked is Emerson's pure spirit, by a copious, sifted series of citations and comments. But we must read as much as possible between the lines, and the picture of the transcendental time (to mention simply one corner) has yet to be painted—the lines have yet to be bitten in. Meanwhile we are held and charmed by the image of Emerson's mind and the extreme appeal which his physiognomy makes to our art of discrimination. It is so fair, so uniform and impersonal, that its features are simply fine shades, the gradations of tone of a surface whose proper quality was of the smoothest and on which nothing was reflected with violence. It is a pleasure of the critical sense to find, with Mr. Cabot's extremely intelligent help, a notation for such delicacies.

We seem to see the circumstances of our author's origin, immediate and remote, in a kind of high, vertical, moral light, the brightness of a society at once very simple and very responsible. The rare singleness that was in his nature (so that he was *all* the warning moral voice, without distraction or counter-solicitation), was also in the stock he sprang from, clerical for generations, on both sides, and clerical in the Puritan sense. His ancestors had lived long (for nearly two centuries) in the same corner of New England, and during that period had preached and studied and prayed and practiced. It is impossible to imagine a spirit better prepared in advance to be exactly what it was—better educated for its office in its faraway unconscious beginnings. There is an inner satisfaction in seeing so straight, although so patient, a connection between the stem and the flower, and such a proof that when life wishes to produce something exquisite in quality she takes her measures many years in advance. A conscience like Emerson's could not have been turned off, as it were, from one generation to another: a succession of attempts, a long process of refining, was required. His perfection, in his own line, comes largely from the noninterruption of the process.

As most of us are made up of ill-assorted pieces, his reader, and Mr. Cabot's, envies him this transmitted unity, in which there was no mutual hustling or crowding of elements. It must have been a kind of luxury to be—that is, to feel—so homogeneous, and it helps to account for his serenity, his power of acceptance, and that absence of personal passion which makes his private correspondence read like a series of beautiful circulars or expanded cards *pour prendre congé*. He had the equanimity of a result; nature had taken care of him and he had only to speak. He accepted himself as he accepted others, accepted everything; and his absence of eagerness, or in other words his modesty, was that of a man with whom it is not a question of success, who has nothing invested or at stake. The investment, the stake, was that of the race, of all the past Emersons and Bulkeleys and Waldos. There is much that makes us smile, today, in the commotion produced by his secession from the mild Unitarian pulpit: we wonder at a condition of opinion in which any utterance of his should appear to be wanting in superior piety—in the essence of good instruction. All that is changed: the great difference has become the infinitely small, and we admire a state of society in which scandal and schism took on no darker hue; but there is even yet a sort of drollery in the spectacle of a body of people among whom the author of *The American Scholar* and of the Address of 1838 at the Harvard Divinity College passed for profane, and who failed to see that he only gave his plea for the spiritual life the advantage of a brilliant expression. They were so provincial as to think that brilliancy came ill recommended, and they were shocked at his ceasing to care for the prayer and the sermon. They might have perceived that he *was* the prayer and the sermon: not in the least a secularizer, but in his own subtle insinuating way a sanctifier.

Of the three periods into which his life divides itself, the first was (as in the case of most men) that of movement, experiment and selection—that of effort, too, and painful probation. Emerson had his message, but he was a good while looking for his form—the form which, as he himself would have said, he never completely found and of which it was rather characteristic of him that his later years (with their growing refusal to give him the *word*), wishing to attack him in his most vulnerable point, where his tenure was least complete, had in some degree the effect of despoiling him. It all sounds rather bare and stern, Mr. Cabot's account of his youth and early manhood, and we get an impression of a terrible paucity of alternatives. If he would be neither a farmer nor a trader he could "teach school"; that was the main resource and a part of the general educative process of the young New Englander who proposed to devote himself to the things of the mind. There was an advantage in the nudity, however, which was that, in Emerson's case at least, the things of the mind did get themselves admirably well considered. If it be his great distinction and his special sign that he had a more vivid conception of the moral life than anyone else, it is probably not fanciful to say that he owed it in part to the limited way in which he saw our capacity for living illustrated. The plain, God-fearing, practical society which surrounded him was not fertile in variations; it had great intelligence and energy, but it moved altogether in the straightforward direction. On three occasions later— three journeys to Europe—he was introduced to a more complicated world; but his spirit, his moral taste, as it were, abode always within the undecorated walls of his youth. There he could dwell with that ripe unconsciousness of evil which is one of the most beautiful signs by which we know him. His early writings are full of quaint animadversion upon the vices of the place and time, but there is something charmingly vague, light, and general in the arraignment. Almost the worst he can say is that these vices are negative and that his fellow townsmen are not heroic. We feel that his first impressions were gathered in a community from which misery and extravagance, and either extreme, of any sort, were equally absent. What the life of New England fifty years ago offered to the observer was the

common lot, in a kind of achromatic picture, without particular in-
tensifications. It was from this table of the usual, the merely typical
joys and sorrows that he proceeded to generalize—a fact that accounts
in some degree for a certain inadequacy and thinness in his enumera-
tions. But it helps to account also for his direct, intimate vision of
the soul itself—not in its emotions, its contortions and perversions,
but in its passive, exposed, yet healthy form. He knows the nature
of man and the long tradition of its dangers; but we feel that
whereas he can put his finger on the remedies, lying for the most
part, as they do, in the deep recesses of virtue, of the spirit, he has
only a kind of hearsay, uninformed acquaintance with the disorders.
It would require some ingenuity, the reader may say too much,
to trace closely this correspondence between his genius and the
frugal, dutiful, happy but decidedly lean Boston of the past, where
there was a great deal of will but very little fulcrum—like a ministry
without an opposition.

The genius itself it seems to me impossible to contest—I mean
the genius for seeing character as a real and supreme thing. Other
writers have arrived at a more complete expression: Wordsworth
and Goethe, for instance, give one a sense of having found their
form, whereas with Emerson we never lose the sense that he is
still seeking it. But no one has had so steady and constant, and above
all so natural, a vision of what we require and what we are capable
of in the way of aspiration and independence. With Emerson it is
ever the special capacity for moral experience—always that and only
that. We have the impression, somehow, that life had never bribed
him to look at anything but the soul; and indeed in the world in
which he grew up and lived the bribes and lures, the beguilements
and prizes, were few. He was in an admirable position for showing,
what he constantly endeavored to show, that the prize was within.
Anyone who in New England at that time could do that was sure
of success, of listeners and sympathy: most of all, of course, when it
was a question of doing it with such a divine persuasiveness. Moreover, the way in which Emerson did it added to the charm—by
word of mouth, face to face, with a rare, irresistible voice and a
beautiful mild, modest authority. If Mr. Arnold is struck with the
limited degree in which he was a man of letters, I suppose it is
because he is more struck with his having been, as it were, a man of
lectures. But the lecture surely was never more purged of its gross-
ness—the quality in it that suggests a strong light and a big brush—
than as it issued from Emerson's lips; so far from being a vulgariza-
tion, it was simply the esoteric made audible, and instead of treating

the few as the many, after the usual fashion of gentlemen on platforms, he treated the many as the few. There was probably no other
society at that time in which he would have got so many persons to
understand that; for we think the better of his audience as we read
him, and wonder where else people would have had so much moral
attention to give. It is to be remembered, however, that during the
winter of 1847–48, on the occasion of his second visit to England, he
found many listeners in London and in provincial cities. Mr. Cabot's
volumes are full of evidence of the satisfactions he offered, the delights and revelations he may be said to have promised, to a race
which had to seek its entertainment, its rewards and consolations,
almost exclusively in the moral world. But his own writings are fuller
still; we find an instance almost wherever we open them.

> All these great and transcendent properties are ours. . . . Let
> us find room for this great guest in our small houses. . . . Where
> the heart is, there the muses, there the gods sojourn, and not in
> any geography of fame. Massachusetts, Connecticut River, and
> Boston Bay, you think paltry places, and the ear loves names of
> foreign and classic topography. But here we are, and if we
> will tarry a little we may come to learn that here is best. . . .
> The Jerseys were handsome enough ground for Washington to
> tread, and London streets for the feet of Milton. . . . That
> country is fairest which is inhabited by the noblest minds.

We feel, or suspect, that Milton is thrown in as a hint that the London streets are no such great place, and it all sounds like a sort of
pleading consolation against bleakness.

The beauty of a hundred passages of this kind in Emerson's
pages is that they are effective, that they do come home, that they
rest upon insight and not upon ingenuity, and that if they are sometimes obscure it is never with the obscurity of paradox. We seem to
see the people turning out into the snow after hearing them, glowing
with a finer glow than even the climate could give and fortified for
a struggle with overshoes and the east wind.

> Look to it first and only, that fashion, custom, authority,
> pleasure, and money, are nothing to you, are not as bandages
> over your eyes, that you cannot see; but live with the privilege
> of the immeasurable mind. Not too anxious to visit periodically
> all families and each family in your parish connection, when
> you meet one of these men or women be to them a divine man;
> be to them thought and virtue; let their timid aspirations find
> in you a friend; let their trampled instincts be genially tempted

out in your atmosphere; let their doubts know that you have doubted, and their wonder feel that you have wondered.

When we set against an exquisite passage like that, or like the familiar sentences that open the essay on "History" ("He that is admitted to the right of reason is made freeman of the whole estate. What Plato has thought, he may think; what a saint has felt, he may feel; what at any time has befallen any man, he can understand"); when we compare the letters, cited by Mr. Cabot, to his wife from Springfield, Illinois (January, 1853) we feel that his spiritual tact needed to be very just, but that if it was so it must have brought a blessing. . . .

Courteous and humane to the furthest possible point, to the point of an almost profligate surrender of his attention, there was no familiarity in him, no personal avidity. Even his letters to his wife are courtesies, they are not familiarities. He had only one style, one manner, and he had it for everything—even for himself, in his notes, in his journals. But he had it in perfection for Miss Fuller; he retreats, smiling and flattering, on tiptoe, as if we were advancing. "She ever seems to crave," he says in his journal, "something which I have not, or have not for her." What he had was doubtless not what she craved, but the letter in question should be read to see how the modicum was administered. It is only between the lines of such a production that we read that a part of her effect upon him was to bore him; for his system was to practice a kind of universal passive hospitality—he aimed at nothing less. It was only because he was so deferential that he could be so detached; he had polished his aloofness till it reflected the image of his solicitor. And this was not because he was an "uncommunicating egotist," though he amuses himself with saying so to Miss Fuller: egotism is the strongest of passions, and he was altogether passionless. It was because he had no personal, just as he had almost no physical wants. "Yet I plead not guilty to the malice prepense. 'Tis imbecility, not contumacy, though perhaps somewhat more odious. It seems very just, the irony with which you ask whether you may not be trusted and promise such docility. Alas, we will all promise, but the prophet loiters." He would not say even to himself that she bored him; he had denied himself the luxury of such easy and obvious short cuts. There is a passage in the lecture (1844) called "Man the Reformer," in which he hovers round and round the idea that the practice of trade, in certain conditions likely to beget an underhand competition, does not draw forth the nobler parts of character, till the reader is tempted to interrupt him with, "Say at once that it is impossible for a gentleman!"

So he remained always, reading his lectures in the winter, writing them in the summer, and at all seasons taking wood walks and looking for hints in old books.

> Delicious summer stroll through the pastures. . . . On the steep park of Conantum I have the old regret—is all this beauty to perish? Shall none re-make this sun and wind; the sky-blue river; the river-blue sky; the yellow meadow, spotted with sacks and sheets of cranberry-gatherers; the red bushes; the iron-gray house, just the color of the granite rocks; the wild orchard?

His observation of nature was exquisite—always the direct, irresistible impression.

> The hawking of the wild geese flying by night; the thin note of the companionable titmouse in the winter day; the fall of swarms of flies in autumn, from combats high in the air, pattering down on the leaves like rain; the angry hiss of the wood-birds; the pine throwing out its pollen for the benefit of the next century (*Literary Ethics*).

I have said there was no familiarity in him, but he was familiar with woodland creatures and sounds. Certainly, too, he was on terms of free association with his books, which were numerous and dear to him; though Mr. Cabot says, doubtless with justice, that his dependence on them was slight and that he was not "intimate" with his authors. They did not feed him but they stimulated; they were not his meat but his wine—he took them in sips. But he needed them and liked them; he had volumes of notes from his reading, and he could not have produced his lectures without them. He liked literature as a thing to refer to, liked the very names of which it is full, and used them, especially in his later writings, for purposes of ornament, to dress the dish, sometimes with an unmeasured profusion. I open *The Conduct of Life* and find a dozen on the page. He mentions more authorities than is the fashion today. He can easily say, of course, that he follows a better one—that of his well-loved .and irrepressibly allusive Montaigne. In his own bookishness there is a certain contradiction, just as there is a latent incompleteness in his whole literary side. Independence, the return to nature, the finding out and doing for oneself, was what he most highly recommended; and yet he is constantly reminding his readers of the conventional signs and consecrations—of what other men have done. This was partly because the independence that he had in his eye was an independence without ill-nature, without rudeness (though he likes that word), and full of gentle amiabilities, curiosities, and tolerances; and partly it is a simple matter of form, a literary expedient, confessing its character—on the part of one who had never really mastered the art of composition—of continuous expression. Charming to many a reader, charming yet ever slightly droll, will remain Emerson's frequent invocation of the "scholar": there is such a friendly vagueness and convenience in it. It is of the scholar that he expects all the heroic and uncomfortable things, the concentrations and relinquishments, that make up the noble life. We fancy this personage looking up from his book and armchair a little ruefully and saying, "Ah, but why *me* always and only? Why so much of me, and is there no one else to share the responsibility?" "Neither years nor books have yet availed to extirpate a prejudice then rooted in me [when as a boy he first saw the graduates of his college assembled at their anniversary] that a scholar is the favorite of heaven and earth, the excellency of his country, the happiest of men." . . .

It has not, however, been the ambition of these remarks to account for everything, and I have arrived at the end without even pointing to the grounds on which Emerson justifies the honors of biography, discussion, and illustration. I have assumed his importance and continuance, and shall probably not be gainsaid by those who read him. Those who do not will hardly rub him out. Such a book as Mr. Cabot's subjects a reputation to a test—leads people to look it over and hold it up to the light, to see whether it is worth keeping in use or even putting away in a cabinet. Such a revision of Emerson has no relegating consequences. The result of it is once more the impression that he serves and will not wear out, and that indeed we cannot afford to drop him. His instrument makes him precious. He did something better than anyone else; he had a particular faculty, which has not been surpassed, for speaking to the soul in a voice of direction and authority. There have been many spiritual voices appealing, consoling, reassuring, exhorting, or even denouncing and terrifying, but none has had just that firmness and just that purity. It penetrates further, it seems to go back to the roots of our feelings, to where conduct and manhood begin; and moreover, to us today, there is something in it that says that it is connected somehow with the virtue of the world, has wrought and achieved, lived in thousands of minds, produced a mass of character and life. And there is this further sign of Emerson's singular power, that he is a striking exception to the general rule that writings live in the last resort by their form; that they owe a large part of their fortune to the art with which they have been composed. It is hardly too much, or too little, to say of Emerson's writings in general that they were not composed at all. Many and many things are beautifully said; he had felicities, inspirations, unforgettable phrases; he had frequently an exquisite eloquence.

> O my friends, there are resources in us on which we have not yet drawn. There are men who rise refreshed on hearing a threat; men to whom a crisis which intimidates and paralyzes the majority—demanding not the faculties of prudence and thrift, but comprehension, immovableness, the readiness of sacrifice, come graceful and beloved as a bride. . . . But these are heights that we can scarce look up to and remember without contrition and shame. Let us thank God that such things exist.

None the less we have the impression that that search for fashion and a manner on which he was always engaged never really came to a conclusion; it draws itself out through his later writings— it drew itself out through his later lectures, like a sort of renunciation of success. It is not on these, however, but on their predecessors, that his reputation will rest. Of course the way he spoke was the way that was on the whole most convenient to him; but he differs from most men of letters of the same degree of credit in failing to strike us as having achieved a style. This achievement is, as I say, usually the bribe or toll money on the journey to posterity; and if Emerson goes his way, as he clearly appears to be doing, on the strength of his message alone, the case will be rare, the exception striking and the honor great.

JOHN JAY CHAPMAN (1862–1933) was an American essayist, poet, and politician. His first book was *Emerson and Other Essays* (1898). He published in all twenty-five volumes of plays, translations, poems, essays, pamphlets, lectures, and a biography of William Lloyd Garrison. He was a friend of William James. In his lifetime his work had a limited appeal because of the diversity of his subjects, his often fragmentary treatment, and the expression of some extreme and even offensive views. His long monographic essay on Emerson has, however, found a permanent place in critical literature.

Emerson

J O H N   J A Y   C H A P M A N

It is unnecessary to go, one by one, through the familiar essays and lectures which Emerson published between 1838 and 1875. They are in everybody's hands and in everybody's thoughts. In 1840 he wrote in his diary:

> In all my lectures I have taught one doctrine, namely, the infinitude of the private man. This the people accept readily enough, and even with commendation, as long as I call the lecture Art or Politics, or Literature or the Household; but the moment I call it Religion they are shocked, though it be only the application of the same truth which they receive elsewhere to a new class of facts.

To the platform he returned, and left it only once or twice during the remainder of his life.

His writings vary in coherence. In his early occasional pieces, like the Phi Beta Kappa address, coherence is at a maximum. They were written for a purpose, and were perhaps struck off all at once. But he earned his living by lecturing, and a lecturer is always recasting his work and using it in different forms. A lecturer has no prejudice against repetition. It is noticeable that in some of Emerson's important lectures the logical scheme is more perfect than in his essays. The truth seems to be that in the process of working up and perfecting his writings, in revising and filing his sentences, the logical scheme became more and more obliterated. Another circumstance helped make his style fragmentary. He was by nature a man of inspirations and exalted moods. He was subject to ecstasies, during which his mind worked with phenomenal brilliancy. Throughout his works and in his diary we find constant reference to these moods, and to his own inability to control or recover them. "But what we want is consecutiveness. 'Tis with us a flash of light, then a long darkness, then a flash again. Ah! could we turn these fugitive sparkles into an astronomy of Copernican worlds!"

In order to take advantage of these periods of divination, he used to write down the thoughts that came to him at such times. From boyhood onward he kept journals and commonplace books, and in the course of his reading and meditation he collected innumerable notes and quotations which he indexed for ready use. In these mines he "quarried," as Mr. Cabot says, for his lectures and essays. When he needed a lecture he went to the repository, threw together what seemed to have a bearing on some subject, and gave it a title. If any other man should adopt this method of composition, the result would be incomprehensible chaos; because most men have many interests, many moods, many and conflicting ideas. But with Emerson it was otherwise. There was only one thought which could set him aflame, and that was the thought of the unfathomed might of man. This thought was his religion, his politics, his ethics, his philosophy. One moment of inspiration was in him own brother to the next moment of inspiration, although they might be separated by six weeks. When he came to put together his star-born ideas, they fitted well, no matter in what order he placed them, because they were all part of the same idea.

His works are all one single attack on the vice of the age, moral cowardice. He assails it not by railings and scorn, but by positive and stimulating suggestion. The imagination of the reader is touched by every device which can awake the admiration for heroism, the consciousness of moral courage. Wit, quotation, anecdote, eloquence, exhortation, rhetoric, sarcasm, and very rarely denunciation, are launched at the reader, till he feels little lambent flames beginning to kindle in him. He is perhaps unable to see the exact logical connection between two paragraphs of an essay, yet he feels they are germane. He takes up Emerson tired and apathetic, but presently he feels himself growing heady and truculent, strengthened in his most inward vitality, surprised to find himself again master in his own house.

The difference between Emerson and the other moralists is that all these stimulating pictures and suggestions are not given by him in illustration of a general proposition. They have never been through the mill of generalization in his own mind. He himself could not have told you their logical bearing on one another. They have all the vividness of disconnected fragments of life, and yet they all throw light on one another, like the facets of a jewel. But whatever cause it was that led him to adopt his method of writing, it is certain that he succeeded in delivering himself of his thought with an initial velocity and carrying power such as few men ever attained. He has the force at his command of the thrower of the discus.

His style is American, and beats with the pulse of the climate. He is the only writer we have had who writes as he speaks, who makes no literary parade, has no pretensions of any sort. He is the only writer we have had who has wholly subdued his vehicle to his temperament. It is impossible to name his style without naming his character: they are one thing.

Both in language and in elocution Emerson was a practiced and consummate artist, who knew how both to command his effects and to conceal his means. The casual, practical, disarming directness with which he writes puts any honest man at his mercy. What difference does it make whether a man who can talk like this is following an argument or not? You cannot always see Emerson clearly; he is hidden by a high wall; but you always know exactly on what spot he is standing. You judge it by the flight of the objects he throws over the wall—a bootjack, an apple, a crown, a razor, a volume of verse. With one or other of these missiles, all delivered with a very tolerable aim, he is pretty sure to hit you. These catchwords stick in the mind. People are not in general influenced by long books or discourses, but by odd fragments of observation which they overhear, sentences or headlines which they read while turning over a book at random or while waiting for dinner to be announced. These are the oracles and orphic words that get lodged in the mind and bend a man's most stubborn will. Emerson called them the Police of the Universe. His works are a treasury of such things. They sparkle in the mine, or you may carry them off in your pocket. They get driven into your mind like nails, and on them catch and hang your own experiences, till what was once his thought has become your character.

"God offers to every mind its choice between truth and repose. Take which you please; you can never have both." "Discontent is want of self-reliance; it is infirmity of will." "It is impossible for a man to be cheated by anyone but himself."

The orchestration with which Emerson introduces and sustains these notes from the spheres is as remarkable as the winged things themselves. Open his works at a hazard. You hear a man talking.

A garden is like those pernicious machineries we read of every month in the newspapers, which catch a man's coat-skirt or his hand, and draw in his arm, his leg, and his whole body to irresistible destruction. In an evil hour he pulled down his wall and added a field to his homestead. No land is bad, but land is worse. If a man own land, the land owns him. Now let him leave home if he dare. Every tree and graft, every hill of melons, row of corn, or quickset hedge, all he has done and all he means to do, stand in his way like duns, when he would go out of his gate.

Your attention is arrested by the reality of this gentleman in his garden, by the firsthand quality of his mind. It matters not on what subject he talks. While you are musing, still pleased and patronizing, he has picked up the bow of Ulysses, bent it with the ease of Ulysses, and sent a shaft clear through the twelve axes, nor missed one of them. But this, it seems, was mere byplay and marksmanship; for before you have done wondering, Ulysses rises to his feet in anger, and pours flight after flight, arrow after arrow, from the great bow. The shafts sing and strike, the suitors fall in heaps. The brow of Ulysses shines with unearthly splendor. The air is filled with lightning. After a little, without shock or transition, without apparent change of tone, Mr. Emerson is offering you a biscuit before you leave, and bidding you mind the last step at the garden end. If the man who can do these things be not an artist, then must we have a new vocabulary and rename the professions.

There is, in all this effectiveness of Emerson, no pose, no literary art; nothing that corresponds even remotely to the pretended modesty and ignorance with which Socrates lays pitfalls for our admiration in Plato's dialogues.

It was the platform which determined Emerson's style. He was not a writer, but a speaker. On the platform his manner of speech was a living part of his words. The pauses and hesitation, the abstraction, the searching, the balancing, the turning forward and back of the leaves of his lecture, and then the discovery, the illumination, the gleam of lightning which you saw before your eyes descend into a man of genius,—all this was Emerson. He invented this style of speaking, and made it express the supersensuous, the incommunicable. Lowell wrote, while still under the spell of the magician:

> Emerson's oration was more disjointed than usual, even with him. It began nowhere, and ended everywhere, and yet, as always with that divine man, it left you feeling that something beautiful had passed that way, something more beautiful than anything else, like the rising and setting of stars. Every possible

criticism might have been made on it but one—that it was not noble. There was a tone in it that awakened all elevating associations. He boggled, he lost his place, he had to put on his glasses; but it was as if a creature from some fairer world had lost his way in our fogs, and it was *our* fault, not his. It was chaotic, but it was all such stuff as stars are made of, and you couldn't help feeling that, if you waited awhile, all that was nebulous would be whirled into planets, and would assume the mathematical gravity of system. All through it I felt something in me that cried, "Ha! ha!" to the sound of the trumpets.

It is nothing for any man sitting in his chair to be overcome with the sense of the immediacy of life, to feel the spur of courage, the victory of good over evil, the value, now and forever, of all great-hearted endeavor. Such moments come to us all. But for a man to sit in his chair and write what shall call up these forces in the bosoms of others—that is desert, that is greatness. To do this was the gift of Emerson. The whole earth is enriched by every moment of converse with him. The shows and shams of life become transparent, the lost kingdoms are brought back, the shutters of the spirit are opened, and provinces and realms of our own existence lie gleaming before us.

It has been necessary to reduce the living soul of Emerson to mere dead attributes like "moral courage" in order that we might talk about him at all. His effectiveness comes from his character; not from his philosophy, nor from his rhetoric nor his wit, nor from any of the accidents of his education. He might never have heard of Berkeley or Plato. A slightly different education might have led him to throw his teaching into the form of historical essays or of stump speeches. He might, perhaps, have been bred a stone-mason, and have done his work in the world by traveling with a panorama. But he would always have been Emerson. His weight and his power would always have been the same. It is solely as character that he is important. He discovered nothing; he bears no relation whatever to the history of philosophy. We must regard him and deal with him simply as a man.

Strangely enough, the world has always insisted upon accepting him as a thinker: and hence a great coil of misunderstanding. As a thinker, Emerson is difficult to classify. Before you begin to assign him a place, you must clear the ground by a disquisition as to what is meant by "a thinker," and how Emerson differs from other thinkers. As a man, Emerson is as plain as Ben Franklin.

People have accused him of inconsistency; they say that he teaches one thing one day, and another the next day. But from the point of view of Emerson there is no such thing as inconsistency. Every man is each day a new man. Let him be today what he is today. It is immaterial and waste of time to consider what he once was or what he may be.

His picturesque speech delights in fact and anecdote and a public which is used to treatises and deduction cares always to be told the moral. It wants everything reduced to a generalization. All generalizations are partial truths, but we are used to them, and we ourselves mentally make the proper allowance. Emerson's method is, not to give a generalization and trust to our making the allowance, but to give two conflicting statements and leave the balance of truth to be struck in our own minds on the facts. There is no inconsistency in this. It is a vivid and very legitimate method of procedure. But he is much more than a theorist: he is a practitioner. He does not merely state a theory of agitation: he proceeds to agitate. "Do not," he says, "set the least value on what I do, or the least discredit on what I do not, as if I pretended to settle anything as false or true. I unsettle all things. No facts are to me sacred, none are profane. I simply experiment, an endless seeker with no past at my back." He was not engaged in teaching many things, but one thing,—Courage. Sometimes he inspires it by pointing to great characters,—Fox, Milton, Alcibiades; sometimes he inspires it by bidding us beware of imitating such men, and, in the ardor of his rhetoric, even seems to regard them as hindrances and dangers to our development. There is no inconsistency here. Emerson might logically have gone one step further and raised inconsistency into a jewel. For what is so useful, so educational, so inspiring, to a timid and conservative man, as to do something inconsistent and regrettable? It lends character to him at once. He breathes freer and is stronger for the experience.

Emerson is no cosmopolitan. He is a patriot. He is not like Goethe, whose sympathies did not run on national lines. Emerson has America in his mind's eye all the time. There is to be a new religion, and it is to come from America; a new and better type of man, and he is to be an American. He not only cared little or nothing for Europe, but he cared not much for the world at large. His thought was for the future of this country. You cannot get into any chamber in his mind which is below this chamber of patriotism. He loves the valor of Alexander and the grace of the Oxford athlete; but he loves them not for themselves. He has a use for them. They are grist to his mill and powder to his gun. His admiration of them he subordinates to his main purpose,—they are his blackboard and diagrams. His patriotism is the backbone of his significance. He came to his countrymen at a time when they lacked, not thoughts, but manliness. The needs of his own particular public are always before him. . . .

No convulsion could shake Emerson or make his view unsteady even for an instant. What no one else saw, he saw, and he saw nothing else. Not a boy in the land welcomed the outbreak of the war so fiercely as did this shy village philosopher, then at the age of fifty-eight. He saw that war was the cure for cowardice, moral as well as physical. It was not the cause of the slave that moved him; it was not the cause of the Union for which he cared a farthing. It was something deeper than either of these things for which he had been battling all his life. It was the cause of character against convention. Whatever else the war might bring, it was sure to bring in character, to leave behind it a file of heroes; if not heroes, then villains, but in any case strong men. On the ninth of April 1861, three days before Fort Sumter was bombarded, he had spoken with equanimity of "the downfall of our character-destroying civilization. . . . We find that civilization crowed too soon, that our triumphs were treacheries; we had opened the wrong door and let the enemy into the castle."

"Ah," he said, when the firing began, "sometimes gunpowder smells good." Soon after the attack on Sumter he said in a public address, "We have been very homeless for some years past, say since 1850; but now we have a country again. . . . The war was an eye opener, and showed men of all parties and opinions the value of those primary forces that lie beneath all political action." And it was almost a personal pledge when he said at the Harvard Commemoration in 1865, "We shall not again disparage America, now that we have seen what men it will bear."

The place which Emerson forever occupies as a great critic is defined by the same sharp outlines that mark his work, in whatever light and from whatever side we approach it. A critic in the modern sense he was not, for his point of view is fixed, and he reviews the world like a searchlight placed on the top of a tall tower. He lived too early and at too great a distance from the forum of European thought to absorb the ideas of evolution and give place to them in his philosophy. Evolution does not graft well upon the Platonic Idealism, nor are physiology and the kindred sciences sympathetic. Nothing aroused Emerson's indignation more than the attempts of the medical faculty and of phrenologists to classify, and therefore limit individuals. "The grossest ignorance does not disgust me like this ignorant knowingness."

We miss in Emerson the underlying conception of growth, of development, so characteristic of the thought of our own day, and which, for instance, is found everywhere latent in Browning's poetry. Browning regards character as the result of experience and as an ever-changing growth. To Emerson, character is rather an entity complete and eternal from the beginning. He is probably the last great writer to look at life from a stationary standpoint. There is a certain lack of the historic sense in all he has written. The ethical assumption that all men are exactly alike permeates his work. In his mind, Socrates, Marco Polo, and General Jackson stand surrounded by the same atmosphere, or rather stand as mere naked characters surrounded by no atmosphere at all. He is probably the last great writer who will fling about classic anecdotes as if they were club gossip. In the discussion of morals, this assumption does little harm. The stories and proverbs which illustrate the thought of the moralist generally concern only those simple relations of life which are common to all ages. There is charm in this familiar dealing with antiquity. The classics are thus domesticated and made real to us. What matter if Æsop appear a little too much like an American citizen, so long as his points tell?

It is in Emerson's treatment of the fine arts that we begin to notice his want of historic sense. Art endeavors to express subtle and ever-changing feelings by means of conventions which are as protean as the forms of a cloud; and the man who in speaking on the plastic arts makes the assumption that all men are alike will reveal before he has uttered three sentences that he does not know what art is, that he has never experienced any form of sensation from it. Emerson lived in a time and clime where there was no plastic art, and he was obliged to arrive at his ideas about art by means of a highly complex process of reasoning. He dwelt constantly in a spiritual place which was the very focus of high moral fervor. This was his enthusiasm, this was his revelation, and from it he reasoned out the probable meaning of the fine arts. "This," thought Emerson, his eye rolling in a fine frenzy of moral feeling, "this must be what Apelles experienced, this fervor is the passion of Bramante. I understand the Parthenon." And so he projected his feelings about morality into the field of the plastic arts. He deals very freely and rather indiscriminately with the names of artists—Phidias, Raphael, Salvator Rosa—

and he speaks always in such a way that it is impossible to connect what he says with any impression we have ever received from the works of those masters.

In fact, Emerson has never in his life felt the normal appeal of any painting, or any sculpture, or any architecture, or any music. These things, of which he does not know the meaning in real life, he yet uses, and uses constantly, as symbols to convey ethical truths. The result is that his books are full of blind places, like the notes which will not strike on a sick piano.

It is interesting to find that the one art of which Emerson did have a direct understanding, the art of poetry, gave him some insight into the relation of the artist to his vehicle. In his essay on Shakespeare there is a full recognition of the debt of Shakespeare to his times. This essay is filled with the historic sense. We ought not to accuse Emerson because he lacked appreciation of the fine arts, but rather admire the truly Goethean spirit in which he insisted upon the reality of arts of which he had no understanding. This is the same spirit which led him to insist on the value of the Eastern poets. Perhaps there exist a few scholars who can tell us how far Emerson understood or misunderstood Saadi and Firdusi and the Koran. But we need not be disturbed for his learning. It is enough that he makes us recognize that these men were men, too, and that their writings mean something not unknowable to us. The East added nothing to Emerson, but gave him a few trappings of speech. The whole of his mysticism is to be found in *Nature,* written before he knew the sages of the Orient, and it is not improbable that there is some real connection between his own mysticism and the mysticism of the Eastern poets.

Emerson's criticism on men and books is like the test of a great chemist who seeks one or two elements. He burns a bit of the stuff in his incandescent light, shows the lines of it in his spectrum, and there an end.

It was a thought of genius that led him to write *Representative Men.* The scheme of this book gave play to every illumination of his mind, and it pinned him down to the objective, to the field of vision under his microscope. The table of contents of *Representative Men* is the dial of his education. It is as follows: Uses of Great Men; Plato, or The Philosopher; Plato, New Readings; Swedenborg, or The Mystic; Montaigne, or The Skeptic; Shakespeare, or The Poet; Napoleon, or The Man of the World; Goethe, or The Writer. The predominance of the writers over all other types of men is not cited to show Emerson's interest in The Writer, for we know his interest centered in the practical man,—even his ideal scholar is a practical man,—but to show the sources of his illustration. Emerson's library was the old-fashioned gentleman's library. His mines of thought were the world's classics. This is one reason why he so quickly gained an international currency. His very subjects in *Representative Men* are of universal interest, and he is limited only by certain inevitable local conditions. *Representative Men* is thought by many persons to be his best book. It is certainly filled with the strokes of a master. There exists no more profound criticism than Emerson's analysis of Goethe and of Napoleon, by both of whom he was at once fascinated and repelled. . . .

Emerson was in no way responsible for the movement, although he got the credit of having evoked it by his teaching. He was elder brother to it, and was generated by its parental forces; but even if Emerson had never lived, the Transcendentalists would have appeared. He was their victim rather than their cause. He was always tolerant of them and sometimes amused at them, and disposed to treat them lightly. . . .

Emerson was divided from the Transcendentalists by his common sense. His shrewd business intellect made short work of their schemes. Each one of their social projects contained some covert economic weakness, which always turned out to lie in an attack upon the integrity of the individual, and which Emerson of all men could be counted on to detect. He was divided from them also by the fact that he was a man of genius, who had sought out and fought out his means of expression. He was a great artist, and as such he was a complete being. No one could give to him nor take from him. His yearnings found fruition in expression. He was sure of his place and of his use in this world. But the Transcendentalists were neither geniuses nor artists nor complete beings. Nor had they found their places or uses as yet. They were men and women seeking light. They walked in dry places, seeking rest and finding none. The Transcendentalists are not collectively important because their *Sturm und Drang* was intellectual and bloodless. Though Emerson admonish and Harriet Martineau condemn, yet from the memorials that survive, one is more impressed with the sufferings than with the ludicrousness of these persons. There is something distressing about their letters, their talk, their memoirs, their interminable diaries. They worry and contort and introspect. They rave and dream. They peep and theorize. They cut open the bellows of life to see where the wind comes from. Margaret Fuller analyzes Emerson, and Emerson Margaret Fuller. It is not a wholesome ebullition of vitality. It is a nightmare, in which the emotions, the terror, the agony, the rapture, are all unreal, and have no vital content, no consequence in the world outside. It is positively wonderful that so much excitement and so much suffering should have left behind nothing in the field of art which is valuable. All that intelligence could do toward solving problems for his friends Emerson did. But there are situations in life in which the intelligence is helpless, and in which something else, something perhaps possessed by a plowboy, is more divine than Plato. . . .

Much of what Emerson wrote about the United States in 1850 is true of the United States today. It would be hard to find a civilized people who are more timid, more cowed in spirit, more illiberal, than we. It is easy today for the educated man who has read Bryce and Tocqueville to account for the mediocrity of American literature. The merit of Emerson was that he felt the atmospheric pressure without knowing its reason. He felt he was a cabined, cribbed, confined creature, although every man about him was celebrating Liberty and Democracy, and every day was Fourth of July. He taxes language to its limits in order to express his revolt. He says that no man should write except what he has discovered in the process of satisfying his own curiosity, and that every man will write well in proportion as he has contempt for the public.

Emerson seems really to have believed that if any man would only resolutely be himself, he would turn out to be as great as Shakespeare. He will not have it that anything of value can be monopolized. His review of the world, whether under the title of Manners, Self-Reliance, Fate, Experience, or what-not, leads him to the same thought. His conclusion is always the finding of eloquence, courage, art, intellect, in the breast of the humblest reader. He knows that we are full of genius and surrounded by genius, and that we have only to throw something off, not to acquire any new thing, in order to be bards, prophets, Napoleons, and Goethes. This belief is the secret of his stimulating power. It is this which gives his writings a radiance like that which shone from his personality. . . .

Emerson himself was the only man of his times who consistently and utterly expressed himself, never measuring himself for a moment with the ideals of others, never troubling himself for a moment with what literature was or how literature should be created. The other men of his epoch, and among whom he lived, believed that literature was a very desirable article, a thing you could create if you were only smart enough. But Emerson had no literary ambition. He cared nothing for belles-lettres. The consequence is that he stands above his age like a colossus. While he lived his figure could be seen from Europe towering like Atlas over the culture of the United States.

Great men are not always like wax which their age imprints. They are often the mere negation and opposite of their age. They give it the lie. They become by revolt the very essence of all the age is not, and that part of the spirit which is suppressed in ten thousand breasts gets lodged, isolated, and breaks into utterance in one. Through Emerson spoke the fractional spirits of a multitude. He had not time, he had not energy left over to understand himself; he was a mouthpiece.

If a soul be taken and crushed by democracy till it utter a cry, that cry will be Emerson. The region of thought he lived in, the figures of speech he uses, are of an intellectual plane so high that the circumstances which produced them may be forgotten; they are indifferent. The Constitution, Slavery, the War itself, are seen as mere circumstances. They did not confuse him while he lived; they are not necessary to support his work now that it is finished. Hence comes it that Emerson is one of the world's voices. He was heard afar off. His foreign influence might deserve a chapter by itself. Conservatism is not confined to this country. It is the very basis of all government. The bolts Emerson forged, his thought, his wit, his perception, are not provincial. They were found to carry inspiration to England and Germany. Many of the important men of the last half century owe him a debt. It is not yet possible to give any account of his influence abroad, because the memoirs which will show it are only beginning to be published. We shall have them in due time; for Emerson was an outcome of the world's progress. His appearance marks the turning-point in the history of that enthusiasm for pure democracy which has tinged the political thought of the world for the past one hundred and fifty years. The youths of England and Germany may have been surprised at hearing from America a piercing voice of protest against the very influences which were crushing them at home. They could not realize that the chief difference between Europe and America is a difference in the rate of speed with which revolutions in thought are worked out.

While the radicals of Europe were revolting in 1848 against the abuses of a tyranny whose roots were in feudalism, Emerson, the great radical of America, the arch-radical of the world, was revolting against the evils whose roots were in universal suffrage. By showing the identity in essence of all tyranny, and by bringing back the attention of political thinkers to its starting-point, the value of human character, he has advanced the political thought of the world by one step. He has pointed out for us in this country to what ends our efforts must be bent.

BARRETT WENDELL (1855–1921) was one of Harvard's most revered teachers. In 1898 he became the first professor at Harvard College to offer American literature as a subject of academic study. Later he moved into the field of comparative literature. His essay on Emerson is from his book *A Literary History of America* (1900).

Ralph Waldo Emerson

BARRETT WENDELL

Emerson's work is so individual that you can probably get no true impression of it without reading deeply for yourself. To many this may be irksome. Like all powerful individualities, his can hardly leave a reader indifferent; you will be either attracted or repelled, and if repelled, the repulsion will very likely make the reading demand a strenuous act of will. But any student of American letters must force himself to the task; for Emerson, thinking, talking, writing, lecturing from that Concord where he lived during the greater part of his life, produced, in less than half a century, work which as time goes on and as the things which other men were making begin to fade, seems more and more sure of survival. America produced him; and whether you like him or not, he is bound to live.

As one grows familiar with his work, its most characteristic trait begins to seem one which in a certain sense is not individual at all, but rather is common to all phases of lasting literature.

Classical immortality, of course, is demonstrable only by the lapse of cumulating ages. One thing, however, seems sure: in all acknowledged classics,—in the great works of antique literature, sacred and profane alike, and, to go no further, in the great poetry of Dante or of Shakespere,—there proves to reside a vitality which as the centuries pass shows itself less and less conditioned by the human circumstances of the writers. No literary expression was ever quite free from historical environment. Homer—one poet or many—belongs to the heroic age of Greece; Virgil, or Horace, to Augustan Rome; Dante to the Italy of Guelphs and Ghibellines; Shakespere to Elizabethan England. But take at random any page from any of these, and you will find something so broadly, pervasively, lastingly human, that generation after generation will read it on with no sense of the changing epochs which have passed since the man who spoke this word and the men for whom it was spoken have rested in immortal slumber. In the work of Emerson, whatever its final value, there is something of this note. Every other writer at whom we have glanced, and almost every other at whom we shall glance hereafter, demands for understanding that we revive our sympathy with the fading or faded conditions which surrounded his conscious life. At best these other works, vitally contemporaneous in their own days, grow more and more old-fashioned. Emerson, on the other hand, from beginning to end, seems constantly modern, with a contemporaneousness almost as perennial as that of Scripture itself. Though his work may lack something of true greatness, it surely seems alive with such unconditioned freedom of temper as makes great literature so inevitably lasting. . . . In essence throughout, Emerson's work bids fair to disregard the passing of time; its spirit seems little more conditioned by the circumstances of nineteenth-century Concord or Boston than Homer's was by the old Ægean breezes.

In form, on the other hand, Emerson's work seems almost as certainly local. Broadly speaking, it falls into two classes,—essays and poems. The essays are generally composed of materials which he collected for purposes of lecturing. His astonishing lack of method is familiar; he would constantly make note of any idea which occurred to him; and when he wished to give a lecture, he would huddle together as many of these notes as should fill the assigned time, trusting with all the calm assurance of his unfaltering individualism that the truth inherent in the separate memoranda would give them all together the unity implied in the fact of their common sincerity. But though this bewildering lack of system for a moment disguise the true character of his essays, the fact that these essays were so often delivered as lectures should remind us of what they really are. The Yankee lecturers, of whom Emerson was the most eminent, were only half-secularised preachers,—men who stood up and talked to ancestrally attentive audiences. And these eager hearers were disposed at once to respect the authority of their teachers, to be on the look-out for error, and to go home with a sense of edification. Emerson's essays, in short, prove to be an obvious development from the endless sermons with which for generations his ancestors had regaled the New England fathers. In much the same way, Emerson's poems, for all their erratic oddity of form, prove on consideration to possess many qualities of temper for which an orthodox mind would have sought expression in hymns. They are designed not so much to set forth human emotion or to give æsthetic delight as to stimulate moral or spiritual ardour. For all his individualism, Emerson could not help being a good old inbred Yankee preacher. . . .

Idealism, of course, is ancestrally familiar to any race of Puritan origin. That life is a fleeting manifestation of unfathomable realities which lie beyond it, that all we see and all we do and all we know are merely symbols of things unseen, unactable, unknowable, had been preached to New England from the beginning. But Emerson's idealism soared far above that of the Christian fathers. Their effort was constantly to reduce unseen eternities to a system as rigid as that which addressed their human senses; and this effort has so far succeeded that to-day those who call God by His name thereby almost clothe Him in flesh and blood, in Jove-like beard and flowing robes, turning Him once more, even though immortally, into a fresh symbol of the infinite divine self which essentially transcends all limitation. To Emerson, on the other hand, the name of God, like the life of Christ, grouped itself with the little facts of every-day existence as simply one more phenomenal symbol of unspeakable, unfathomable, transcendental truth. There is for ever something beyond; you may call it God, you may call it Nature, you may call it Over-Soul; each name becomes a fresh limitation, a mere symbolic bit of this human language of ours. The essential thing is not what you call the everlasting eternities; it is that you shall never cease, simply and reverently, with constantly living interest, to recognise and to adore them.

Now, in contrast with this infinite eternity of divine truth, no man, not even Christ himself, is free from the almost equally infinite limitations of earthly life. The essence of truth is that it comprehends and comprises all things, phenomena and ideals alike; and we men, great or small, ourselves on any eternal scale little more wonderful than are the leaves of grass which spring and wither in the field, can perceive at any moment only one aspect of this truth. Look at the moon; when it is full you shall see it as a silvery disk in the heavens; again it is shrunk to a sickle; and yet again you shall see no moon at all. By and by you learn a little of the secret law which reveals the same satellite first in one of its protean forms and then in another throughout the changing months of our fleeting human years. Gaze next into the infinities, whereof the system is so unspeakably further from simplicity than the motions of any moon or planets. At one moment you shall see them in one aspect, at the next in another, and so on till life and eternity shall merge. Nay, you shall have less true knowledge of them than if for a little while one should revisit the glimpses of the moon, and, seeing only a curved line dimly gleaming in sunset skies, should return to the shades with news that there is no moon left but a sinking new one.

Would you strive to reconcile one with another the glories of eternity? strive, with your petty human powers, to prove them consistent things?— . . .

In Emerson's calm impatience of philosophic system there is a fresh touch of that unhesitating assurance with which he brushed aside the most sacred of Christian institutions, when for a moment it threatened to limit him. "See," he seems to bid you, "and report what you see as truly as language will let you. Then concern yourself no more as to what men shall say of your seeing or of your saying." For even though what you perceive be a gleam of absolute truth, the moment you strive to focus its radiance in the little terms of human language, you must limit the diffusive energy which makes it radiant. So even though your gleams be in themselves consistent one with another, your poor little vehicle of words, conventional and faint symbols with which mankind has learned to blunder, must perforce dim each gleam by a limitation itself irreconcilable with truth. Language at best was made to phrase what the cant of our passingly fashionable philosophy has called the knowable, and what interested Emerson surged infinitely throughout the unknowable realms.

Take that famous passage from his essay in "Society and Solitude," on "Civilisation":—

> "'It was a great instruction,' said a saint in Cromwell's war, 'that the best courages are but beams of the Almighty.' Hitch your wagon to a star. Let us not fag in paltry works which serve our pot and bag alone. Let us not lie and steal. No god will help. We shall find all their teams going the other way,—Charles's Wain, Great Bear, Orion, Leo, Hercules; every god will leave us. Work rather for those interests which the divinities honor and promote,—justice, love, freedom, knowledge, utility."

In one sense this seems hodge-podge; in another, for all its lack of lyric melody, it seems an almost lyric utterance of something which all men may know and which no man may define. "Hitch your waggon to a star" has flashed into the idiom of our speech; but if you try to translate it into visual terms you must find it a mad metaphor. The waggon is no real rattling vehicle of the Yankee country, squalid in its dingy blue; nor is the star any such as ever twinkled through the clear New England nights. No chain ever forged could reach far on the way from a Concord barn to Orion. Yet behind the homely, incomplete symbol there is a thought, an emotion, flashing swifter than ever ray of starry light, and so binding together the smallest things and the greatest which lie within our human ken that for an instant we may feel them both alike in magnitude, each alike mere symbols of illimitable truth beyond, and both together significant only because for an instant we have snatched them together, almost at random, from immeasurable eternity.

For phenomena, after all, are only symbols of the eternities, and words at their best are trivial, fleeting, conventional symbols of little nobler than these mere phenomena themselves:—

> "Good as is discourse, silence is better, and shames it. The length of the discourse indicates the distance of thought betwixt the speaker and the hearer. If they were at a perfect understanding in any part, no words would be necessary thereon. If at one in all parts, no words would be suffered."

So in a way of his own Emerson disdained words. This peculiarity appears perhaps most clearly when he is avowedly dealing with matters of fact. In 1856 he published a book named "English Traits," in which he recorded the impressions made on him by two visits to England, some fifteen years apart. His subject here is what he had observed as a traveller; his treatment of it falls into unsystematic notes, each phrased in terms of unqualified assertion. As you read, you find few statements which do not seem full of shrewd, suggestive truth:—

> "Man in England," he says, for example, "submits to be a product of political economy. On a bleak moor a mill is built, a banking house is opened, and men come in as water in a sluiceway, and towns and cities rise. Man is made as a Birmingham button. The doubling of the population dates from Watt's steam-engine. A landlord who owns a province, says, 'The tenantry are unprofitable; let me have sheep.' He unroofs the houses and ships the population to America."

Again, a little later we read:—

> "There is an English hero superior to the French, the German, the Italian, or the Greek. When he is brought to the strife with fate, he sacrifices a richer material possession and on more purely metaphysical grounds. He is there with his own consent, face to face with fortune, which he defies. On deliberate choice and from grounds of character, he has elected his part to live and die for, and dies with grandeur."

Each of these statements seems true, and they are not really incompatible; but each needs the other to qualify the impression of universality which Emerson somehow conveys with every sentence. Qualification he rarely stoops to. All he says is true, all incomplete, all suggestive, all traceable to the actual facts of that complex England which gave rise to all. And just as Emerson writes about England, with its wealth and its manufactures, its aristocracy and its cockneys, its "Times" and its trade and its Stonehenge, so he writes elsewhere of God, of the eternities, of Concord farmers, of the Over-Soul, of whatever else passes before his untiring earthly vision.

A dangerous feat, this. Any one may attempt it, but most of us would surely fail, uttering mere jargon wherein others could discern little beyond our several limitations. As we contemplate Emerson, then, our own several infirmities slowly reveal to us more and more clearly how true a seer he was. With more strenuous vision than is granted to common men, he really perceived in the eternities those living facts and lasting thoughts which, with all the careless serenity of his intellectual insolence, he rarely troubled himself intelligibly to phrase.

Sometimes these perceptions fairly fell within the range of language; and of language at such moments Emerson had wonderful mastery. Open his essays at random. . . . Emerson was face to face with perceptions for which language was never framed; and then comes his half-inspired jargon. Yet, through it all, you grow more and more to feel that with true creative energy he was always striving to make verbal images of what to him were true perceptions; and more deeply still you grow aware that in his eager contemplation of truth he suffered astonishingly little of himself to intervene between perception and expression. So long as what he said seemed for the moment true, he cared for little else.

Again, one grows to feel more and more in Emerson a trait surprising in any man so saturated with ideal philosophy. As the story of Brook Farm indicated, the Transcendental movement generally expressed itself in ways which, whatever their purity, beauty, or sincerity, had not the grace of common sense. In the slang of our day, the Transcendentalists were cranks. With Emerson the case was different; in the daily conduct of his private life, as well as in the articulate utterances which pervade even his most eccentric writings, you will always find him, despite the vagaries of his ideal philosophy, a shrewd, sensible Yankee, full of a quiet, repressed, but ever present sense of humour which prevented him from overestimating himself, and compelled him when dealing with phenomena to recognise their relative practical value. He was aware of the Over-Soul, in whose presence Orion is no better than a team which should plod before a Concord haycart. He was equally aware that a dollar is a dollar, and a cent a cent, and that dollars and cents are convenient things to have in pocket. When you think of him as a lecturer or as a writer of books, then, you find all the old contradiction in a new form. You go to him as a prophet; you find a kindly gentleman with a good-natured smile lurking in the corners of his lips, who seems to tell you: "Dear me, I am no more of a prophet than you are. We are all prophets. If you like, I will look into the eternities with great pleasure, and tell you what I see there; but at the end of the business I shall present you with a little bill. If you will pay it, I shall receipt it, and dine a trifle better in consequence."

He was the prophet of Transcendentalism, if you like; but, after all, his general manner and temper were less prophetic than those of conventional parsons who thunder forth divine authority. He was farther still from the authoritative prophets of antiquity. He did not passionately seek God and phrase his discoveries in the sacred mysteries of dogma. He was rather a canny, honest Yankee gentleman, who mingled with his countrymen, and taught them as well as he could; who felt a kindly humour when other people agreed with him, and troubled himself little when they disagreed; who hitched his waggon to star after star, but never really confused the stars with the waggon.

And so descending to Concord earth, we find in him a trait very characteristic of the period when he happened to live, and one at which he himself would have been the first good-humouredly to smile. He was born just when the Renaissance of New England was at hand, when at last the old tripod of theology, classics, and law was seen not to be the only basis of the human intellect, when all philosophy and letters were finally opening to New England knowledge. With all his contemporaries he revelled in this new world of human record and expression. To the very end he never lost his consequent, exuberantly boyish trick of dragging in allusions to all sorts of personages and matters which he knew only by name. . . .

It is now nearly twenty years since Emerson's life gently faded away, and it is a full sixty since his eager preaching or prophecy of individualistic idealism stirred renascent New England to its depths. We have been trying to guess what Emerson may mean in permanent literature. To understand what he means historically, we must remind ourselves again of the conditions which surrounded his maturity. When he came to the pulpit of the Second Church of Boston, the tyranny of custom, at least in theoretical matters, was little crushed. Heretical though Unitarianism was, it remained in outward form a dominant religion. Statesmanship and scholarship, too, were equally fixed and rigid; and so, to a degree hardly conceivable today, was the structure of society. Even today untrammelled freedom of thought, unrestrained assertion of individual belief, sometimes demands grave self-sacrifice. In Emerson's day it demanded heroic spirit.

To say that Emerson's lifelong heroism won us what moral and intellectual freedom we now possess would be to confuse the man with the movement of which he is the great exemplar. As the years pass, however, we begin to understand that no other American writings record that movement half so vitally as his. As our individual freedom becomes more and more surely established, we may delight in Emerson more or less. According as our individuality responds or not to the idealism which touched him, we may find him repellent or sympathetic; and although it may hardly be asserted, it may fairly be surmised, that even in Emerson's most memorable utterances the future may find no considerable truth not better phrased by others. For in his effort to express truth, just as in his whole knowledge of life, he was limited by the national inexperience which throughout his time still protected New England. Yet whether or no, in generations to come, Emerson shall prove to have made lasting contributions to human wisdom, one thing which will remain true of him should commend him to the regard of all his countrymen who love spiritual freedom. We may not care for the things he said, we may not find sympathetic the temper in which he uttered them, but we cannot deny that when, for two hundred years, intellectual tyranny had kept the native American mind cramped within the limits of tradition, Emerson fearlessly stood forth as the chief representative of that movement which asserted the right of every individual to think, to feel, to speak, to act for himself, confident that so far as each acts in sincerity good shall ensue.

Whoever believes in individualism, then, must always respect in Emerson a living prophet; and, just as surely, those who find prospect of salvation only in obedience to authority must lament the defection from their ranks of a spirit which, whatever its errors, even they must admit to have been brave, honest, serene, and essentially pure with all that purity which is the deepest grace of ancestral New England.

1901-1925

GEORGE EDWARD WOODBERRY (1855–1930), American man of letters and professor of comparative literature at Columbia, was a highly respected and influential teacher. He wrote a biography of Hawthorne (1902), several books of poetry, and books of literary criticism, *America in Literature* (1903) and *Appreciation of Literature* (1907). His biography of Emerson (1907) in the *English Men of Letters* series is still valuable as criticism of high quality. The following is the chapter on Emerson's poetry.

The Poems

GEORGE EDWARD WOODBERRY

Emerson, as has been said, was fundamentally a poet with an imperfect faculty of expression. By no means a perfect master of prose, he was much less a master of the instrument of verse; yet the same qualities appear in his work of both kinds, and as the excellence of his prose lies in the perfect turn of short sentences and in brief passages of eloquence, so the excellence of his verse lies in couplets and quatrains and brief passages of description or feeling. He owes much in both kinds to his quotability, or the power with which his thought in its best and most condensed expression sinks into the mind and haunts the memory. He was indifferent to the technical part of verse, but this was because of an incapacity or lack of gift for it; he was not careless, and his verse was brooded over, turned in his mind and rewrought in his study, and what he published was generally the last and long deferred result of such power of expression as he was capable of; he was inartistic by necessity. He had no constructive, but only an ejaculatory, genius; and all that belongs to construction and depends upon it, such as dramatic power, for example, he was deficient in. His verse on the prosaic level of simple observation is descriptive, and becomes lyrical when melted by tenderness of feeling or set aglow by patriotic fervour or fired and expanded by a philosophical thought. The movement is, on the lowest plane, often Wordsworthian, and in the lesser odes has the fall and terminal slides of the eighteenth century, and at the highest is apt to be of the sort that is best called runic. The technical quality of it is immaterial, and should be neglected and forgotten, so far as possible; its value lies in its original power of genius and owes little to the forms. The matter itself is often dark and even unintelligible without a previous understanding of the thought which is the key to the meaning; and this key must be sought in the *Essays*.

The *Poems* are a more brief and condensed form of the *Essays*, in many respects a far finer form, and for that reason they appeal less broadly to men. The thought gains in brilliancy and external beauty by being given under the forms of imagination; and besides this it is mixed in the poems with Emerson's personality in a more intimate and familiar way, and is blended with his daily life and human concerns. The *Poems* are autobiography in a very strict sense. Here, in verse, Emerson was most free; he did not consult his audience at all, as in prose he was more or less bound to do, and he was really not aware of any audience, but wrote purely to please himself. He was the very type of a private man at heart, and always mixed with the world under protest and by the strict compulsion of life. He would have preferred to remain in his garden and the adjoining fields and woods, to live with nature and to the soul, and let the world go by. He managed his life so as to command much leisure of this sort, to be a vagabond of the day with the plants and birds, the woods and quiet streams, the sky and the distant mountain, and to come home laden with natural thoughts as a bee with honey, or laden only with the peace of his own soul. He spent much time in this loitering and revery and apparent emptiness of mind, happy with the heat and the quiet and the bloom of things, or pleased with the snowy silence under the winter pines; and the *Poems* are the fruit of this long leisure, slowly matured from the spontaneous germs but tended with all a poet's love for his own. As has been noticed he had formed an ideal poet, who stood for this poet in him, another and higher self, and named him Osman, and quoted from him in his prose; but in his verse he was that poet, and gave him other names there; and this self, secret and private and most dear to him, whose life was that of the roamer of nature, is the bard who uses the wind, the pine tree, and Monadnock, snowstorm and seashore, the chemic heat and the solar blaze, as the strings of his lyre.

He was a poet of both the soul and Nature, but in his verse Nature enters more largely and for its own sake. Even in his prose no passages are more felicitous or more sweetly abide in the memory than his incidental description of landscape or the weather. The weather was always interesting to him, and some of his happiest lines contain no more than the qualities of the atmosphere. His senses were deeply engaged with the visible and audible world. He was a minute observer, and loved Nature in detail, one might almost say without selection at all. The "turtle proud with his golden spots" is as dear as a nightingale to him. This gives that homely quality to his local description which is a large part of its power to please and to cling to the mind. In marking the traits of the spring he notices the footprint left in thawing ground and the loosened pebble that "asks of the urchin to be tost"; and in the lament for the death of his little boy he recalls the painted sled, the "ominous hole he dug in the sand," the poultry yard, the shed, the wicker wagon frame that needed mending; by such everyday and prosaic detail he arrives at a truth of rendering that is invaluable to him in describing the New England scene. This quality tells, especially, in all that portion of his verse which is in low relief, and in the simplest and easily intelligible poems such as the fable of the squirrel and the anecdote of the titmouse; and by it he is quite the equal of Whittier for local colour and of Thomson for general truth to the actual features of a near scene. In this sort of description he keeps near the ground and loves veracity and enjoys the thing he sees, and imagination seldom enters to touch or transform the object of sense; but if it does so enter, it appears in an original and surprising way, of which there is no better instance than the following transformation of the phenomenon of the gradual lengthening of the days as spring comes on:—

> "I saw the bud-crowned Spring go forth,
> Stepping daily onward north
> To greet staid ancient cavaliers
> Filing single in stately train.
> And who, and who are the travellers?
> They were Night and Day, and Day and Night,
> Pilgrims wight with step forthright.
> I saw the Days deformed and low,
> Short and bent by cold and snow;
> The merry Spring threw wreaths on them,
> Flower-wreaths gay with bud and bell;
> Many a flower and many a gem,
> They were refreshed by the smell,
> They shook the snow from hats and shoon,
> They put their April raiment on;
> And those eternal forms,
> Unhurt by a thousand storms,
> Shot up to the height of the sky again,
> And danced as merrily as young men."

Imagination with Emerson usually is set in motion by ·some philosophic thought or by the presence of something elemental in the scene. His mind expands with the greatness of what is before him, and reaches a loftier height even when he is still in the region of description, as, for example, in the *Snow Storm,* equally admirable as a picture of human home and of the wild grandeur of Nature; but the best instance of imaginative description on a grand scale is the *Sea Shore*, in which a noble eloquence, which was born in prose and is more often to be found there as it might be in Hooker or More, has taken eagle's wings to itself and soars with swift circles each higher by a flight. It is a sublime passage, and has scriptural quality, and the English poems that can be so described are numbered on the fingers of one hand; it is so biblical that it seems more like prose than verse. To give a loose to his genius in this way Emerson requires the amplest sphere, the scenery of space, and the stage of long-lapsing time. A good example in the purely physical sphere is the image of the earth swimming in space, of which he was fond:—

> "this round, sky-cleaving boat
> Which never strains its rocky beams;
> Whose timbers, as they silent float,
> Alps and Caucasus uprear,
> And the long Alleghanies here,
> And all town-sprinkled lands that be,
> Sailing through stars with all their history."

Nature as an element, however, is more apt to take on the atomic form in this verse and to be chemistry. Emerson always thinks of the process of Nature as a dance of atoms, and he reduces to the same image all her matings and pairings, her correspondences and flow under every aspect, and sees the sphere in all its parts as rhythmical movement, and tune, and rhyme, as if the stars still sang together as at creation and the life of the universe were a Bacchic dance. He conceives the energy of Nature as a Dionysiac force, with overflow and intoxication in it, and his imaginative symbols for it are all of this order. This incorporation of the atomic theory in his thought of the world, and also the large prominence he gives to the idea of evolution in general, and his use of scientific terms of detail, give to his poetry a characteristic tone and colour sympathetic with the age. Science, indeed, may be said to enter into the surfaces and imagery of his poetry as an integral part; few poets have used it so much or so organically in their verse, or so coloured their minds with it; but it is the spectacle and not the reason of science which is thus used. The mazy dance and Bacchanalia of Nature, however, do not yield to the verse such elements of beauty and charm as are found in her ordinary aspect of "the painted vicissitude" of the soul. The scenes of pastoral interwoven in *Wood-Notes* and *May-Day* have both poetical sweetness and the wild flavour of Indian temperament that befits them in fresh American verse still near to the forest primeval. A grave classic beauty belongs to some of the single images flashed suddenly out, such as that supreme one,—

> "O tenderly the haughty day
> Fills his blue urn with fire."

At the other extreme is *Hamatreya,* in which the melancholy of the Earth-might and the shadow of the grave over life is caught in the old race mood of our blood; no poem is more purely Saxon in feeling and in the fall of the short runic lines; they might have been written in the eighth century, so true they ring. Occasionally Nature is used as a pure symbol, of which the happiest instance is *Two Rivers,* admirable for the harmonizing of the unseen river of the eye with the river of the senses, so that the stream of eternity seems but the immortalization of the stream of the meadows, and to flow as it were out of it. The best are those in which the subject is confined to simple Nature and the thought flowing out of it simply, of which the type is *The Rhodora.*

In a second group stand the poems of feeling both personal and patriotic. The first section of these consists of the love poems, simple and sweet and quite natural, such as *To Ellen in the South,* the poems that have for their motive Emerson's personal habits and ways, such as *My Garden, Good-by, The Apology,* with which may be classed also *Terminus,* and lastly the poems of lament for his son and his brothers. These are all plain reading, and in the poems of bereavement there is the greatest intimacy that he ever allowed his readers with his private life. He was fond of children, in a gentle and fatherly way; but the quality of his fondness would not be known without the *Threnody,* in which the home-life of the boy, the child in the house, is so pathetically set forth with sad insistence on little things and the day's common history, while the father's grief and question are so tenderly expressed. In the second part the poem becomes philosophical, and has the interest of showing what comfort Emerson found in his divine theory before the actual presence and under the pressure of the sharpest trial of impersonal religion, and in what spirit he met it and was freed from it. Of the passages that refer to his brothers, *The Dirge* is the poem by which they are remembered, and among English household poems it excels in reality of affection, in domestic beauty, and in simpleness; it has the tones of his voice in it. The patriotic poems have enthusiasm in a high degree and are especially rich in great single lines and apothegms, like nuggets, which have been caught up by the people and will long

be memorable. The dicta belong to the old spirit of the plain democracy of New England, they still feel the ardour of the Revolution,
and most of them fall within the sphere of the rights of man; these
poems, nevertheless, are local rather than national, and are the fruit
of Concord and Boston, whose memories and ideals they apply to
the times and questions of the Civil War. They are entirely intelligible in themselves and require no comment. With them belongs
the hymn which has been adopted into church services and ex-
presses the old New England feeling for the congregational meeting-
house with words in which all, without distinction of sect or creed,
can join.

The philosophical section of Emerson's poems is the larger and
the characteristic part, though it is that which offers the greatest
obstruction to his general acceptance; both the matter and the mode
are too lofty for the ordinary reader, but to him who finds in them
an appeal they yield a nobility and beauty and a certain glory, as
of the largeness and brightness of Nature herself, such as he will
not find elsewhere. The poems which are most exclusively philosophical and bare in sentiment, such as the lines often prefixed to particular essays and designated *Elements,* are the least interesting;
next to these are the poems each of which is devoted to some one
idea of his philosophy such as *Xenophanes, Guy, Astrœa, To Rhea,
Initial, Dœmonic and Celestial Love,* and a few others, which are
intelligible only by the key of the *Essays* and are seldom poetically
successful. The philosophy becomes poetical in proportion as personality and the actual scene of Nature enter into it as imagery
and solving powers, and as the ideas are stated less in an intellectual
and definite, more in a living and suggestive way. The element of
autobiography, especially, adds force and interest. Of the poems
where Emerson is himself most present, the *Ode to Beauty* is among
the first, and best presents him as a lover of beauty with a truth that
makes the phrase apply to him as rightfully as to Keats, however
less rich was his sense of beauty and however poor he was in the
passion for beauty. *Give All to Love* is a companion piece and full
of individuality. The most interesting and characteristic in their
peculiarity are the two in which he elaborates by imagery his doctrine of experience, of the thirst for all natures that he may pass
through them as if in an Indian transmigration, and draw from
Nature the whole of her being and the meaning of all life, becoming
one with the infinite diversity of all,—*Mithridates* and *Bacchus.* The
last is, perhaps, his most original poem, and is a marvellous parable
of the wine of being, equal in universality to the stream of the *Two*

Rivers and far excelling the latter in imaginative grasp and compass; it is distinguished, too, for its enthusiasm, an example of the "mania" that Emerson counselled as the mood of life, and showing an unsuspected power of abandonment in himself.

This doctrine of experience, it should be observed, here definitely includes all sorts of experience, and with it should be joined the idea that evil itself is a discipline in good and can work no final harm,—one of the most difficult of doctrines for Emerson's disciples. This is the "knowledge" of *Uriel*. Uriel was a name for himself, and the fable of the poem refers to the time of his Divinity School Address. The special expression is in the quatrain:—

> "Line in nature is not found;
> Unit and universe are round;
> In vain produced, all rays return;
> Evil will bless, and ice will burn."

It is echoed in *The Park:*—

> "Yet spake yon purple mountain,
> Yet said yon ancient wood,
> That Night or Day, that Love or Crime,
> Leads all souls to the Good."

It rests on the basis of the philosophy of Identity, of which *Bramah* is the poetical text, a poem rightly selected by the popular instinct as the quintessence of Emerson, that which is most peculiarly his own. In that cryptic expression, as in a divine cypher, he has condensed all he knows; the rest of his writings are only its laborious commentary and explanation.

Most personal, too, are the admirable poems on the poet and his art, *Merlin* and *Saadi*, both other names for himself. Such a theory of life as he held more appropriately finds a career in poetical inspiration and enthusiasm than elsewhere, and seems more true there. In both these poems he repeats the counsels of freedom, self-reliance, privacy, spontaneity, joyfulness, surprise, and ease, and the blessedness of poverty, which are found scattered less effectively throughout his works. In one the Saxon strength, in the other the Oriental colour, bring into play the two most effective literary traditions to which he was under obligation, and afford that distance of artistic atmosphere which is so often an element in romantic charm; Hafiz is in his poetry what Plotinus is in his prose, a far horizon line, which helps to give that suggestion of eternity in his thought, of universality in his truth, which characterize his writing. He seems always to use the iron pen. In *Saadi* he wears the Persian poet's guise, and in *Merlin* the old harper's, and imposes the illusion on the mind as when he makes the pine wood and Monadnock speak; and it is always the same voice. He knew as little of Persian as he knew of Buddhism; but his half knowledge gave to literature *Saadi* in one case and *Bramah* in the other, and this is more than the learning of all others has yet accomplished for poetry. In the ideal of the poet here set forth his personal expression of philosophy had its most individual form, was most blended with himself; in two other poems, *The Problem* and *Each and All*, which contain much personality also, the philosophy is rendered in purely poetical ways.

The last group is composed of those poems in which the philosophy is put forth in a universal statement of large comprehension. The leading thought is here of the opposition of Nature and man, of the inadequacy of the creature of the Universe. Nature is represented as the Great Mother and man as her child. The burden of the verse is that man is a weakling. His state is accounted for by his division from Nature. One easily recognizes the doctrine as a phase of the general social theory of the eighteenth century most associated with the name of Rousseau. But to Emerson this is his substitute for sin and the Fall of Man; it is not that man has fallen off from God, but from Nature. There is a passage in *Wood-Notes* which states the sense clearly:—

> "But thou, poor child! unbound, unrhymed,
> Whence camest thou, misplaced, mistimed,
> Whence, O thou orphan and defrauded?
> Is thy land peeled, thy realm marauded?
> Who thee divorced, deceived, and left?
> Thee of thy faith who hath bereft,
> And torn the ensigns from thy brow,
> And sunk the immortal eye so low?
> Thy cheek too white, thy form too slender,
> Thy gait too slow, thy habits tender
> For royal man;—they thee confess
> An exile from the wilderness,—
> The hills where health with health agrees,
> And the wise soul expels disease. . . .
> There lives no man of Nature's worth
> In the circle of the earth;
> And to thine eye the vast skies fall,
> Dire and satirical,

On clucking hens and prating fools,
On thieves, on drudges, and on dolls.
And thou shalt say to the Most High,
'Godhead! all this astronomy,
And fate and practice and invention,
Strong art and beautiful pretension,
This radiant pomp of sun and star,
Throes that were, and worlds that are,
Behold! were in vain and in vain;—
It cannot be,—I will look again.
Surely now will the curtain rise,
And earth's fit tenant me surprise;—
But the curtain doth *not* rise,
And Nature has miscarried wholly
Into failure, into folly.' "

There is a passage to the same effect in *Blight*. Out of this view arises the capital idea of Emerson's poetry, the promise of the coming of the ideal man, who shall achieve the reconcilement and be himself equal to Nature, the purified and perfect soul. It is clearly a Messianic idea. The most noble expression of it is in the *Song of Nature,* and the passage though long is necessary to exhibit the idea properly:—

"But he, the man-child glorious,—
Where tarries he the while?
The rainbow shines his harbinger,
The sunset gleams his smile.

"My boreal lights leap upward,
Forthright my planets roll,
And still the man-child is not born,
The summit of the whole.

"Must time and tide forever run?
Will never my winds go sleep in the west?
Will never my wheels which whirl the sun
And satellites have rest?

"Too much of donning and doffing,
Too slow the rainbow fades,
I weary of my robe of snow,
My leaves and my cascades;

"I tire of globes and races,
Too long the game is played;
What without him is summer's pomp,
Or winter's frozen shade?

"I travail in pain for him,
My creatures travail and wait;
His couriers come by squadrons.
He comes not to the gate.

"Twice I have moulded an image,
And thrice outstretched my hand,
Made one of day and one of night
And one of the salt sea-sand.

"One in a Judæan manger,
And one by Avon stream,
One over against the mouths of Nile,
And one in the Academe.

"I moulded kings and saviours,
And bards o'er kings to rule;—
But fell the starry influence short,
The cup was never full.

"Yet whirl the glowing wheels once more,
And mix the bowl again;
Seethe, Fate! the ancient elements,
Heat, cold, wet, dry, and peace and pain.

"Let war and trade and creeds and song
Blend, ripen race on race,
The sunburnt world a man shall breed
Of all the zones and countless days."

The same idea is substantially contained in *The Sphinx*, in which the portrait of man as he is bears the same lineaments, and the deliverance is represented as the poet's solving of the riddle of Nature by guessing one of her meanings, according to the doctrine of the microcosm which is so constant in the *Essays*. The poem, which is less difficult than it appears, contains many of Emerson's characteristic sayings, and what may be regarded as the most condensed of his great affirmations, comprehending like *Bramah* his whole mind—

"Ask on, thou clothed eternity.
Time is the false reply."

The *Poems* contain so many thoughts by the way, so many scattered beauties and felicities, that any general view is inadequate to indicate fully their value. There is wealth of detail. No expression of the subjectivity of Nature equals for refinement and sublimation the lines in *Monadnock:*—

"And that these gray crags
Not on crags are hung,
But beads are of a rosary
On prayer and music strung."

The moral dicta, too, that strew the pages, are among the most prized of his lines, and some have passed into undying permanence; of them perhaps the greatest is the quatrain on duty, "So nigh is grandeur to our dust," and one on sacrifice:—

" 'Tis man's perdition to be safe,
When for the truth he ought to die."

And in closing the little volume one remembers, too, whole poems left neglected in this sketch; but among the best, *Hermione, The Romany Girl, Days, The Day's Rations, Forerunners,* each of which has a unique and memorable quality and sets forth some view of his philosophy in a characteristic way and poetically.

Emerson's poetry does not make a wide appeal; it has been for a select audience, and perhaps it may always be so; yet to some minds it seems of a higher value than his prose. He was more free, more completely enfranchised, in poetry. He was farther away from his books, from which, however afterward certified by intuitions, he did in fact derive his ideas. The ideas are old; nothing is fresh there except the play of his mind about the ideas. Indeed, it is an obvious observation that one difficulty about intuition as expounded by Emerson is that it gives out no new ideas, but only rubs up old ones and makes them shine in a way which after all is still familiar. Emerson is farther away from his origins of thought when he goes into the woods. He is also a more natural man there, and leaves the minister, too, well behind him. There are many of the poems in which there is no touch of clergy. The poems began, too, at the moment of his first liberation. He had written verse before, and from boyhood had always practised it; but the lines were practically without merit and of no worth to the world. When he was thirty-three years old, at the time he left the church, his mind, which up to that moment had been slow in unfolding, suddenly matured; in the ten years following he did all his thinking, and it may be fairly said that he had no new ideas after he was forty years old; from then on he repeated and rearranged the old. There were favourable circumstances for development in the beginning of this period. The taking such a step, decisive and important as it was, gave of itself a certain maturity of character; the renewed health with which he returned from abroad was a great gain in conditions; the need he was under to justify the step by work outside the church, and the sense he had—and it was great—of the disparagement of his talents and labours, the ostracism of the University and the unfriendliness of the respectable and educated class in the community about him, the feeling of being set aside—all this combined to stir the energy of his mind to the utmost. He did his best writing, *Nature,* then, and his earlier Addresses are in some ways much superior to the *Essays* in style; they are more fluid, and if more contemporary, they are better adapted to readers.

It was natural that his poetic instinct should share this general quickening of his powers and higher level of attainment. One circumstance especially favoured its development: he was now for the first time in a home of his own in the country, with leisure in many hours at least, and filled with what was to him the new delight of real acquaintance with nature in the fields and woods. His poetry suddenly changed its quality and became quite another thing from what it had been; and concurrently with his development of thought on the side of prose, in the same ten years he composed this group of poems, giving a very different expression to the same ideas and blending with them his own life in nature. In this poetic outlet of his genius he found a new liberty; in his prose he was still much engaged to his past, and always dragged the chain of "the moral sentiment"; here he was free, and his nature disclosed unsuspected and fundamental vigours, and at times even what he would have called dæmonic power. There is a vehemence, a passion of life, in *Bacchus* that no prose could have clothed. The whole world takes on novelty in the verse; on all natural objects there is a lustre as if they were fresh bathed with dew and morning, and there is strange colouring in all; not that he is a colour poet; he does not enamel his lines as the grass is enamelled with wild flowers; but the verse is pervaded with the indescribable colouring of mountain sides, and the browns and greens of wide country prospects. This lustre of nature is one of his prime and characteristic traits. There is, too, a singular nakedness of outline as of things seen in the clarity of New England air. His philosophy even helps him to melt and fuse the scene at other times, and gives impressionist effects, transparencies of nature, unknown aspects, the stream of the flowing azure, the drift of elemental heat over waking lands, the insubstantial and dreaming mountain mass: all this is natural impressionism in the service of philosophy. His persons, too, are mythic and heroic, and the very names yield up poetry,—Merlin, Xenophanes, Bacchus, Uriel, Saadi, Merops, Bramah. The *Poems* are full of surprise, also; many are original and unique in their originality, so that there is no other poem of that sort in the world. In the *Poems,* as a whole, there are these great and significant qualities, where the theme is most impersonal and abstract; and, besides, about this strange and various rendering of nature, there are in the margin, as it were, scenes of human life and common days exquisitely plain, tender, and truthful. The range is wide, the moods are many; Saxon and Arab blend, the chant of the hammer here, and there the Persia of the mind; here poems that are atmospheric in lustre and purity, and again poems that contain the sum of human destiny,—Bramah, the Messianic child of Nature, the Sphinx.

It is futile to make deductions and notice that with all this fine quality there is defect of art and defect of taste, the harshness and roughness of the New England land itself, and downright commonplace and doggerel; for it is not with deductions that the poems please, they either please so that the defects are forgotten, or they please not at all. If one is in an artistic mood and cannot lay it off, these poems shall seem impossible,—ding-dong and huddle and muddle, a blend of the nebulous and the opaque, sweet bells jangled out of tune and harsh; but if he follows one of Emerson's wisest counsels, and remembers that to fail in appreciation of another is only to surrender to one's own limitations and put a term to one's own power, then another hour will come when all that seems grotesque and so unequal shall take on again majesty and mystery and brightness, the fascination of a new, strange, and marvellous world, the glow, the charm; and the reader shall, like—

> "The lone seaman all the night
> Sail astonished amid stars."

Such are the two moods in which Emerson is read, but there is no mixing of the two. There is something of the same doubleness of impression in the *Essays,* but it is there much less radical. And since the appreciation of Emerson is largely one of temperament, if I may speak personally as perhaps I ought, I own that I have little intellectual sympathy with him in any way; but I feel in his work the presence of a great mind. His is the only great mind that America has produced in literature. His page is as fresh in Japan and by the Ganges as in Boston; and it may well be that in the blending of the East and West that must finally come in civilization, the limitations that awaken distrust in Occidental mind may be advantages when he is approached from the Oriental slope of thought, and his works may prove one of the reconciling influences of that larger world. His material is permanent; there will always be men in his stage of mental culture or, at least, of his religious development; his literary merit is sufficient to secure long life to his writings. For these reasons his fame seems permanent, and with it his broad contact with the minds of men. However unconvincing he may be in detail, or in his general theory and much of his theoretic counsel, he convinces men of his greatness. One has often in reading him that feeling of eternity in the thought which is the sign royal of greatness. It is in his poems that I feel it most, and find there the flower of his mind.

WILLIAM CRARY BROWNELL (1851–1928) was for the last forty years of his life editor and literary adviser of the publishing firm of Charles Scribner's Sons. His book *French Traits* (1889) has been ranked with Emerson's *English Traits*. In all, Brownell wrote nine books, mainly on style, literature, and the character of American civilization. His *American Prose Masters* (1909), from which the following is taken, was reprinted in 1963 and edited by Howard Mumford Jones.

Emerson

W. C. BROWNELL

The perspective of time, doubtless for the most part in substantial alliance with equity, diminishes many imposing literary figures, but it has already enlarged Emerson's. His fame grows. More and more generally, and more and more distinctly, it is discerned as our answer to the literary challenge of the world. Emerson is of the company of Plato and Pascal, of Shakespeare and Goethe, emulating easily their cosmic inclusivenes. And he is ours—absolutely and altogether our own. If he is not typically, he is peculiarly, American. No other country could have produced him. And his own may take a legitimate satisfaction in the consciousness that its greatest is also one of its most characteristic minds. Especially may the American lover of literature joy in finding this intellectual pre-eminence illuminating the firmament of letters, rather than arising in some field of activity more commonly associated with our character and achievements.

II

Except a childhood recollection of Lincoln speaking from a hotel balcony on his way to his first inauguration—of his towering size, his energy in gesture and emphasis, his extraordinary *blackness,* his angularity of action, and a certain imposing sincerity of assertion, the last very likely an imputation of later years—I have no memory of any of our public men more vivid than that of hearing in early youth a lecture by Emerson. Surely when Lowell called Lincoln "the first American" he forgot Emerson. Or he was thinking of Lincoln's representative character in, rather than of, his country. Politics is "too much with us." The first American both in chronology and in completeness appeared in the field of letters, and—if we are, as of course Lowell meant, to consider personal greatness in the comparison and thus exclude Cooper—in the efflorescence of New

England culture. Naturally I do not in the least recall the topic of Emerson's lecture. I have an impression that it was not known at the time and did not appear very distinctly in the lecture itself. The public was small, attentive, even reverential. The room was as austere as the chapel of a New England Unitarian church would normally be in those days. The Unitarians were the intellectual sect of those days and, as such, suspect. Even the Unitarians, though, who were the aristocratic as well as the intellectual people of the place, found the chapel benches rather hard, I fancy, before the lecture was over, and I recall much stirring. There was, too, a decided sprinkling of scoffers among the audience, whose sentiments were disclosed during the decorous exit. Incomprehensibility, at that epoch generally, was the great offence; it was a sort of universal charge against anything uncomprehended, made in complete innocence of any obligation to comprehend. Nevertheless the small audience was manifestly more or less spellbound. Even the dissenters—as in the circumstances the orthodox of the day may be called—were impressed. It might be all over their heads, as they contemptuously acknowledged, or vague, as they charged, or disintegrating, as they—vaguely—felt. But there was before them, placidly, even benignly, uttering incendiarism, an extraordinarily interesting personality. It was evening and the reflection of two little kerosene lamps, one on either side of his lectern, illuminated softly the serenest of conceivable countenances—nobility in its every lineament and a sort of irradiating detachment about the whole presence suggestive of some new kind of saint—perhaps Unitarian. There was nothing authoritative, nothing cathedral in his delivery of his message, the character of which, therefore, as a message was distinctly minimized; and if nevertheless it was somehow clear that its being a message was its only justification, it was in virtue of its being, so to say, blandly oracular. It was to take or to leave, but its air of almost blithe aloofness in no wise implied anything speculative or uncertain in its substance—merely, perhaps, a serene equability as to *your* receptivity and its importance to *you*. Communication was manifestly the last concern of the lecturer. That was conspicuously not his affair. If, in turning over the leaves of his manuscript, he found they had been misplaced and the next page did not continue his sentence, he proceeded unmoved, after an instant's hesitation, with what it recorded. The hiatus received but the acknowledgment of a half smile—very gentle, wise, and tolerant. Nothing could better emphasize the complete absence of pretension about the entire performance, which thus reached a pitch of sim-

plicity as effective as it was unaffected. "It makes a great difference
to the force of a sentence," he says somewhere, "if there is a man
behind it." Such lyceum technic cannot be considered exemplary.
But in this case the most obvious fact about the lecture was that
there *was* a man behind it. Conventions of presentation, of delivery,
of all the usually imperative arts of persuasion—even of communication, as I say—seemed to lose their significance beside the personal
impressiveness of the lecturer.

This, at all events, is true of the literature he produced—of his
works in both prose and poetry. His life, his character, his personality—quite apart I mean from the validity of his precepts—have the
potency belonging to the personality of the founders of religions
who have left no written words. All the inconsistencies, the contradictions, the paradoxes, the inconsequences, even the common-
places of his writings are absorbed and transfigured by his personal
rectitude and singleness. One feels that what he says possesses a
virtue of its own in the fact of having been said by him. He has
limitations but no infirmities. He is no creature of legend. From
cradle to grave his life was known, intimately known, of all men.
There is a wealth of recorded personal reminiscence about him and
one may soberly say there has been found "no fault in him." Everything testified of him explicitly attests this. "I never heard of a crime
which I might not have committed," he says (or cites), in speaking
of "Faust." But this was the sportiveness of his obsessive intellect.
As a matter of fact he never committed any—not even the most venial
error. Nor was his blamelessness in the least alloyed with weakness.
His energy was as marked as his rectitude. He had the dauntless
courage of the positively polarized—as he might say—and in no wise
illustrated the negative virtues of passivity. He is of our time, of our
day, he lived and wrote but yesterday at Concord, Massachusetts,
he passed through the most stirring times, he shared, with whatever
spiritual aloofness, the daily life of his fellows and neighbors and
was part and parcel of a modern American community for nearly
four score years, and never in any respect or in the slightest degree,
in any crisis or any trivial detail of humdrum existence, failed to
illustrate—to incarnate—the ideal life. Introducing his lectures on
"The Ideal in Art," Taine exclaims eloquently: "It seems as if the
subject to which I am about to invite your attention could only be
treated in poetry." Similarly, one feels in approaching any consideration of Emerson that his character is such as to implicate a lyric
strain. Criticism is exalted into pure appreciation. Not only is there
no weakness, no lack of heroic ideality in his life and conduct, but

neither is there in his writings. Not only every poem, every essay, but every sentence, one may almost say, is fairly volatile in its aspiration toward the ideal. His practical admonitions and considerations—and his works are full of these—all envisage the empyrean. His homeliest figures and allusions direct the mind to the zenith and never stop at the horizon. And this incarnation of the ideal is a Massachusetts Yankee, for he was absolutely nothing else. I know of nothing in the history of literature, or in history itself, more piquant as an indifferent, more inspiring as a patriotic, critic would say. Emerson is, as I have said, our refutation of alien criticism, grossly persuaded of our materialism and interestedness. To "mark the perfect man" has been left to America and American literature.

III

Note moreover that Emerson's moral greatness—most conspicuous of all facts about him, as I think it is—receives its essentially individual stamp, aside from its perfection, from its indissoluble marriage with intellect. When he left his church he took his pulpit with him. He preached throughout his life. And he did nothing but preach; even his poetry is preaching. Of course, his sermons are lay sermons. There is, I think, rather a marked absence of the religious element in them. But the ethical note sounds through them all. He discovers the moral in the bosom of the rose, and of art itself finds its chief value to be the teaching of history. His distinction, his true originality, is missed if this is not perceived. As a man of letters, an artist, a poet, a philosopher, a reformer, he has limitations that it is impossible to deny. As a preacher—a lay preacher—he is unsurpassed. Since the days of the Hebrew prophets, whom temperamentally he in no wise resembled, there has been no such genius devoted to the didactic. He was quite conscious of his mission. "I have my own spirits in prison," he says, "spirits in deeper prisons whom no man visits if I do not." Confident in his sublimated pantheism, feeling himself an organic constituent of the universal substance, the authenticity of his didactic title was, one may almost say, more a matter of consciousness than of assumption with him. His capacity was not so much representative as original. He was not so much a delegate of the divine as a part of it, and consequently scorned credentials as he did exposition and spoke *ex proprio vigore*.

His distinction *as* a preacher, however, is not the authority with which he speaks—others have spoken as authoritatively—but that, though preaching always, his appeal is always to the mind. He never pleads, adjures, warns, only illuminates. He may talk of other gods, his Zeus is intellect. The hand may be Isaiah's, the voice is that of the intelligence. "The capital secret of the preacher's profession," he says, "is to convert life into truth." These five words define his own work in the world with precision. And his instrument, his alembic, for this conversion was the intellect. Treating moral questions, or questions which by extension are to be so called, almost exclusively, he treats them without reference to any criterion but that of reason. Pure intellect has never received such homage as he pays it. Its sufficiency has never seemed so absolute to any other thinker. "See that you hold yourself fast,"—by the heart, the soul, the will? No,—"by the intellect," is the climax of one of his earliest and most eloquent preachments. The strain is recurrent throughout his works. "Goethe can never be dear to men," he says, with his extraordinary penetration. "His is not even the devotion to pure truth: but to truth for the sake of culture." He would have blandly scouted Lessing's famous preference for the pursuit over the possession of truth, and was far from "bowing humbly to the left hand" of the Almighty and saying, "Father, forgive: pure truth is for Thee alone." He never pursued truth—or anything. He simply uttered it, with perfect modesty but also with absolute conclusiveness. He never pretended to completeness, to the possession of all truth. "Be content with a little light, so it be your own," he counsels the youthful "scholar." He was imperturbably content with his; it was indubitably his own, and he trusted it implicitly. To increase one's store of light he prescribes a "position of perpetual inquiry" and commends not study but examination, exclaiming eloquently, "Explore, and explore!" What with? Under whose guidance? That of your intellect of course. He is in essential agreement with Carlyle, in calling the light of the mind "the direct inspiration of the Almighty"—except that he would have substituted Nature for the Almighty, to whom his references are as few as Carlyle's are frequent.

Moreover it was the pure, as distinguished from the practical, intellect that he worshipped. Naturally, since it was this that he possessed. He himself admits, or rather proclaims, that his "reasoning faculty is proportionally weak." Logic was apparently discovered by Aristotle and Emerson is a pure Platonist. He cites the Stagirite when it serves his Platonist purpose—for example, the beautifully Platonist definition of art as "the reason of things without their substance"—but he has no native sympathy with him. He is in fact Plato *redivivus* in his assumption that conceptions as such justify and prove themselves; or rather, that all kinds of proof are imperti-nent. Logic, indeed, has been superstitiously overvalued. It has been responsible for an enormous amount of absolutely artificial error, as one need go no farther than to remember Aristotle's despotic rule during the Middle Ages—still persisting in both Roman and Protestant ecclesiasticism—to recall. At the same time, quite apart from its pretensions as a science, it has the supreme value of being the only test which we may apply to the verification of our other-wise unestablished intuitions. The rôle of verification, however, is altogether too humble to win respect from such an Olympian spirit as Emerson. He speaks always as little like the logicians as the scribes. Not only his practice—which others have shared—but his theory, in which he is unique among the serious philosophers of the modern world, is quite definitely that of the seer. However blandly, however shrewdly, he unfolds his message, he has consciously and explicitly as well as inferentially the attitude of merely transmitting it. More—far more—than that, for with his inveterate didacticism he insists that this attitude be universal. Abstract yourself sufficiently, he seems to say to his audience, and let the god speak through you. Then all will be well. To what purpose? Well, to no purpose, except the end of the formulation of truth. Truth he viewed almost as a commodity. If you could but get enough life converted into truth, there would be nothing left to ask for. That would be the legitimate end and conclusion of effort, because—though of course he never stooped to assign any reason for assuming the all-sufficiency of truth —since error is blindness, once perceived it won't be followed. He is, I confess, a little exasperating in his airy avoidance of this "con-clusion of the whole matter." Even artistic completeness—for which, however, he had no sense—seems to require it. Logic also; axio-matically the highest good is goodness. But doubtless there are plenty of people to draw conclusions. Emerson was concerned mainly with premises—even major premises. The utilities he in gen-eral abhorred. There were in effect too many people to attend to them; to say nothing of the notorious fact that they would take care of themselves. The important thing was, as one may say, to illustrate Tennyson's exquisite image,

"Now lies the earth all Danaë to the stars,"

and let the divine interpenetrate and fecundate human deliverances on any subject—as little alloyed as possible with any ratiocination or other obstruction of pure transmission. In Emerson's case we know who the god was—even his name and address. His utterances are too highly differentiated for mistake. The divine voice is of course one. All things are one to Emerson. But the one in this instance seems sufficiently distinguished from its other articulatenesses to involve a polytheistic rather than a generally immanent explanation. To us the god is inescapably Emerson himself; it is at least excusable, practically, to identify what you find in no other conjunction. Naturally the inference is that we are all gods, and no doubt Emerson would willingly have adopted, with whatever modifications, the current "panentheism" which unites his pantheism with theism, for though he never lost sight of the existence of the many he always saw them as ultimately resident in the one. In this case we have only to say that Emerson was a most superior kind of god, or in other words—hardly more specific perhaps, but more in accord with current parlance—that he was a man of genius. However, genius too has its privileges, whether divine in the transcendental or in the merely literary sense. And one of them is notoriously independence of logic. Of this practical privilege he took the amplest advantage. "We cannot spend the day in explanation," he says theoretically. There is no syllogism in all his essays—not even, I fancy, a "therefore." There is no attempt to argue, to demonstrate even statements and positions that almost seem to cry out for such treatment. It is all distinctly facultative, but all instinct with the authority of the Hebrew prophets, the *ex cathedra* tone of the inspired or even the possessed. As I have intimated, the contrast between this tone—this assumption—and the frequently homely, workaday, Yankee expression of it is particularly picturesque. In general the prophets are in the distance—enwrapped in the mists of legend or enlarged in the mirage of remoteness.

Naturally, thus, his inconsistencies are striking—even glaring—but they are not as significant as superficially they may be esteemed. They are in the first place often superficial in themselves, and anyone who takes the trouble—as, in his lofty way, Emerson would have scorned, did in fact scorn, to do—can reconcile them by the exercise of attentive discrimination and, above all, of cordial good faith. I say "cordial," because goodwill is needful to illuminate even essential perspicacity when on the surface of things the case might so easily be adversely adjudicated. In reading over the Essays recently I must confess I have been extraordinarily impressed by the frequency of these apparent inconsistencies. One grows tired of noting them. Cumulatively they convey the impression of irresponsibility. Consistency, one says vainly to oneself, is the vice of feeble minds; indulged to this extent, it almost suggests the sportiveness of

literary bohemia. *But,* after a time—an apprenticeship one may say—
you perceive that inconsistency is inseparable from Emerson's
method. If a record had been kept of the oracles of Delphi, would
they have been found to hang together? Besides, the Pythia, however abstractly, dealt with the concrete. She was not consigned, like
Emerson, to the oracular in general, so to speak—the oracular
apropos of every imaginable abstract consideration. On the whole
it seems too much to ask that the oracular should also be consistent.
Too much ingenuity would be requisite to make it so, and the
association of ingenuity with oracle involves a contradiction in terms.
The mouthpiece of the god is not concerned about matching its
inspirations. If ever there existed a seer whose mental activity was
in a perpetual state of ferment, Emerson was such a one. Yet he
conceived of himself as a passive medium of transmission for divine
messages to humanity. He conceived thus of everyone worth attention at all in the intellectual world, and even commended the attitude to the humblest of his audiences. Why not, indeed, if the
farmer to whom he lent a volume of Plato returned it with the reassuring remark, "He seems to have a good many of my idees"?

We speak of a mercurial temperament, but really temperament
is a constant quantity compared with the intellect, pure and simple,
unbalanced by, unweighted with, its steady pull and pressure. Logic
itself hardly takes its place as a check on the irresponsible and the
experimental. And, as I say, Emerson eschewed logic. Obviously
either logic or feeling is requisite for the control of intellectual
caprice—a phenomenon mainly noticeable in the unsentimental and
the active-minded: precisely Emerson's category. And the thinker
who frames a system or even compasses a coherent body of doctrine
is probably indebted even more than to his logic to those general
appetences that make up a temperamental personality. Left to itself,
without concern for consequences either to logic or predilection, the
intellect is tremendously adventurous, and as hospitable to the
strange and the subversive as the nomad or the outlaw. Emerson
had a splendid scorn for the consequences of any of his thinking.
His thinking was in truth a series of perceptions, so directly visible
to his mind—undirected by any bent, unsteadied by any controlling
prejudice, so unselected temperamentally that is to say—as to need
no matching or comparison, no holding in abeyance, no tentative
consideration preliminary to complete adoption. With him modification means a new view, more light, still another perception. Philo-
sophically thus, and constitutionally, this preacher of individuality
is himself the most impersonal of individuals. Everyone in his

entourage, everyone who came in contact with him, noted, in the measure of his powers of analysis, the absence in him of the element of personality—the element *par excellence* that centralizes, unifies, and renders communicable any set of ideas, or even any particular point of view. . . . He is himself as elusive as his philosophy is fluid. His own introspection, busy enough with his mind and seeing the universe in as well as through it, pauses at the threshold of his nature and, instinctively shrinking from looking for fixity in anything so subtly undetermined, even professes ignorance of its constitution. The matter, however, was probably simpler than with his mystic turn he was ready to admit. His nature was flooded with light, but it lacked heat. It had animation without ardor, exaltation without ecstasy.

His deification of intellect, indeed, inevitably involves a corresponding deficiency in susceptibility, and defective sympathies are accordingly—and were as a matter of fact with him—as characteristic of Emerson's order of moral elevation as is this one enthusiasm to which his susceptibility limited him. Distinctly he lacked temperament. His was a genial but hardly a cordial nature—in personal relations, indeed, more amiable even than genial. As he says, "the intellect searches out the absolute order of things as they stand in the mind of God, and without the colors of affection." "Something is wanting to science until it has been humanized," he asserts, but by humanization he means "union with intellect and will"—quite formally neglecting the susceptibility, the necessary transition between the two. Will comes next to intellect in his esteem—he praises action on occasion—but it is a distant second. Virtue itself, he says, "is vitiated by too much will." He was poise personified, and both will and feeling impair equilibrium. The ether that he breathed habitually was too rarefied a medium for the affections to thrive in. He was in love only with the ideal—and the ideal as he conceived it, that is, "the absolute order of things." In all human relations, even the closest, a certain aloofness marks his feeling. As to this the testimony is unanimous. It was far from being shyness in the sense of diffidence. He did not know what diffidence was. On the contrary, it proceeded from an acute sense of self-respect. Mr. Cabot's Memoir contains a delicious letter to Margaret Fuller, who sighed for more reciprocity in him. Plainly he was to be neither wheedled nor bullied into intimacy. He was himself quite conscious of his innate unresponsiveness—as indeed what was there that escaped his all-embracing, all-mirroring consciousness? He was twice married, and received his life long the deferential devotion of family and friends.

But he undoubtedly felt that "my Father's business"—or his equivalent for it—had claims upon his preoccupation superior to theirs. The essence of love is self-abandonment, and such an attitude is quite foreign to him. It was in fact inconsistent with his idea of the dignity and importance of his own individuality, which he cherished with a singleness quite exactly comparable with the saint's subordination of all earthly to divine affection. He did not care enough for his friends to discriminate between them—which I imagine is the real reason for the extraordinary estimate of Alcott that has puzzled so many of his devotees. Aloofness is no respecter of persons. Seen from a sufficient height ordinary differences tend to equalization. He shrank even from having followers and all his friends felt his detachment. He was silent for the most part in company—not constrained, not abstracted, just resting, one fancies, in a temporary surcease of meditative activity. And at home, he says, "Most of the persons I see in my own house I see across a gulf."

Such temperamental composure it is perhaps that saves him from the fanaticism regnant around him through much of his life, and more or less directly derived from the disintegration of conservatism whose elements he had himself set free. We owe him our intellectual emancipation in all of its results, no doubt. But he himself never lost his equilibrium. His enthusiasms did not enthrall him, nor did he ever become the slave even of his own ideas. Of theories he had practically none. And his lack of fixity was not only too integral for fanatical determination but too frigid for volcanic disturbance. Common sense—of the recognizably Yankee variety—was less his balance-wheel than a component part of his nature, and gives to his intellect its marked turn for wisdom rather than speculation. It is this element in his writings that prevents his oracular manner from arousing distrust and makes his paradoxical color seem merely the poetizing of the literal. On all sorts of practical things he says the last word—the last as well as the *fin mot*. With the eloquence and enthusiasm of youth—no writer is so perennially young—he had the coolness of age; and this coolness is as marked in his earliest as in his latest writings, which indeed show increased mellowness and a winning kind of circumspect geniality. But, to adopt the terms he himself would have sanctioned, if not employed, his susceptibility was really stirred by the reason alone—the self-knower, the organ of immediate-beholding—and was in no wise responsive, even in dealing with the most practical matters, to the conclusions of the understanding, or the report of the senses. "There is no doctrine of the Reason," he exclaims with tender fervor, "which will bear to be taught by the Understanding." Being thus stimulated in the main by only a portion (to speak anciently again) of his beloved intellect, his feelings really glowed, one may say, within extraordinarily narrow limits. When he could exercise his *Vernunft* in complete neglect of his *Verstand* he reached the acme of his exaltation. The direct perception of truth—meaning, of course, moral truth—suffused him with something as near the ecstasy he so often seems to aspire to without ever quite reaching, as his extremely self-possessed temperament would suffer. "God, or pure mind," is one of his phrases, incidental but abundantly defining his conception of Deity, and it is this central conception that colors his philosophy and on its religious side makes it so strictly ethical.

Professor Woodberry—whose "Life of Emerson" is in my judgment not only a masterly study of a difficult subject but one of our few rounded and distinct literary masterpieces—maintains that Emerson is essentially religious. I cannot myself see it. Perhaps it is a question of definition, but surely it is an accepted idea that religion is a matter of the heart, and one is confident that no religious or other emotion ever seriously disturbed the placid alternation of systole and diastole in Emerson's. It is fortunate probably that it is so little a matter of the intellect; otherwise the mass of mankind whom it guides and consoles in one way or another, *tant bien que mal,* would distinctly be losers. The wise and prudent themselves, as a matter of fact, to which class Emerson eminently belonged, have mainly manifested a susceptibility to it in virtue of that side of their nature which they share with the babes to whom it has been revealed. What the unaided intellect has ever done for it, except by way of occasionally divesting it of the theology it had previously encumbered it with, is difficult to see. Certainly no secular writer, even, ever cared less about it, however defined—unless it be religious to aggrandize the moral sentiment and insist on it as the *summum bonum* and the *suprema lex* of life—than Emerson. Matthew Arnold called it "the most lovable of things," though in describing it as "morality touched by emotion" he seemed to many to eliminate its divine and therefore most characteristic sanction. With Emerson neither morality nor anything else is "touched by emotion" in any other sense than that of exaltation. He counsels the "scholar" to be "cold and true." And though on the other hand he is in constant communication with the divine element in nature, what he understands by this is not the power that makes for righteousness, but mind—universal mind, whose sole manifestation is not goodness, or beauty, but truth, of which goodness is altogether a concomitant, and beauty a mere manifestation. "No law can be sacred to me but that of my own nature. Good and bad are but names very readily transferable to this or that; the only right is what is after my constitution, the only wrong what is against it.". . .

OSCAR W. FIRKINS (1864–1932) was professor of comparative literature at the University of Minnesota. He wrote biographies of Jane Austen and William Dean Howells. His book *Ralph Waldo Emerson*, from which the following was taken, was published in 1915.

Emerson as Prose-Writer

OSCAR W. FIRKINS

. . .

III. CLEARNESS

Dr. Garnett writes of the individual sentence in Emerson: "His thought is transparent and almost chillingly clear." For most men, the clarity is hardly of the sort that regulates the temperature. It is true, nevertheless, that for Emerson, as for Browning and Meredith, around the *fact* of obscurity an *illusion* of greater obscurity has grown up. The trouble with Emerson is more often strangeness than dimness; the indistinctness of the moral Monadnock or Agiochook which he points out to us is due rather to the distance of the peak than to the haze in the atmosphere. He is obscure to-day because time has shortened the distance. "Self-Reliance" and "Compensation" have tinctured the air, and the study of the parents has borne fruit in the swifter intuitions of the children. Fifty years of approach have lightened many difficulties, and one reflects curiously that fifty years of recession, should they occur, might involve our grandchildren in the same perplexities which befogged our grandsires.

IV. COHERENCE

The articulation of the sentences within the paragraph is a point on which the public has been grossly misled. Among the grossest of its deceivers is Emerson himself whose declaration that each of his sentences was an "infinitely repellent particle" deserves incarceration in the same pound with the assertion that he did not know what an argument meant. His paragraphs will usually bear analysis; they sustain analysis better—sometimes—than perusal; and a second reading strengthens their coherence. In other words, a distinction must be made between the *cogency* and the *transparency* of the sequence; the connection between two thoughts is often inti-

155

mate enough, but the passage as Mr. Macy suggests is underground.

The absence or rarity of connecting particles in Emerson's style is sometimes rashly assumed to be an evidence of an equal want of sequence in the thought. But here a misunderstanding exists which the citation of two passages from Macaulay—a writer of impeccable sequence—may aid us to disentangle. The first is from the description of the Puritans:

"Events which short-sighted politicians ascribed to earthly causes, had been ordained on his account. For his sake empires had risen, and flourished, and decayed. For his sake the Almighty had proclaimed his will by the pen of the Evangelist, and the harp of the prophet. He had been wrested by no common deliverer from the grasp of no common foe. He had been ransomed by the sweat of no vulgar agony, by the blood of no earthly sacrifice. It was for him that the sun had been darkened, that the rocks had been rent, that the dead had risen, that all nature had shuddered at the sufferings of her expiring God."

The second passage treats of government in relation to the claims of the Jews (connectives underscored):

"*If* it be right that the property of men should be protected, and *if* this can only be done by means of government, *then* it must be right that government should exist. *Now* there cannot be government unless some person or persons possess political power. *Therefore* it is right that some person or persons possess political power. *That is to say,* some person or persons must have a right to political power."

It is clear that the first of these passages is devoid of formal articulations, that the second is sown with them and profits much by their support, and that, nevertheless, the earlier passage exhibits a solidarity with which its successor cannot pretend to compete. If you carry irregular or nondescript objects, toys, kitchen utensils, pine knots, some kind of external ligature, rope, basket, knapsack, becomes indispensable. But if you carry planed blocks of equal size, the mere likeness is a substitute for cohesion, and the armful is commodious without aids.

Now the Emersonian paragraph, without obeying any rigid law and with no scant measure of elasticity, *tends* to assume the form of the first citation from Macaulay; it *tends* to furnish several illustrations or several restatements of one law. Hence, to the extent of this tendency, the absence of connectives fails to injure coherence.

The prevalent impression that the Emersonian paragraph is a dust-heap—gold-dust, indeed, but for all that a heap—is due partly no doubt to the frame of his epigrams. It is thoughtlessly assumed that fitness for effective detachment must imply as a corollary unfitness for effective union. But the analogy of matter—and of society, also, for that matter—shows that independence and adaptiveness (or sociability) are far from inconsistent properties. A square or a diamond stands out in effective distinctness, when isolated, but it blends admirably with figures of its class in a checkerboard, a chimney-piece, or a mosaic pavement. Take, for instance, the apparently abrupt and unaccommodating dictum, "Imitation is suicide," and see how deftly it is wrought into the solid fabric of a sentence such as this: "There is a time in every man's education when he arrives at the conviction that envy is ignorance; that imitation is suicide; that he must take himself for better for worse as his portion; that though the wide universe is full of good, no kernel of nourishing corn can come to him but through his toil bestowed on that plot of ground which is given to him to till."

While due allowance, therefore, should be made for Emerson's reluctance to advertise—or even sometimes to announce—the articulation of successive sentences, it is time surely to bury the legend that he worked in pellicles, that his composition is a fall of snowflakes. The whole fascination of life for him lay in the disclosure of identity in variety, that is, in the concurrence, the *running together,* of several distinct images or ideas. It would be suggestive, and not wholly inaccurate, to aver that he *thought* in *paragraphs.*

The theory of formlessness in the compositions as a whole may be promptly put aside. Those who prefer to read Emerson's essays backward may be left without question to the unhindered enjoyment of this innocent form of calisthenics. But the true critic will perceive that method, in some form or degree, is universal in Emerson. We should say that his aptitude for method was mediocre, permitting him, in lucky subjects and genial moods, to approach excellence, and in refractory subjects or unruly moods, to sink to the plane of badness. At its lowest, however, it is far above chaos.

On this topic on which honest investigation is as rare as loose talk is plentiful, a few specifications will be in place.

First, the method deteriorates in advancing life.

Second, the pure or abstract essays are of looser fabric than the works strongly tinctured with concrete fact or practical import.

Third, Emerson had a good eye for simple likeness and direct contrast. When his matter is capable of subjection to these obvious principles, his success in organization is considerable.

Fourth, Emerson frequently numbers his points, a practice which is thought to be the acme, almost the pedantry, of order.

Fifth, Emerson failed to distinguish sharply between related ideas; the same thought sometimes occurs twice in one essay, or two thoughts which are kinsmen and should be neighbors are kept apart by comparatively alien ideas.

Sixth, Emerson's wish to get his whole philosophy into each essay tended toward sameness and promiscuity at once; it made the *essays similar* and the *paragraphs diverse.*

Seventh, Emerson's feeling for conclusions was strong; what he found hard was to make his conclusion his stopping-place. Too many essays resemble "Compensation" in having what might be called recurving tips: they end, so to speak, in a footnote.

It may be added, in conclusion, that, in both the paragraph and the essay, the order is better than it seems to be, and this absence of the *look* of order must be counted as an æsthetic defect. The æsthetic sense has more to do with our judgments of the merits of plans than we should willingly suppose, and Emerson's building, even when sound, rarely produces the *effect* of architecture.

v. English

Emerson's relation to the grammar of his native tongue may be defined as a constitutional negligence superimposed upon an inculcated carefulness. He was normally a loose writer, who had taken to heart in childhood a stringent tradition. Hence a general effect and air of strictness in his work, accompanied by frequent occasions when his English—to use a homely term—stretches itself. His grammar could unbend at intervals, as his Puritanism countenanced a rare cigar or glass of wine.

He uses unfamiliar preterites and participles, which are rather antiquated than inaccurate; "sprung" and "begun" in the past tense and the once fashionable "having drank" and "have rode." Carlyle perhaps is responsible for his predilection for quaint comparatives, "liker," "perfecter," "easilier," and for matronly and buxom superlatives, "subtilest," "cheerfulest," "learnedest," "willingliest." He never hesitates to invest an adjective that chances to end in "ly" with all the prerogatives of an adverb, and uses "orderly" and "masterly" and even "jolly" as modifiers of verbs with the most edifying intrepidity. He uses that snare for the unwary, the hanging or unattached participle, the participle in disjunction from a noun, with a freedom which places him at a bound on a level with the noblest of the English classics. He disappoints us a little by a pretty strict loyalty to the orthodox tradition in the matter of "shall" and "will," but regains our regard by an explicit, though rare, surrender to the enticements of the split infinitive. In the "Journals" we find "to not exasperate," and in "Society and Solitude" "to fairly disengage." A phrase like "intended to have dispatched this letter" awakens in him no debile compunctions, and he writes "thou from speech refrained" with the aplomb of the callous transgressor.

His use of pronouns is untainted by purism. The "and which" or "but which" error, whereby a "which" clause or "who" clause is yoked in morganatic connection with an unpretending participle or adjective receives his unqualified sanction; and the "but I" for "but me," in phrases like "which have no watchman, or lover, or defender, but I," could not escape his patronage. The zealots for "It is I" will read with pain the following double-edged solecism in the "Journals": "he is me, and I am him." If he disappoints us a little by the delicate exactness of some uses of "every," he manifests a consoling readiness to use the pronominal "either" of three, four, five, six, as many persons as you please. Give him time—plenty of time—and he will even add to each a plural verb: "Each of these are free." He clinches his emancipation from rule by the following couplet from "The Celestial Love":—

"There need no vows to bind
Whom not each other seek, but find."

There is an unusual idiom of which he is curiously fond, "too" in correlation with "than." "The poet stands too high than that he should be a partisan." He uses "not but" pleonastically for "only": "they have not but 350 or less pages." Once he even rises to the audacious "off of."

The reader will bear in mind that these solecisms occur *rari natantes* in the text, and that an aggregation like the foregoing unduly magnifies their importance. They point significantly, however, to Emerson's native insensibility to linguistic or logical precision, a defect which his eminent rhetorical precision—the precision which sifts words and pares sentences—brings out in emphatic relief.

vi. Diction

In view of Emerson's predilection for the slang-like,—we mean for the homely, the brusque, the metaphorical, and the exaggerated,—his almost total avoidance of slang is an honor to his taste.

He seldom admits it even in the company of that priceless antiseptic, the quotation mark. He hated vulgarity while he loved its concomitants.

Mr. Cabot and Professor Woodberry tell us that he was indifferent to the French language and literature, but the frequency of French citations in the "Journals" and the rather noticeable sprinkling of French words in his English would support a quite contrary conjecture. . . . He dignifies his page with an occasional Latin phrase, or indulges his ear, more rarely, with some flute-like vocable from Italy. The single German word recorded in our notebook is *kleinstadlich.*

He has a relish for unfamiliar words, words of recent coinage or of his own make, or that closely similar type of words to which age has brought a second childhood. One regrets his countenance of new words ending in "ize"—a suffix which with its graceless kindred "ist," "ism," deserves to be paralleled with Attila and Alaric, Genseric and Rollo, and other captains of hordes of invading barbarians—or barbarisms, at the reader's pleasure. Emerson uses "Copernicize," "rhetoricize," "anthropize," "contemporize," and even, to the final overturn of one's nerves, "apathize." He does not shrink from "analogizing," as these examples prove, and ventures once upon "gigantizing." After this, "Birminghamize" will be a mere peccadillo, and a fondness for the prefix "dis," shown in "disentitle" and "disimagine," will unite with his partiality for "ize" to produce the impressive compound, "disindividualize." "Ize," of course, debouches into "ization," and we have "Africanization," which is pardonable, and "Jonathanization" (Americanization) which is "recommended to mercy." There are occasional Grecisms of heavy build,— "anthropometer," "dispathy," "lotophagous"; and there are Latin derivatives, sometimes a trifle plethoric, "circumlation," "omnivolence," "plenipotence," "pleniloquence," "enumerable," "miniminity," "necessitative," "consuetude," "exanimate," and "longanimity" (the last two not unusual in literature, of course, but curious and characteristic). Other Latinisms are of slenderer and more pleasing fabric, "pudency" (dear to Emerson), "impressional," "routinary," "reverable," "aversation," "intensate," "edificant." One could spare "opprobriate" and "jeopardous," and "the tempers of angels" would be disturbed by "scribaceousness."

There is a class of homely improvisations which are sometimes attractive if the usage is solitary. "Selfism" is pedantic and "prigism" is cumbrous, but "fromness" is happily pictorial, and "otherest," in the sense of "most different," is a godsend. "Hasters" and "seemer" (one who seems) may be received with tempered gratitude, but "framable" is, or might be, useful, and "bugdom" and "flydom" are delectable inventions. To "ungod" is a term that throws one into consternation; it seems born of the Promethean Caucasus or of the Satanic (and Miltonic) Inferno.

Rarely a word is found of vulgar or flaunting connotations; "negrofine" is oleaginous, and "recentness" has the smartness and cheapness of fresh paint. The word "daguerred" (photographed) seems not so much up to date as in advance of date.

Emerson's position, in diction as in grammar, may be described as license invading scrupulosity, or, if one pleases, conscientiousness in the earliest stage of disintegration.

STUART P. SHERMAN (1881–1926) wrote many books that dealt with American life and letters, among them *The Genius of America* (1923), *Points of View* (1923), and *The Main Stream* (1927). Persuaded that American writers of his day had turned their backs on their American inheritance, Sherman took a stand for what he considered to be the American tradition and its bearers. Towards the end of his life, however, he seemed to attempt to reach out sympathetically towards the new writers. As editor of *Books*, the literary supplement of the New York *Herald Tribune*, he contributed weekly articles which made the publication the leading critical journal of the time. The essay on Emerson is from *Americans* (1922), but it originally was the Introduction to *Essays and Poems of Emerson* (1921), edited by Sherman.

The Emersonian Liberation

STUART P. SHERMAN

There is some disposition at present to look upon Emerson's ambition as extravagant and to regard his work as a closed chapter in the intellectual life of America. It is even asserted that he never much affected the thinking of his countrymen. Says a recent writer, "What one notices about him chiefly is his lack of influence upon the main stream of American thought, such as it is. He had admirers and even worshippers, but no apprentices." But this judgment will not stand examination. Emerson was a naturalist with a fresh vision of the natural world: he had Thoreau for an apprentice, and between them they established relations with the natural world, which successive naturalists like John Burroughs and John Muir have maintained and broadened to the dimensions of a national tradition. Emerson was a poet with a fresh vision of the poetic field in America: he had Whitman for a disciple, and a large part of what passes with us as poetry to-day, whatever is indigenous and racy of the soil and native character and ideals, is ultimately traceable to their inspiration. Emerson is our great original force in criticism; he left the imprint of his spirit upon Lowell, who said: "There is no man living to whom, as a writer, so many of us feel and thankfully acknowledge so great an indebtedness for ennobling impulses." Whatever is finely academic, high-bred, and distinguished in our critical literature to-day has felt the influence of Emerson and Lowell. "To him," according to Lowell, "more than to all other causes together did the young martyrs of our Civil War owe the sustaining strength of thoughtful heroism that is so touching in every record of their lives." By his aid innumerable preachers and teachers have found a way to translate the message of ancient scriptures into the language of modern men. Every American who pretends to know anything whatever of the American classics has at one time or other read the *Essays;* and the "idealism" which was once thought to be characteristic of the American people is most readily formulated in a half dozen of his "familiar quotations," which every one knows, whether he has read a line of Emerson or not. Directly and indirectly Emerson probably did as much as any other writer in our history to establish what we mean by "a good American"; and that, in the long run, is the most important sort of influence that can be exerted by any writer in any country.

That his influence abroad has been considerable may be briefly suggested by the reminder that he touched deeply such various men as Carlyle, Matthew Arnold, Nietzsche, and M. Maeterlinck. When Arnold visited America in 1883, he lectured on Emerson, on whom thirty years earlier he had written a sonnet of ardent admiration and homage. The lecture, the fruit of his ripest critical reflection, was not altogether satisfactory to his American audience. It impressed them as quite inadequately appreciative of their chief literary luminary. For Arnold very firmly declared that Emerson is not to be ranked with the great poets, nor with the great writers of prose, nor with the great makers of philosophical systems. These limitations of Emerson's power are commonly quoted as if detraction were the main burden of Arnold's message. As a matter of fact they are preliminary to his deliberate and remarkable declaration that in his judgment Emerson's essays are the most important work done in prose in our language during the nineteenth century. This is high praise from an exacting critic who was little given to the use of superlatives in any case, least of all in the case of American authors.

For what merit does Emerson deserve this preeminent place? Because, says Arnold, in a phrase full of significance, because "he is the friend and aider of those who would live in the spirit." Let us unfold a little the implications of this phrase and make its application more precise. Important as Emerson may have been to young Englishmen in the first half of the last century, he was still more important to young Americans. Helpful as he may become to European minds, he will always remain peculiarly the friend and aider of those who would live in the spirit amid an enviroment which, as is generally thought, tends powerfully to confirm on the one hand the hard and merely practical genius of the Yankee, and, on the other hand, the narrow and inflexible righteousness of the merely traditional Puritan, the Puritan who feels no longer the urgency and progressive force of new moral life within him. To the posterity of Franklin and Edwards, Emerson is the destined and appropriate counsellor because he brings them undiminished the vital force of their great moral traditions while at the same time he emancipates them from the "dead hand," the cramping and lifeless part of their past. To children of the new world, Emerson is a particularly inspiring friend, because with deep indigenous voice he frees them from unmanly fear of their elders, lifts from their minds the overawing prestige of Europe, liberates the powers and faith of the individual man and makes him "at home" in his own time and place.

A great part of our lives, as we all recognize in what we call our educational period, is occupied with learning how to do and to be what others have been and have done before us. We come abreast of our predecessors by imitating them, and are grateful to the masters when they reveal to us their secrets, to the older men when they give us the benefit of their experience. But presently we discover that the world is changing around us, and that the secrets of the masters and the experience of our elders do not wholly suffice—much though they aid us—to establish us effectively in our younger world. We discover within us needs, aspirations, powers of which the generation that educated us seems unaware, or towards which it appears to be indifferent, unsympathetic, or even actively hostile. We perceive gradually or with successive shocks of surprise that many things which our fathers declared were true and satisfactory are not at all satisfactory, are by no means true, for us. Then it dawns upon us, perhaps as an exhilarating opportunity, perhaps as a grave and sobering necessity, that in a little while we ourselves shall be the elders, the responsible generation. Our salvation in the day when we take command will depend, we are constrained to believe, upon our disentanglement from the lumber of heirlooms and hereditary devices, and upon the discovery and free wise use of our own faculties. The vital part of education begins in the hour when consciousness of self-dependence breaks upon the mind. That is the hour for Emerson.

He appeals to unfolding minds because he is profoundly in sympathy with the modern spirit. By this phrase we mean primarily the disposition to accept nothing on authority, but to bring all reports to the test of experience. The modern spirit is first of all a free spirit open on all sides to the influx of truth. But freedom is not its only characteristic. The modern spirit is marked further by an active curiosity which grows by what it feeds upon, and goes ever enquiring for fresher and sounder information, not content till it has the best information to be had anywhere. But since it seeks the best, it is, by necessity, also a critical spirit, constantly sifting, discriminating, rejecting, and holding fast that which is good only till that which is better is within reach. This endless quest, when it becomes central in a life, requires labor, requires pain, requires a measure of courage; and so the modern spirit, with its other virtues, is an heroic spirit. As a reward for difficulties gallantly undertaken, the gods bestow on the modern spirit a kind of eternal youth with unfailing powers of recuperation and growth. This spirit—free, actively curious, upward-striving, critical, courageous, and self-renewing— Emerson richly possesses; and that is why he is so happily qualified to be a counsellor of youth in the period of intellectual emancipation.

There are many prophets abroad in the land today, offering themselves as emancipators, who have only very partially comprehended their task. By the incompleteness of their message they bring the modern spirit itself into disrepute. They understand and declare that the modern spirit is free and curious. They have failed to recognize that it is also critical and upward striving. When the well-born soul discards the "old clothes" of outworn custom and belief, it seeks instinctively for fresh raiment; but these Adamites would persuade it to rejoice in nakedness and seek no further. They know that man is an animal; but it escapes their notice that man is an animal constituted and destined by his nature to make pilgrimages in search for a shrine, and to worship, till he finds it, the Unknown God. Because they understand so ill the needs and cravings of man, they go about eagerly hurrying him from a predicament into a disaster. They conceive that they have properly performed the emancipative function when they have cut the young generation loose from the old moorings, and set it adrift at the mercy of wind and tide. . . .

There is a familiar saying of Emerson's which would epitomize, if it were understood, most of what is important and dynamic in all the Emersonian messages. Taken from its context in the essay on "Civilization," it has perhaps been more widely quoted than anything else that he uttered. Unfortunately one never hears it quoted with any sense of what it means in the thought of Emerson, where its position is absolutely central. The saying is this: "Hitch your wagon to a star." If one asks a man from whose lips it has glibly slipped what "Hitch your wagon to a star" means, he replies, "Aim high," a useful enough maxim of archery, but as a moral precept dreadfully trite and unproductive. What Emerson really means is: Put yourself in connection with irresistible power. In the physical world, let water turn your mill, let steam pull your cars, let the atmospheric electricity carry your words around the world. "That is the way we are strong, by borrowing the might of the elements." Likewise in the moral world, go where the gods are going, take the direction of all good men and let them bear you along, strike into the current of the great human traditions, discover the law of your higher nature and act with it. Presently you will notice that you are no longer fuming at obstacles and fretting at your personal impotence, but are borne forward like one destined.

At just this point many stern critics have cried out against Emerson as a moral teacher, and have charged him with counselling an optimistic passivity. Emerson bids us go with the current. The stern critic snatches at a figure and comes away with an error. Have not all the orthodox doctors taught that the good man goes *against* the current? Such misapprehension is the penalty for being a poet— for not sticking faithfully to the technical jargon. Without resorting to that medium, however, it should be possible to clear Emerson of the charge of counselling a foolish optimism, an indiscreet or base passivity. It should, at any rate, be possible to clear him in the eyes of any one whose morals have, like his, a religious basis—for example, in the eyes of the sad and strenuous author of that great line: "*In la sua volontade è nostra pace*—In his will is our peace." The point is, that Emerson does not urge us to confide in all currents, to yield to all tendencies. It is only after we have arrived by high thinking at a proud definition of man that we are to take for our motto: "I dare do all that may become a man." It is only after we have discovered by severe inquisition the law of our higher self that we are to trust our instincts and follow our nature. We are to be confident and passive. Yes: when we are doing the will of God.

What made Emerson's teaching take hold of his contemporaries, what should commend it to us today, is just its unfailingly positive character, the way it supplements by the restoration of classical virtues our Christian gospel of long-suffering. There is a welcome in it for life, even before the quality is disclosed: "Virtue is uneducated power." There is a place in it for manly resistance: "Be as beneficent as the sun or the sea, but if your rights as a rational being are trenched on, die on the first inch of your territory." There is the strong man's relish for difficulty and hostility: "We must have antagonisms in the tough world for all the variety of our spiritual faculties or they will not be born." There is precept for use of the spur: "He that rides his hobby gently must always give way to him that rides his hobby hard." There is warrant for choosing one's path: It is a man's "essential virtue to carry out into action his own dearest ends, to dare to do what he believes and loves. If he thinks a sonnet the flower and result of the world, let him sacrifice all to the sonnet." Even in his definition of friendship, Emerson drives at action: "He is my friend who makes me do what I can." It is obvious that he restores ambition, an aspect of magnanimity, to its proper place in the formation of the manly character, ambition to bring one's life to its fullest fruit.

This accounts for his extraordinary emphasis upon the virtue of courage: "It may be safely trusted—God will not have His work made manifest by cowards." Read from that cue, and presently you fancy that all forms of virtue appeared to him as aspects and phases of courage. He has praise for the courage of nonconformity, the courage of inconsistency, the courage of veracity, the courage to mix with men, the courage to be alone, the courage to treat all men as equals—but at this thought he remembers his proud conception of man, his imagination kindles, and he cries: "Shall I not treat all men as gods?" and, elsewhere, "God defend me from ever looking at a man as an animal." It sounds like extravagance. It may turn out to be a maxim of the higher prudence. Treating men like worms has been tried—without particularly gratifying results. Why not explore the consequences of assuming that men have a nobler destiny? If you are educating a prince, all the classical manuals enjoin it upon you to treat him like a prince. Why should not this hold of uncrowned sovereigns in general? Courage to do these extraordinary things Emerson learned of his Aunt Mary Moody Emerson, who taught him in his boyhood to face whatever he feared. Such courage he praised in his last word on Carlyle, "He never feared the face of man.". . .

D. H. LAWRENCE (1885–1930). Lawrence came to Taos, New Mexico, in 1922 on the invitation of Mabel Dodge (Luhan). He left in March 1923, but returned a year later, and remained there until October. He came a third time in April 1925 and stayed until September. His *Studies in Classic American Literature,* which he began to write in 1917, was published in 1923 (though an earlier version under another title was published in 1918–19). Lawrence's views on Emerson, however, appeared in a review of Stuart Sherman's *Americans,* in the *Dial* for May 1923. The following is taken from this review.

Emerson

D . H . L A W R E N C E

Emerson. The next essay is called "The Emersonian Liberation". Well, Emerson is a great man still: or a great individual. And heroes are heroes still, though their banners may decay, and stink.

It is true that lilies may fester. And virtues likewise. The great Virtue of one age has a trick of smelling far worse than weeds in the next.

It is a sad but undeniable fact.

Yet why so sad, fond lover, prithee why so sad? Why should Virtue remain incorruptible, any more than anything else? If stars wax and wane, why should Goodness shine for ever unchanged? That too makes one tired. Goodness sweals and gutters, the light of the Good goes out with a stink, and lo, somewhere else a new light, a new Good. Afterwards, it may be shown that it is eternally the same Good. But to us poor mortals at the moment, it emphatically isn't.

And that is the point about Emerson and the Emersonian Liberation—save the word! Heroes are heroes still: safely dead. Heroism is always heroism. But the hero who was heroic one century, uplifting the banner of a creed, is followed the next century by a hero heroically ripping that banner to rags. *Sic transit veritas mundi.*

Emerson was an idealist: a believer in "continuous revelation", continuous inrushes of inspirational energy from the Oversoul. Professor Sherman says: "His message when he leaves us is not, 'Henceforth be masterless', but, 'Bear thou henceforth the sceptre of thine own control through life and the passion of life'."

When Emerson says: "I am surrounded by messengers of God who send me credentials day by day," then all right for him. But he cosily forgot that there are many messengers. He knew only a sort of smooth-shaven Gabriel. But as far as we remember, there is Michael too: and a terrible discrepancy between the credentials of the pair of 'em. Then there are other cherubim with outlandish names bringing very different messages than those Ralph Waldo got: Israfel, and even Mormon. And a whole bunch of others. But Emerson had a stone-deaf ear for all except a nicely aureoled Gabriel *qui n'avait pas de quoi.*

Emerson listened to one sort of message and only one. To all the rest he was blank. Ashtaroth and Ammon are gods as well, and hand out their own credentials. But Ralph Waldo wasn't having any. They could never ring *him* up. He was only connected on the Ideal phone. "We are all aiming to be idealists," says Emerson, "and covet the society of those who make us so, as the sweet singer, the orator, the ideal painter."

Well, we're pretty sick of the ideal painters and the uplifting singers. As a matter of fact we have worked the ideal bit of our nature to death, and we shall go crazy if we can't start working from some other bit. Idealism now is a sick nerve, and the more you rub on it the worse you feel afterwards. Your later reactions aren't pretty at all. Like Dostoievsky's Idiot, and President Wilson sometimes.

Emerson believes in having the courage to treat all men as equals. It takes some courage *not* to treat them so now.

"Shall I not treat all men as gods?" he cries.

If you like, Waldo, but we've got to pay for it, when you've made them *feel* that they're gods. A hundred million American godlets is rather much for the world to deal with.

The fact of the matter is, all those gorgeous inrushes of exaltation and spiritual energy which made Emerson a great man, now make us sick. They are with us a drug habit. So when Professor Sherman urges us in Ralph Waldo's footsteps, he is really driving us nauseously astray. Which perhaps is hard lines on the professor, and us, and Emerson. But it wasn't I who started the mills of God a-grinding.

I like the essay on Emerson. I like Emerson's real courage. I like his wild and genuine belief in the Oversoul and the inrushes he got from it. But it is a museum-interest. Or else it is a taste of the old drug to the old spiritual drug-fiend in me.

We've got to have a different sort of sardonic courage. And the sort of credentials we are due to receive from the god in the shadow would have been real bones out of hell-broth to Ralph Waldo. *Sic transeunt Dei hominorum.*

So no wonder Professor Sherman sounds a little wistful, and somewhat pathetic, as he begs us to follow Ralph Waldo's trail.

1926-1971

LEWIS MUMFORD (1895–   ), American philosopher and historian, is best known for his writings on regional and city planning. His *Technics and Civilization* (1934), *The Conduct of Life* (1951), and *The Myth of the Machine* (1967) have been highly influential in arousing public awareness of the importance of ecology. He has also been a keen student of American literature and civilization. His biography, *Herman Melville* (1929), helped to bring about a rediscovery of Melville's genius. Mumford's *The Golden Day* (1926), from which the following chapter on Emerson is taken, has been widely read as an expression of the American heritage.

The Morning Star

LEWIS MUMFORD

I

No one who was awake in the early part of the Nineteenth Century was unaware that in the practical arrangements of life men were on the brink of a great change. The rumble of the industrial revolution was heard in the distance long before the storm actually broke; and before American society was completely transformed through the work of the land-pioneer and the industrial pioneer, there arose here and there over the land groups of people who anticipated the effects of this revolution and were in revolt against all its preoccupations. Some of these groups reverted to an archaic theocracy, like that of the Mormons, in which a grotesque body of beliefs was combined with an extraordinary amount of economic sagacity and statesmanship; some of them became disciples of Fourier and sought to live in coöperative colonies, which would foster men's various capacities more fully than the utilitarian community. . . .

The period from 1830 to 1860 was in America one of disintegration and fulfillment: the new and the old, the crude and the complete, the base and the noble mingled together. Puritan fanatics like Goodyear brought to the vulcanization of rubber the same intense passion that Thoreau brought to Nature: sharp mountebanks like Barnum grew out of the same sort of Connecticut village that nourished an inspired schoolmaster like Bronson Alcott: genuine statesmen like Brigham Young organized the colonization of Utah whilst nonentities like Pierce and Buchanan governed the whole country. During this period, the old culture of the seaboard settlement had its Golden Day in the mind; the America of the migrations, on the other hand, partly because of weaknesses developed in the pioneer, partly because of the one-sided interests of the industrialist, and partly because of the volcanic eruption of the Civil War had up to 1890 little more than the boomtown optimism of the Gilded Age to justify its existence. . . .

There were no Carlyles or Ruskins in America during this period; they were almost unthinkable. One might live in this atmosphere, or one might grapple with the White Whale and die; but if one lived, one lived without distrust, without inner complaint, and even if one scorned the ways of one's fellows, as Thoreau did, one remained among them, and sought to remedy in oneself the abuses that existed in society. Transcendentalism might criticize a fossilized past; but no one imagined that the future could be equally fossilized. The testimony is unqualified. One breathed hope, as one might breathe the heady air of early autumn, pungent with the smell of hickory fires and baking bread, as one walked through the village street.

"One cannot look on the freedom of this country, in connection with its youth," wrote Emerson in The Young American, "without a presentiment that here shall laws and institutions exist in some proportion to the majesty of Nature. . . . It is a country of beginnings, of projects, of vast designs and expectations. It has no past: all has an onward and prospective look." The voice of Whitman echoed Emerson through a trumpet: but that of Melville, writing in 1850, was no less sanguine and full-pulsed: "God has predestinated, mankind expects, great things from our race; and great things we feel in our souls. The rest of the nations must soon be in our rear. We are the pioneers of the world; the advance guard, sent on through the wilderness of untried things, to break a new path in the New World that is ours. In our youth is our strength; in our inexperience, our wisdom."

"Every institution is the lengthened shadow of a man." Here and there in America during its Golden Day grew up a man who cast a shadow over the landscape. They left no labor-saving machines, no discoveries, and no wealthy bequests to found a library or a hospital: what they left was something much less and much more than that—an heroic conception of life. They peopled the landscape with their own shapes. This period nourished men, as no other has done in America before or since. Up to that time, the American communities were provincial; when it was over, they had lost their base, and spreading all over the landscape, deluged with newcomers speaking strange languages and carrying on Old-World customs, they lost that essential likeness which is a necessary basis for intimate communication. The first settlement was complete:

agricultural and industrial life were still in balance in the older parts of the country; and on the seas trade opened up activities for the adventurous. When Ticknor was preparing to go to Germany, in the first decade of the century, there was but one German dictionary, apparently, in New England. Within a generation, Goethe was translated, selections from the European classics were published; and importations of the Indian, Chinese and Persian classics widened the horizon of people who had known India only by its shawls, China only by its tea. . . . When all is reckoned . . . there is nothing in the minor writers that is not pretty fully recorded by Emerson, Thoreau, Whitman, Melville, and Hawthorne. These men, as Mr. D. H. Lawrence has well said, reached a verge. They stood between two worlds. Part of their experience enabled them to bring the protestant movement to its conclusion: the critical examination of men, creeds, and institutions, which is the vital core of protestantism, could not go much further. But already, out of another part of their experience, that which arose out of free institutions planted in an unpreëmpted soil, molded by fresh contact with forest and sea and the more ingenious works of man, already this experience pushed them beyond the pit Melville fell into, and led them towards new institutions, a new art, a new philosophy, formed on the basis of a wider past than the European, caught by his Mediterranean or Palestinian cultures, was capable of seizing. . . .

II

All the important thinkers who shared in this large experience were born between 1800 and 1820; their best work was done by the time the Civil War came; if not beyond the reach of its hurt, they at all events could not be completely overthrown or warped by it. The leader of these minds, the central figure of them all, was Ralph Waldo Emerson. He was the first American philosopher with a fresh doctrine: he was the first American poet with a fresh theme: he was the first American prose writer to escape, by way of the Elizabethan dramatists and the Seventeenth Century preachers, from the smooth prose of Addison or the stilted periods of Johnson. He was an original, in the sense that he was a source: he was the glacier that became the white mountain torrent of Thoreau, and expanded into the serene, ample-bosomed lake of Whitman. He loses a little by this icy centrality: he must be climbed, and there is so much of him that people become satisfied with a brief glimpse, and forget that they have not reached the summit which dominates the lower peaks and platforms. His very coldness seems familiar to academic minds; and for too long they appropriated him, as one of them: they forgot that his coldness is not that of an impotence, but of an inner intensity: it burns! The outward manner of his life was mild: there are summer afternoons when from the distance Mont Blanc itself seems little more than a cone of ice-cream; and his contemporaries forgot that this sweet man carried a lash, a lash that would not merely drive the money-changers from the temple but the priests.

Emerson was a sort of living essence. The preacher, the farmer, the scholar, the sturdy New England freeholder, yes, and the shrewd Yankee peddler or mechanic, were all encompassed by him; but what they meant in actual life had fallen away from him: he represented what they stood for in eternity. With Emerson's works one might reconstruct the landscape and society of New England: a few things would be left out from Nature which Thoreau would have to supply for us—a handful of flora and fauna, and the new Irish immigrants who were already building the railroads and who finally were to take possession of Boston—but what remained would still be everything of importance in the New England scheme of things. The weaknesses of New England are there, too: its bookishness, its failure, as Margaret Fuller said of Emerson, to kiss the earth sufficiently, its impatience to assume too quickly an upright position, its too-tidy moral housekeeping. Strong or weak, Emerson was complete: in his thought the potentialities of New England were finally expressed.

It is almost impossible to sum up Emerson's doctrine, for he touched life on many sides, and what is more, he touched it freshly, so though he is a Platonist, one will not find Plato's doctrines of Art in his essay on Art; and though he was in a very derivative way a Kantian, one will not find Kant's principles at the bottom of his ethics. With most of the resources of the past at his command, Emerson achieved nakedness: his central doctrine is the virtue of this intellectual, or cultural, nakedness: the virtue of getting beyond the institution, the habit, the ritual, and finding out what it means afresh in one's own consciousness. Protestantism had dared to go this far with respect to certain minor aspects of the Catholic cult: Emerson applied the same method in a more sweeping way, and buoyed up by his faith in the future of America—a country endowed with perhaps every advantage except venerability—he asked not merely what Catholic ritual means, but all ritual, not merely what dynastic politics means but all politics; and so with every other important aspect of life. Emerson divested everything of its associations, and seized it afresh, to make what associations it could with the life he had lived and the experience he had assimilated. As a result, each part of the past came to him on equal terms: Buddha had perhaps as much to give as Christ: Hafiz could teach him as much as Shakespeare or Dante. Moreover, every fragment of present experience lost its associated values, too: towards the established hierarchy of experiences, with vested interests that no longer, perhaps, could exhibit the original power of sword or spade, he extended the democratic challenge: perhaps new experiences belonged to the summit of aristocracy, and old lines were dying out, or were already dead, leaving only empty venerated names.

Emerson saw the implications of this attempt to re-think life, and to accept only what was his. He did not shrink from them. "Nothing is at last sacred but the integrity of your own mind. . . . I remember an answer which when quite young I was prompted to make to a valued adviser, who was wont to importune me with the dear old doctrines of the church. On my saying, 'What have I to do with the sacredness of traditions, if I live wholly from within?' my friend suggested,—'But these impulses may be from below, not from above.' I replied, 'They do not seem to me to be such; but if I am the Devil's child, I will live then from the Devil.' No law can be sacred to me but that of my Nature."

"Life only avails, not the having lived." There is the kernel of the Emersonian doctrine of self-reliance: it is the answer which the American, in the day of his confidence and achievement, flung back into the face of Europe, where the "having lived" has always been so conspicuous and formidable. In a certain sense, this doctrine was a barbarism; but it was a creative barbarism, a barbarism that aimed to use the old buildings not as a shell, but as a quarry; neither casting them aside altogether, nor attempting wretchedly to fit a new and lush existence into the old forms. The transcendental young photographer, in Hawthorne's House of the Seven Gables, suggested that houses should be built afresh every generation, instead of lingering on in dingy security, never really fitting the needs of any family, but that which originally conceived and built it. An uncreative age is aghast at this suggestion: for the new building may be cruder than the old, the new problem may not awaken sufficient creative capacities, equal to the previous one: these are the necessary counsels of prudence, impotence.

In the heyday of the American adventure, neither Emerson nor Hawthorne was afraid. Emerson re-thought life, and in the mind he coined new shapes and images and institutions, ready to take the place of those he discarded. A building was perishable; a custom might fall into disuse; but what of it? The mind was inexhaustible; and it was only the unawakened and unimaginative practical people who did not feel that these dearly purchased trinkets might all be thrown into the melting pot and shaped over again, without a penny lost. It was not that nakedness itself was so desirable; but clothes were cheap! Why keep on piecing together and patching the old doctrines, when the supply never could run out, so long as life nourished Emersons? "We shall not always set so great a price," he exclaimed, "on a few texts, a few lives. We are like children who repeat by rote the sentences of grandames and tutors, and, as they grow older, of the men of talents and character they chance to see,—painfully recollecting the exact words they spoke; afterwards, when they come into the point of view which these had who uttered these sayings, they understand them, and are willing to let the words go; for at any time, they can use words as good when the occasion comes. . . . When we have new perceptions, we shall gladly disburden the memory of its hoarded treasures, as of old rubbish."

III

The Platonism of Emerson's mind has been overemphasized; or rather, it has been misconstrued to mean that he lived in a perpetual cloud-world. The truth is, however, that Emerson's Platonism was not a matter simply of following Plato: it was a matter of living like Plato, and achieving a similar mode of thought. Critics have too often spoken of Plato's forms as if they were merely a weak escape from the urgent problems of Fifth-Century Athens; and of Emerson's, as if they were a neurotic withdrawal from the hurly-burly of American life. They were both, in a sense, a withdrawal; but it was a withdrawal of water into a reservoir, or of grain into a bin, so that they might be available later, if they could not be effectively distributed at once. Both Plato and Emerson had mixed with the life about them and knew its concrete details: both were conscious of the purely makeshift character of existing institutions; both were aware that they were in a period of transition. Instead of busying himself with the little details of political or economic readjustment, each sought to achieve a pattern which would permit the details to fall into place, and so make possible a creative renovation. Emerson wrote about Man the Reformer; but he never belonged to any political sect or cult. The blight of Negro slavery awakened his honest anger, and his essay on the Know-nothings is an excellent diatribe;

but even this great issue did not cause him to lose his perspective: he sought to abolish the white slaves who maintained that institution.

In coupling Emerson's name with Plato's I have hinted that Emerson was a philosopher; I see no reason to qualify this hint, or to apologize for the juxtaposition. He has been more or less grudgingly given such a place by current philosophic commentators, because on a superficial examination there is no originality in his metaphysics: both Plato and Kant had given an independent reality to the world of ideas, and the habit of treating existing facts as symbols is so ancient it became a shocking novelty when reëmployed in our own time by Dr. Sigmund Freud. The bare metaphysical outlines of Emerson's work give no insight, however, into the body of his thought as a whole. The content of Emerson's philosophy is much richer, I think, than that of any of his contemporaries; and he is denied a high place in philosophy largely because the content is so rich that it cannot be recognized, in the attentuated twilight of academic groves, as philosophy. Hegel and Comte and Spencer, Emerson's contemporaries, had all found formulæ which led them into relations with a vast mass of concrete facts: the weakness of their several philosophies was due to severe defects of personality— they were sexually neurotic, like Comte, with his pathetic apotheosis of Clothilde, or they were querulous invalids, like Spencer, who had never been able to correct by a wider experience the original bias given to his mind by his early training as a railroad engineer. Emerson had the good fortune to live a healthy and symmetrical life: he answered Tolstoi's demand for essential greatness—he had no kinks. In him, philosophy resumed the full gamut of human experience it had known in Pythagoras and Plato.

Emerson's uniqueness, for his time, consists in the fact that he appreciated not merely the factual data of science, and the instrumental truth of scientific investigation: he also recognized the formative rôle of ideas, and he saw the importance of "dialectic" in placing new patterns before the mind which did not exist, ready-made, in the order of Nature. "All the facts of the animal economy, sex, nutriment, gestation, birth, growth, are symbols of the passage of the world into the soul of man, to suffer there a change, and reappear a new and higher fact." The occasion for, or the efficacy of, this passage into the soul of man was denied by the externalism of Nineteenth Century empiricism; obscurely, it was the ground for contention between religion and science, a quarrel which religion lost by holding fast to a purely superstitious empiricism. If instrumental truths are the only order of truth, all religion is a superstition, all poetry a puerility, and all art itself is a weak anticipation of photography and mechanical drawing.

Emerson's affirmation of both physics and dialectic, of both science and myth, an affirmation which justified the existence of the artist, the poet, the saint, was of prime importance; for he did not make the mistake of disdaining the order and power that science had achieved within its proper department. Emerson was a Darwinist before the Origin of Species was published, because he was familiar with the investigations which were linking together the chain of organic continuity, and he was ready to follow the facts wherever they would lead him. Agassiz, Cambridge's great man of science, accepted the facts, too; but he was afraid of them; insulated in his evangelical Christianity, he insisted that the facts did not exist in Nature but in the mind of God. Emerson was untroubled by Agassiz's reluctance: the function of "God" was perpetually being performed for him in the passage of the world into the soul of man; and there was nothing in his philosophy to make him deny an orderly sequence in Nature. For Emerson, matter and spirit were not enemies in conflict: they were phases of man's experience: matter passed into spirit and became a symbol: spirit passed into matter and gave it a form; and symbols and forms were the essences through which man lived and fulfilled his proper being. Who was there among Emerson's contemporaries in the Nineteenth Century that was gifted with such a complete vision? To withhold the name of philosopher from the man who saw and expressed this integral vision of life so clearly is to deny the central office of philosophy.

Emerson's thought does not seal the world up into a few packets, tied with a formula, and place them in a pigeonhole. In the past, it was not limited to a phase of Christianity, nor a phase of classic culture: it roamed over a much wider area, and as he himself suggested, used Plato and Proclus, not for what they were, but as so many added colors for his palette. The past for Emerson was neither a prescription nor a burden: it was rather an esthetic experience. Being no longer inevitable in America, that is, no longer something handed down with a living at Corpus Christi or a place at court, the past could be entertained freely and experimentally. It could be revalued; and the paradox of Brahma became as acceptable as the paradox that the meek shall inherit the earth.

The poet, for Emerson, was the liberator; and in that sense, he was a great poet. With him one does not fel that our "civilization nears its meridian, but rather that we are yet only at the cock-crowing and the morning star." The promise of America, of an unspotted

Nature and a fresh start, had seeped into every pore of Emerson's mind. "Do not set the least value on what I do," he warns, "nor the least discredit on what I do not, as if I pretended to settle anything as true or false. I unsettle all things. No facts to me are sacred; none are profane; I simply experiment, an endless seeker, with no Past at my back. . . . Why should we import rags and relics into the new hour? . . . Nothing is secure but life, transition, the energizing spirit. No love can be bound by oath or covenant to secure it against a higher love. No truth so sublime but it may be trivial tomorrow in the light of new thoughts. People wish to be settled: only as far as they are unsettled is there any hope for them."

The vigor of this challenge, the challenge of the American wilderness, the challenge of the new American society, where the European lost the security of his past in order to gain a better stake in the future—who but can feel that this is what was distinguished and interesting in our American experience, and what was salutary, for all its incidental defects, in the dumb physical bravado of the pioneer? Two men met the challenge and carried it further: Thoreau and Whitman. They completed the Emersonian circle, carrying the potted flower of the scholar's study out into the spring sunshine, the upturned earth, and the keen air.

JAMES TRUSLOW ADAMS (1878–1949) was editor of the *Dictionary of American Biography* and author of many books, including *The Founding of New England* (1921) and *The Epic of America* (1931). His essay on Emerson appeared in the *Atlantic Monthly* (October 1930). Other critics before Adams, as we have seen, attacked Emerson for "shallow optimism" and for insistence on intuition and spontaneity, but perhaps not as sharply.

Emerson Re-read

J A M E S   T R U S L O W   A D A M S

1

Except in tales of romance it is not given to us to be able to pass through postern doors or forest glades and find ourselves in lands of leisure where it is always afternoon. If one seeks the King of Elfland's Daughter it must be between the pages of a book. Nevertheless, one can change one's stage and ways of life and amplify one's days. Some months ago by a simple shift in space I so wrought a change in time that, for a while at least, I have been able without sense of haste or pressure to browse again among the books I read and marked as a boy, books which for more years than I like to count had stood untouched upon my shelves, open apparently to the reaching hand, but in reality, owing to lack of time, as remote as boyhood's days themselves.

A week ago, I picked up one of the oldest of these, oldest in possession, not in imprint—the *Essays* of Emerson. In an unformed hand there was the inscription on the flyleaf, "James Truslow Adams, 1896." I was then seventeen, and had evidently read him earlier, for at the beginning of a number of the essays, notably "Self-Reliance," are marked the dates of reading, "1895, '96, '96, '96." The volume, one of that excellent, well-printed series which in those halcyon days the National Book Company used to sell for fifty cents, is underlined and marked with marginal notes all through. The passages are not all those I should mark to-day, but at sixteen and seventeen it is clear I was reading Emerson with great enthusiasm, and again and again.

In the past few days I have gone through five volumes of his work and found the task no light one. What, I ask myself, is the trouble? It is obviously not that Emerson is not "modern," for the other evening I read aloud, to the mutual enjoyment of my wife and myself, the *Prometheus Chained* of Æschylus, which antedates

Emerson by some twenty-five hundred years. I turn to Paul More's *Shelburne Essays,* Volume XI, and read the statement that "it becomes more and more apparent that Emerson, judged by an international or even by a true national standard, is the outstanding figure of American letters."

I pause and ponder. "International," even "true national," standards are high. Whom have we? Lowell as a critic? One thinks of, say, Sainte-Beuve, and a shoulder shrug for Lowell. Lowell as poet, Whittier, Longfellow, Bryant? *Exeunt omnes,* except as second-rate by world standards. The troop of current novelists and poets are much the same here as in a half-dozen other countries. Hawthorne? A very distinctive, and yet a minor voice, in the international choir. Poe? Again a minor, and scarcely distinguishable as a "national." Whitman? One thinks of Whitman five hundred years hence in world terms, and shakes one's head. The choice is narrowing fast. Is Mr. More right? Yet the Emerson who evidently so stirred me at sixteen leaves me cold to-day at fifty. It is something to be looked into. I try, at fifty, to reappraise my Emerson. I take up the volumes again to see wherein the trouble lies.

First of all it occurs to me to test him by his own appraisals of others, and I turn to his volume on *Representative Men.* The list of names is itself of considerable significance—Plato, Swedenborg, Montaigne, Shakespeare, Napoleon, Goethe. Four of these are evidently so obvious as to tell us nothing of the mind choosing them. The case is a good deal like that of the Pulitzer Jury in biography, which is forbidden to award prizes for lives of Lincoln or Washington. The essential point is, what has Emerson to say of these men?

I confess that, when after these thirty years or more I turn from reading about Emerson to reading him himself, I am rather amazed by what seems to me the shallowness of these essays. In fact, I believe that even Mr. More considers the Plato a very unsatisfactory performance. Emerson babbles of "the Franklin-like wisdom" of Socrates, and, indeed, I think we could look for as sound an essay from an intelligent undergraduate. The Shakespeare is almost equally naïve and unsatisfying, and Emerson's final judgment is that the dramatist was merely a "master of the revels to mankind," the purveyor of "very superior pyrotechny this evening," and that the end of the record must be that with all his ability he "led an obscure and a profane life, using his genius for the public amusement." This essay throws much light on Emerson if little on Shakespeare. Nor does he show more real understanding of his other great men. He can say that Napoleon left no trace whatever on Europe, that "all passed away like the smoke of his artillery." Of Goethe's greatest poem, the *Faust,* Emerson notes mainly its "superior intelligence." One suspects that he chose these four names unconsciously because they were high in the world's record of the great, not because he understood the men or their work.

When he turns from these names, almost imposed upon him, to another of his independent choosing, it is illuminating that the one he dwells on with greatest admiration is Swedenborg. This fact is significant. For him, the Swedish mystic is "a colossal soul," the "last Father in the Church," "not likely to have a successor," compared with whom Plato is a "gownsman," whereas Lycurgus and Caesar would have to bow before the Swede. Emerson quotes from him as "golden sayings" such sentences as "in heaven the angels are advancing continually to the spring-time of their youth, so that the oldest angel appears the youngest," or "it is never permitted to any one in heaven, to stand behind another and look at the back of his head: for then the influx which is from the Lord is disturbed." Nor should we forget that entry in Emerson's *Journals* in which he noted that "for pure intellect" he had never known the equal of—Bronson Alcott!

It is true that these essays are not Emerson's best, but they were written when he was over forty years old and at the height of his fame and mental maturity, and they help us to understand our problem. They are typical products of the American mind. Conventional praise is given to the great names of Europe, with comment that indicates lack of understanding of the great currents of thought and action, while Mrs. Eddy and Brigham Young peer over the writer's shoulders. We begin to see how deeply Emerson was an American.

His national limitation is noteworthy in another important source of influence in a mature culture, that of art. Music appears to have been outside his life and consideration. Of painting he could write that, having once really seen a great picture, there was nothing for one to gain by looking at it again. In sculpture he finds a "paltriness, as of toys and the trumpery of a theater." It "is the game of a rude and youthful people, and not the manly labor of a wise and spiritual nation," and he quotes with approval Isaac Newton's remark about "stone dolls." Art is not mature unless it is "practical and moral," and addresses the uncultivated with a "voice of lofty cheer." All art should be extempore, and he utters a genuine American note in his belief that it will somehow come to us in a new form, the religious heart raising "to a divine use the railroad, the insurance office, the joint-stock company, our law, our primary assemblies, our commerce, the galvanic battery, the electric jar, the prism, and the chemist's retort." "America is a poem in our eyes; its ample geography dazzles the imagination, and it will not wait long for metres." A century later, and we realize that something more is needful for the imagination than an ample geography.

His doctrine that art should be extempore stems from his general belief that knowledge comes from intuition rather than from thought, and that wisdom and goodness are implanted in us—a fatally easy philosophy which has always appealed to the democratic masses, and which is highly flattering to their self-esteem. Wordsworth had led the romantic reaction by making us see the beauty and value in the common things of everyday life, but the philosophy of Emerson has a different ancestry. The two when joined are a perfect soil for democratic belief, and democratic laxity in mind and spirit, far as that might be from Emerson's intention and occasional statements. The more obvious inferences are dangerous, for although a cobbler's flash of insight *may* be as great as the philosopher's lifetime of thought, such is of the rarest occurrence, and preached as a universal doctrine it is a more leveling one by far than universal suffrage.

2

As the ordinary unimportant man, such as most of us are, reads Emerson, his self-esteem begins to grow and glow. "The sweetest music is not in the oratorio, but in the human voice when it speaks from its instant tones of tenderness, truth, or courage." Culture, with us, he says, "ends in headache." "Do not craze yourself with thinking, but go about your business anywhere. Life is not intellectual or critical, but sturdy." "Why all this deference to Alfred and Scanderbeg and Gustavus? As great a stake depends on your private act today as followed their public and renowned steps." "We are all wise. The difference between persons is not in wisdom but in art." "Our spontaneous action is always the best. You cannot with your best deliberation and heed come so close to any question as your spontaneous glance shall bring you whilst you rise from your bed."

There is a kernel of noble thought in all this, but it is heady doctrine that may easily make men drunk and driveling, and I think we are coming near to the heart of our problem. The preaching that we do not have to think, the doctrine of what I may term, in Emerson's phrase, "the spontaneous glance," is at the bottom of that appalling refusal to criticize, analyze, ponder, which is one of the chief characteristics of the American people to-day in all its social, political, and international affairs. Many influences have united to bring about the condition, and Emerson cannot escape responsibility for being one of them.

On the other hand, a new nation, a common man with a fleeting vision of the possibility of an uncommon life, above all the youth just starting out with ambition and hope but little knowledge or influence as yet, all need the stimulation of a belief that somehow they *are* important and that not only may their private acts and lives be as high and noble as any, but that the way is open for them to make them so. This is the one fundamental American doctrine. It is the one unique contribution America has made to the common fund of civilization. Our mines and wheat fields do not differ in kind from others. With Yankee ingenuity we have seized on the ideas of others and in many cases improved their practical applications. The ideas, however, have largely come from abroad. The use of coal as fuel, the harnessing of steam and electricity for man's use,—the foundations of our era,—originated in Europe. Even the invention of the electric light was only in part American. But the doctrine of the importance of the common man is uniquely an American doctrine. It is something different, on the one hand, from the mere awarding to him of legal rights and, on the other, from the mere career open to the talents.

It is a doctrine to which the heart of humanity has responded with religious enthusiasm. It, and not science, has been the real religion of our time, and, essentially, the doctrine is a religious and not a philosophical or scientific one, equally made up as it is of a colossal hope and a colossal illusion. This does not invalidate it. Like all religions it will have its course to run and its part to play in the moulding of man to something finer. It is one more step up, and we need not deny it merely because of the inherent falsity of that gorgeous preamble which proclaims to the world, "All men are created equal." In spite of the self-assertion of the so-called masses, that is a statement which, deep in their hearts, it is as difficult for the inferior as the superior genuinely to believe. It is an ideal, which, like every religious ideal, will be of far-reaching influence, but which must be made believable emotionally. Emerson's greatness lies in his having been the greatest prophet of this new religion, an influence that might well continue to be felt on the two classes that need the doctrine most—the common man striving to rise above the mediocre, and the youth striving to attain a courageous and independent maturity.

Another strain in Emerson, that of the poet and mystic, has also to be reckoned with in making up the man's account. His insistence upon values in life, culminating in the spiritual, is one sorely needed in the America of our day as of his. We are, perhaps, further from the ideal he drew in his "American Scholar" than were the men of his own time. His large hope has not been fulfilled. There is a delicate beauty in his spiritual outlook on life, a beauty akin to that of many an old fresco in Umbria or Tuscany. Unfortunately, there were fundamental flaws in the work of the Italian artists, flaws not of spiritual insight or of artistic craftsmanship, but of wet plaster or of wrong chemical combinations in materials, so that little by little their painting has crumbled and faded. If Emerson's mysticism led him too easily toward Swedenborg rather than toward Plato, and if the beauty of his spiritual interpretation of the universe does not carry that conviction or mould his readers as it should, may we not wonder whether there were not some fundamental flaws in the mind of the man that may explain his decreasing influence, just as in examining a wall where a few patches of dim color are all that remain of a Giotto we have to consider, not the artist's love of the Madonna, but his lack of knowledge of the mechanics of his art? Of this we shall speak presently.

The quintessence of Emersonianism is to be found in the first and second series of *Essays,* and it may be noted that it was these, as my pencilings show, which I myself read most as a boy, and of them, it was such essays as "Self-Reliance," in which the word is found in its purest form, that I read over and over. What do I find marked as I turn the old pages? "Trust thyself: every heart vibrates to that iron string." "Whoso would be a man must be a nonconformist." "Nothing at last is sacred but the integrity of your own mind." "I do not wish to expiate, but to live. My life is not an apology, but a life. It is for itself and not for a spectacle." "What I must do is all that concerns me, not what the people think." "The great man is he who in the crowd keeps with perfect sweetness the independence of solitude." "Always scorn appearances and you always may. The force of character is cumulative." "Life only avails and not the having lived." "Insist on yourself; never imitate." "Nothing can bring you peace but yourself."

This is high and worthy doctrine, the practice of which will tax a man's strength and courage to the utmost, and such sentences as the above have proved the strongest influences in the making of literally countless adolescent Americans, stimulating their ambition in the noblest fashion. Unfortunately this part of Emerson's teaching has had less influence than the other. The average American soon slips into preferring "we are all wise" to "scorn appearances." Insisting on being one's self is strenuous and difficult work anywhere, more so in America than any other country I know, thanks to social opinion, mass ideals, and psychologized advertising of national products. Emerson deserves full meed of praise for preaching the value of individualism, but it may be asked, granting that nearly all intelligent, high-minded American youths for nearly a century have, at their most idealistic stage, come under the influence of Emerson's doctrine, why has the effect of his teaching been so slight upon their later manhood? Does the fault lie in them or in the great teacher, for, in such sentences as we have quoted above, I gladly allow that the sage of Concord *was* a great teacher.

The answer, I think, is that the fault lies to a great extent in Emerson himself. His doctrine contains two great flaws, one positive, the other negative, and both as typically American as he himself was in everything. That he had no logically articulated system of thought is not his weakest point. He once said that he could not give an account of himself if challenged. Attempts have been made to prove that his thought was unified and coherent. One may accept these or not. It matters little, for it is not, and never has been, as a consistent philosopher that Emerson has influenced his readers. It has been by his trenchant aphorisms which stir the soul of the young and the not too thoughtful, and set the blood to dancing like sudden strains of martial music. It is in these, and not in any metaphysical system about which philosophers might argue, that we find the fatal flaws and influences I have mentioned.

The first, the positive one, in spite of his high doctrine of self-reliance and individualism, is that Emerson makes life too easy by his insistence on intuition and spontaneity. The style and construction of his writings deliberately emphasize the import of the aphorisms. The occasionally qualifying context sinks into insignificance and out of memory as does the stick of a rocket in the darkness of night. We see and recall only the dazzling shower of stars. If this is now and then unfair to Emerson's thought, he has himself to blame. He took no pains to bind his thought together and loved the brilliancy of his rocket-stars of "sayings." We have already quoted some of these on the point we are now discussing. All teaching is "Intuition." In "Spontaneity or Instinct" he finds "the essence of genius, the essence of virtue, and the essence of life." "It is as easy for the strong man to be strong, as it is for the weak to be weak." "All good conversation, manners, and action, come from a spontaneity which forgets usages, and makes the moment great." "No man need be perplexed by his speculations. . . . These are the soul's mumps and measles and whooping-coughs." "Our moral nature is vitiated by any interference of our will. . . . There is no merit in the matter. Either God is there or he is not there. We love characters in proportion as they are impulsive and spontaneous. The less a man thinks or knows about his virtues the better we like him." A page or two back we noted his theory of spontaneity in art and intellect.

3

This, as we have said, unless the occasional qualifications are as greatly emphasized as the sayings themselves, is extremely dangerous doctrine. Of all the youths who have read Emerson in their impressionable years, a certain proportion have subsequently retrograded in the spiritual and intellectual scale, and a certain proportion have advanced. Of the difficulty with the master felt by the latter we shall speak presently, but for the first group this doctrine of spontaneity, so emphasized by Emerson, offers all too soft a cushion upon which to recline. Act and do not think. Culture is headache. Perplexities are the soul's mumps and measles. Radiant sentence after sentence, graven with clear precision on the cameo of the mind. It has been said that, of all the sages, Emerson requires the least intellectual preparation to read. He is, indeed, in some respects, and those in which he exerts most influence, fatally easy. Fatally easy and alluring to the busy hundred-per-cent American is this doctrine of intuition and spontaneity. It is a siren voice, a soft Lydian air blown across the blue water of the mind's tropical sea. For a century the American has left the plain hard work of life to his foreign serfs. The backbreaking toil of digging trenches, laying rails, puddling iron in the furnaces, has been delegated successively to the Irish, the Italians, the Slavs. But thinking is intellectually, willing is spiritually, as backbreaking as these. The ordinary American prefers also to abandon them and to take for himself the easier task of solving the economic problems and puzzles in which he delights. Intuition and spontaneity—fatal words for a civilization which is more and more coming to depend for its very existence on clear, hard, and long-sustained "thinking-through." It is this positive flaw in Emerson's teaching that has made the effect of his really noble doctrines of so little influence upon the boys who have worshiped him this side idolatry at sixteen and then gone into the world and found every invitation to retreat from the high ground rather than to advance.

What now of those others, those who also worshiped Emerson in youth, who have fought the world, and who find him declining in influence over their lives the more they advance? With them we reach Emerson's negative flaw.

What a gulf between the man of fifty and the boy of sixteen! As one has in those intervening years studied the history of the past, watched the daily life of the people of a score of nations, seen wars and famines take their toll of millions, and, nearer one's own heart, watched the physical pain of those closest to one's self, stood at grave after grave, found, too, perhaps, that one has wrought evil when most striving to do good, one has come to feel the whole mystery of that problem of Evil—of sin, of suffering, of death. One may yet carry a brave heart and hold one's self erect, but one is no longer content with a philosophy of shallow optimism, a "God's in his heaven—all's right with the world."

I think that here is where Emerson fails us as we grow older and wiser. The trumpet blasts of self-reliance which so thrilled us at sixteen sound a little thin and far-off now. We needed them when they first smote our ear and we are deeply grateful, but we have fought the fight, we have tried to be ourselves, we have tried to live our life for itself and not for a spectacle, and now we are older. We have lived, loved, suffered, enjoyed, fought, and to some extent won. The world has been rich in interest—and in suffering. There are hopeful signs on every side. There is sunlight as well as darkness, but there *is* darkness. One has been close to failure and looked it in the eye. There have been the brows we could not soothe through years of suffering, the waxen faces we kissed for the last time before we laid them away, the mysterious darkness coming toward ourselves like the shadow of a cloud on a summer landscape, but inevitably to overtake us. When we turn again to the great teacher of our youth, what does he say to help or hearten us? Nothing.

Owing largely to material circumstance and a vast and uninhabited continent, the prevailing mood of the American people came to be one of shallow and unlimited optimism, the waves of which flowed over even the sectional Calvinism of New England. Nature ceased to be the evil enemy of man's spirit and gave him her fairest gifts, as Mephistopheles bestowed his Helen on the tortured Faust. With material abundance, spiritual evil ceased to appear important and a golden age seemed dawning, as youth came to Faust in that most un-American legend.

For its hundred and fifty years America has been scarcely touched by suffering. Pestilence? None. Think of the Black Death and other great plagues that have swept over Europe. Famine? None. Think of India and China. War? Scarcely more than one. In the Revolution only an infinitesimal part of the population was in the army for any length of time. The War of 1812 was a ripple, almost all at sea, and the deaths were negligible to the population. The Indian Wars? Skirmishes by paid troops. The Mexican War? A junket which never came home to the people. The Civil War? Yes, but even that did not come home to the whole civilian popula- tion, except in the South, as have the wars which have flowed in torrents over Europe. Compare it with the Thirty Years' War, in which, to say nothing of the rest of Europe, the population of Ger- many, from the ravages of the sword, famine, disease, and emigra- tion, sank from 16,000,000 to 6,000,000, and in which of 35,000 vil- lages in Bohemia less than 6,000 were standing at the end, and in which nine tenths of the entire population of the Palatinate dis- appeared. The Spanish War was a holiday affair except for a few homes. In the last Great War we lost by death a mere 126,000 as compared with 8,500,000 in the Old World. In civil life our history has been one long business boom, punctuated by an occasional panic, like a fit of indigestion for a man who continually overeats. We have never suffered like the rest of humanity, and have waxed fat without, as yet, having to consider the problems forced upon others, until we have ceased to believe in their reality. The dominant American note has thus been one of a buoyant and unthinking optimism. America is a child who has never gazed on the face of death.

Emerson somewhere speaks of "the nonchalance of boys sure of a dinner." Can any words better express the American attitude toward the universe, and, in spite of his spirituality and the some- what faded fresco of his mysticism, does Emerson himself really give us anything deeper? Man, acording to him, "is born to be rich." Economic evils trouble our sage not at all. The universe, for him, is good through and through, and "success consists in close application to the laws of the world, and, since those laws are intellectual and moral, an intellectual and moral obedience." One thinks of Jay Gould and the career of many a magnate of to-day! "In a free and just commonwealth, property rushes from the idle and imbecile, to the industrious, brave, and persevering." As I am certainly not idle (I am working on a holiday to write this), and as Americans would not admit that theirs is not a just and free commonwealth, imbecility is the only third horn of the trilemma on which to impale myself if property has not rushed toward me. "Do not skulk," the sage tells every man in "a world which exists for him." At fifty, we have found, simply, that the world does *not* exist for us. "Love and you shall be loved. All love is mathematically just, as much as the two sides of an algebraic problem." One rubs one's eyes. "There is a soul at the center of nature and over the will of every man, so that none of us can wrong the universe." Man may, he says, "easily dismiss all particular uncertainties and fears, and adjourn to the sure revelation of time the solution of his private riddles. He is sure his welfare is dear to the heart of being." Is he so sure? Alas, no longer.

4

As I think over my most recent visit to Rome, where two thousand years of human history, happiness, and suffering have left their monuments, and Heaven knows how many thousand unmarked before, I contrast it with a visit to Emerson's house at Concord on an October day many years ago. It is a charming, roomy old house, and in it Emerson was able to live with a large library and three servants on two thousand a year. In the ineffable light of an American autumn, as I saw it, it was a place of infinite peace. Concord in 1840 was an idyllic moment in the history of the race. That moment came and passed, like a baby's smile. Emerson lived in it. "In the morning," he wrote, "I awake, and find the old world, wife, babies, and mother, Concord and Boston, the dear old spiritual world, and even the dear old devil not far off."

It is true that he has very occasional qualms and doubts. He even wonders in one essay whether we must presuppose some "slight treachery and derision" in the universe. As we turn the pages, we ask ourselves with some impatience, "Did this man never really suffer?" and read that "the only thing grief has taught me, is to know how shallow it is. That, like all the rest, plays about the surface, and never introduces me into the reality, for contact with which, we would even pay the costly price of sons and lovers."

One ends. Perhaps Mr. More is right. Perhaps Emerson *is* the outstanding figure in American letters. Who else has expressed so magnificently the hope, and so tragically illustrated the illusion, of our unique contribution to the world? My own debt to the sage is unpayable. He was one of the great influences in my early life, as, in his highest teaching, he should be in that of every boy. It seems almost the basest of treason to write this essay, and I would still have every youth read his Emerson. But what of America? What of the hope and the illusion? A century has passed. Is no one to arise who will fuse them both in some larger synthesis, and who, inspiring youth, will not be a broken reed in maturity? Are our letters and philosophy to remain the child until the Gorgon faces of evil, disaster, and death freeze our own unlined ones into eternal stone? Is it well that the outstanding figure in American letters should be one whose influence diminishes in proportion as the minds of his readers grow in strength, breadth, and maturity? And, speaking generally, is this not true of Emerson? Does any man of steadily growing character, wealth of experience, and strength of mind find the significance and influence of Emerson for him growing as the years pass? Does he turn to him more and more for counsel, help, or solace?

There is but one answer, I think, and that is negative. Unlike the truly great, the influence of Emerson shrinks for most of us as we ourselves develop. May the cause not lie in the two flaws I have pointed out, flaws in the man as in his doctrine in spite of the serene nobility of so much of his life? If with all his wide and infinitely varied reading, noted in his *Journals*, we find his culture a bit thin and puerile, is it not because he himself trusted too much to that theory of spontaneity, of the "spontaneous glance," rather than to the harder processes of scholarship and thinking-through coherently; and if we find him lacking in depth and virility, is it not because he allowed himself to become a victim to that vast American optimism with its refusal to recognize and wrestle with the problem of evil? One turns to Æschylus and reads:—

> . . . affliction knows no rest,
> But rolls from breast to breast its vagrant tide.

One does not need to be a pessimist, merely human, to find here the deeper and more authentic note.

If Emerson is still the outstanding figure in American letters, is that not the equivalent of saying that America a century after the *Essays* appeared has not yet grown to mental maturity, and that the gospel it preaches is inspiring only for unformed adolescence,—of whatever age,—without having risen to a comprehension of the problems of maturity? In Europe, the past has bequeathed not only a wealth of art, but a legacy of evil borne and sorrow felt. Perhaps American letters, like American men, will not grow beyond the simple optimism and, in one aspect, the shallow doctrine of Emerson until they too shall have suffered and sorrowed. Emerson, in his weakness as in his strength, is American through and through. He could have been the product, in his entirety, of no other land, and that land will not outgrow him until it has some day passed through the fires of a suffering unfelt by him and as yet escaped by it.

ROBERT E. SPILLER (1896–   ) was chairman of the editorial board of *Literary History of the United States* (1948), for which he wrote the chapter on Emerson as a comprehensive view of Emerson's work. Spiller, professor of English, emeritus, at the University of Pennsylvania, has been co-editor of *The Early Lectures of Ralph Waldo Emerson* (1959, 1964), and has written *The Cycle of American Litreature* (1955) and many other critical works in the field of literary history. Some of his essays have been collected in *The Oblique Light* (1968). The following, from the above-mentioned chapter, is concerned with Emerson's poetry.

Ralph Waldo Emerson: Man Thinking

ROBERT E. SPILLER

A half century after the United States had been baptized in political independence, the time had come for confirmation in freedom of the soul. Ralph Waldo Emerson, of Concord, Massachusetts, declared the ceremony performed and became spokesman for his time and country.

His preeminence has caused our literary historians some embarrassment. America was ready for a Shakespeare, a Dante, or a Dostoevski to give literary voice to her achieved majority. She was given an apologist—an Aristotle, a Paul, a Bacon. In the wise and temperate Emerson, the heat became radiant light. It was he who brought into its first sharp focus the full meaning of two centuries of life on the Atlantic seaboard of this continent; of the economic and spiritual revolutions which had unsettled the Old World and settled the New; of the experiment in democracy which was to make a Holy Commonwealth into a world power.

He did this in two ways: by carrying to its ultimate statement the individual's revolt from authority, which marked the transition from the medieval world to the modern; and by formulating the dichotomy between the vision of a Jonathan Edwards and the common sense of a Benjamin Franklin, a conflict and a balance which has always provided the creative tension in American life. But he translated these discoveries neither into formal philosophy nor into fully formed art. His logic and his metaphysics remained without system; his art, like that of all great American romantics, retained its organic freedom.

As Emerson had no Boswell, he must speak for himself, and he spent his life in doing so. Upon an audience he played with the sure hands of a master organist; but the oft shuffled manuscripts in his study were cold. "We do not go to hear what Emerson says," wrote Lowell, "so much as to hear Emerson." A tall blond figure in black, he leaned forward across the reading desk in shy Yankee awkwardness and searched the hearts of his hearers with sincere blue eyes and controlled voice.

"Where do we find ourselves?" he asks in his essay on "Experience," and he gives his answer: "On its own level, or in view of nature, temperament is final." The inner wholeness of the man is his true self; his life "is a train of moods like a string of beads"; temperament, the iron wire on which the beads are strung. Striving to give expression only and always to this central self, Emerson has left a handful of essays and poems which are to many an essential part of their religious literature; but the man himself evades discovery. "So much of our time is preparation," he explains, "so much is routine, and so much retrospect, that the pith of each man's genius contracts itself to a very few hours."

Preparation—routine—retrospect; these are the entries on the calendar, the frame of life for a reticent New England man who is Emerson the seer. He devoted thirty-three years to what he thought of later as "preparation" before he published his first book in 1836; some two decades provided the "very few hours" when his genius was at high pitch and all of his great work was produced from the essential stability and calm of "routine"; and finally there were almost thirty years of "retrospect" before his death in 1882. The central twenty years have left us our impression of a man who always stood firm on moral ground and admonished his fellows to turn their eyes from evil, to have faith in themselves and in one another, and to seek God through Nature. But the Emersonian confidence and calm were not achieved, nor were they maintained, without struggle, doubt, and self-examination. . . .

IV

The "new art" of Emerson is contained in five volumes—all, except some of the poems, written within the decade 1844–54, none published immediately. They are *Poems* (1847), *Representative Men* (1850), *English Traits* (1856), *The Conduct of Life* (1860), and *May-Day* (1867). That in this period he passed from a state of romantic tension to one of "classic" or organic restraint more suitable to the New England disposition is attested by his own statement in a lecture on "Art and Criticism" delivered in 1859:

"The art of writing is the highest of those permitted to man as drawing directly from the Soul, and the means or material it uses are also of the Soul. . . . Classic art is the art of necessity; organic; modern or romantic bears the stamp of caprice or chance." Even though he retained the doctrinal foundations of his thought in historical romanticism, Emerson developed his arts of poem and lecture-essay in this, his own, definition of the classic, by admitting the need for moral restraint in art.

His poetry was written in his own study, the product of walks in the Concord fields or to his "garden," the wood lot on Walden Pond which he allowed Thoreau to use for his cabin. The prose was a reworking of lectures delivered in England (1847–48) and in the "West" from Pittsburgh to Cincinnati, to St. Louis and Chicago (1850–53). During these years he was away almost as much as he was at home, and Lidian made out as best she could, caring for the children and the big white house, aided by the townsfolk and by Henry Thoreau, the master's delegate in residence to tend the fires and the garden.

Had he never written a word of prose, Emerson's achievement as an experimental and epigrammatic poet would give him a primary place in our literature. In his youth he was the admitted poet of the family, but even he refrained from taking his nonsense and imitative verses too seriously. When the time came to woo Lydia* Jackson, not only to himself but to Concord, he had attained to better perspective. "I am a born poet," he wrote, "of a low class without doubt yet a poet . . . in the sense of a perceiver and dear lover of the harmonies that are in the soul and in matter, and specially of the correspondence between these and those"; but he was "uncertain always whether I have one true spark of that fire which burns in verse."

A born poet he most assuredly was, in theory as well as fact. Before the publication of his *Poems* in 1847, the United States had had but one true student and experimenter in the art, Edgar Allan Poe. Bryant, Halleck, and Freneau either had shown no deep interest in the theory and technique of poetry or had conformed to the romantic modes of Wordsworth and Byron, and to the traditions of the English lyric. The early verse of Whittier, Simms, Longfellow, Lowell, and Holmes had accepted similar models without fresh exploration of anything but the American scene. Poe alone had sought to rediscover the nature and function of poetry in itself. Emerson's originality is as profound as that of Poe, and the theories of the two supplement each other. Poe sought an aesthetic base for

*Emerson preferred to call her Lidian, and that apparently became her name. —Ed.

the art; Emerson, a moral. Poe explored mainly the possibilities of rhythm; Emerson, of symbol. Together they directed the course of American poetry since their time by turning from borrowed conventions and by seeking once more the springs of poetry. Walt Whitman and Emily Dickinson were further to exploit these breaks with the past; others would follow.

Part of Emerson's sense of inadequacy was caused by his high ideals for the poet. He is the seer, but he is more. He is also "the sayer, the namer, and represents beauty. He is sovereign and stands on the center. . . . He is a beholder of ideas and an utterer of the necessary and causal." His office is that "of announcement and affirming." He does not make his poem, "for poetry was all written before time was. . . . The men of more delicate ear write down these cadences." By characteristic overstatement, Emerson would thus make the role of the poet seem almost passive. He is an Aeolian harp that "trembles to the cosmic breath" (a favorite image). But he is also Merlin, the traditional bard, the wise man, the magician, whose "blows are strokes of fate." In the distribution of functions among men, he is the man speaking, the scholar who has an assigned course of action—to express the message he receives. By this test Plato at times seems almost to qualify as poet, and Sir Thomas Browne, Zoroaster, Michelangelo, and the authors of the Vedas, the Eddas, the Koran. George Herbert stands the test and Milton, next to Shakespeare the prince of poets because of his genius "to ascend by the aids of his learning and his religion—by an equal perception, that is, of the past and the future—to a higher insight and more lively delineation of the heroic life of man." And the Persian Saadi becomes for Emerson the prototype of the poet because

> He felt the flame, the fanning wings,
> Nor offered words till they were things.

Herein lies the insight which caused his spontaneous acceptance of *Leaves of Grass* in 1855. Whitman's words were things.

If the recording of celestial music had been to Emerson the only function of the poet, his verse might have been more melodic than it is. Rather in his prose, especially when it was prepared to be spoken, he came closest to achieving rhythmic freedom, as did Melville, whose philosopher in *Mardi* chants only when he is seized with the frenzy of prophetic vision. Before it was pruned and sharpened by gnomic insight, Emerson's style might flow with the current of his eloquence and climb by the measured but open periods of the Song of Solomon, the Sermon on the Mount, or Whitman's sweeping rhythms. In an unpublished passage from the introductory lecture to the early course on "Human Culture," he used the techniques which Whitman was later to exploit. Freed from the paragraph of prose as well as the meter of verse, his periodic lines are held to a frame by parallel phrasing, assonance, alliteration, and return:

> The philosopher laments the inaction of the higher faculties.
> He laments to see men poor who are able to labor.
> He laments to see men blind to a beauty that is beaming on every side of them.
> He laments to see men offending against laws and paying the penalty, and calling it a visitation of Providence. . . .
> He laments the foreign holdings of every man, his dependence for his faith, for his political and religious estimates and opinions, on other men, and on former times.
> And from all these oppressions is a wise Culture to redeem the Soul.

But Emerson asked more than this of the poet. The active function of poetry, as he saw it, was to make manifest and specific the correspondence between the real and the ideal, a task which rhythm alone could not accomplish. From the English metaphysical poets in prose and verse, Herbert, Donne, Milton, Browne, he learned the connotative value of the individual word, the possibilities for luster and surprise in the image. He turned to them rather than to the contemporary romantics who had acquiesced too easily in a passive pantheism. Milton and Herbert rather than Wordsworth and Coleridge felt God intensely and struggled to restore him to this world. These elder poets had striven, as did Emerson, to reconcile an intense religious faith with an equally intense challenge of science, and his method was theirs. In this, he stood alone in his times among British and American poets, for not even Matthew Arnold appreciated the full worth of the symbol, however much he struggled with the "two worlds" between which he stood. The mystic and the scientist must become one, and the symbol is the only means for the accomplishment of the union. This Emerson fully appreciated, and it is his gift to modern poetry. From Bacon he took the Aristotelian view that "poetry, not finding the actual world exactly conformed to its idea of good and fair, seeks to accommodate the show of things to the desires of the mind, and to create an ideal world better than the world of experience." To this he added the Swedenborgian view that nature must serve man for symbols, that by seeing through the phemonenon to the essence, the poet might transform the evidence of his senses to a higher use and reestablish the correspondence between the natural and the moral laws. "The act of imagination is ever attended by pure light. It infuses a certain volatility and intoxication into all Nature." The poet is "an exact reporter of the essential law," but he is active rather than passive because he restores the harmonies of the Over-Soul through the counterpoint of experience; he supplies from his intuition the true, rather than the apparent, natural image. "The mind, penetrated with its sentiment or its thought, projects it outward on whatever it beholds." The result is a beauty not of the senses but of the moral sentiment.

The critic should not be misled by Emerson's frequent references to poetry as music, for his own verse rarely sings. "That which others hear," he confessed, "I see." Even in his poem on "Music," the images are almost all visual, and "Merlin's Song" is "of keenest eye" before it is of "truest tongue." His dissonant rhymes and limping rhythms are parts of a deliberate effort to achieve freedom of movement, and they receive at least some authority from their models. Butler used "slanted" or imperfect rhymes, Milton incomplete lines, and Shakespeare, in his later plays, a roving accent. Emerson asked for all these freedoms together. He made excessive use of rhyme, because to him it was the favorite instrument of rhythm in Nature (although again his examples are visual: reflections in a pond or the repeating forms of shadows). He also adopted the eight-syllable line because he was convinced by the theory of O. W. Holmes that periodicity in poetry is determined by human respiration. He never broke loose in his poetry as did Whitman, into the more natural freedom of colloquial speech. But within his limits, all of which he believed are imposed by Nature rather than tradition, he trusted the song as he heard it, even though his hearing was not always true. His rhymes are often little more than assonances; his meter, counted syllables that sometimes miss the count, letting the accent fall where it may.

With the visual image, Emerson's muse can safely be trusted. In his "Mottoes"—verses distilled to provide texts for his essays—he committed Wordsworth's fault of trying to deal too directly with thought. But where the image is given full play, as in "The Sphinx" (his own favorite), "Days" (perhaps his most successful), "Hamatreya" (his most direct), "Uriel," "Brahma," "The Snow-Storm" and the first part of "Merlin," it achieves an intricate pattern of conceit worthy of Herbert or Donne, but fresh from his own experience. Here the poet exerted his full prerogatives with volatile nature, using the evidences of the pines, the sea, the stars to its own purposes and revealing the correspondence of the law of things to the law of God. In other poems like "Woodnotes," "Threnody," and his odes, he achieves sureness and freedom in some passages, but falls into rhymed prose in others; and sometimes, as in "The Rhodora," the message is too explicit, the effect didactic.

At his best, Emerson's keen sensitivity to the larger aspects of nature, his mastery and daring with the visual image, his deep appreciation of the connotative value of single words (a gift not shared even by Poe and not approached by any other contemporary except Emily Dickinson who followed his course in both theory and technique), place him among the most original and provocative if not the most even poets in the language. Add to these qualities the intrinsic value of what he has to say, and his poetry becomes one of the treasures of our literature, greater in some respects than his essays because, when he allows himself full scope, he speaks from and for himself a universal language, without reference to a particular audience even by inference. His art is organic in that it reproduces the organism of moral law as reflected in nature; it is classic, as he would have it, only when his daring experiments achieve unity and, as in "Days," his intricate and climbing images merge into a single symbol of revelation. . . .

JONATHAN BISHOP (1927–   ) is associate professor of English at Cornell University. His book *Emerson on the Soul* (1964) is one of the best studies of Emerson published in the twentieth century. The following is from the concluding chapter.

Emerson as Prophet

JONATHAN BISHOP

The new Emerson I have just finished schematizing is an appealing figure. He may seem easier to sympathize with, to "approve of," than the radical transcendentalist. It is easier to believe in the existence of a slight Soul. The lack of pretension, the relative absence of what was incredible in the early vatic stance, is truly admirable. We confront, in the mature ideas and the mature tone, much that effortlessly coincides with the best of a literary and social tradition we can still imaginatively share. The history of American culture since Emerson died would support a high valuation for his later self. When subsequent generations continued to value his first ideas, they understood them as they were diffused through and modified by the image of a gentlemanly and modestly optimistic scholar who remained behind after his radical identity lapsed. And now that "Emerson" exists, if he exists at all, as a certain subtle flavor of intellect, it is to the finished ironies and mature acknowledgments that one can most readily turn to exemplify what remains to be admired by men of the world. His later stance allowed Emerson a more relaxed appreciation of the serial impulses of the mind, a certain freedom to notice what interested him in the world for its own sake, regardless of its ultimate reference to the unused or unusable powers of the Soul. His renderings of the details of experience become more understandable because more casual. The potluck of the day turned out to be easier to put in convincing words than the entirety gestured at in the old phrase of the Mt. Auburn experience, "It was Day." All expression, after all, is of parts, of particles. We would probably find it easier to convince a contemporary skeptic that Emerson deserves attention as a man of letters by bringing forward the passages that show a man of infinite literary tact, a mind capable of sophisticated address, than by holding his unwilling attention to the old expressions of enthusiastic hope. The talent of Emerson is easier to communicate without the labor of explanation than his genius.

In spite of this, it is, I believe, the early doctrine that we should attend to most seriously. We are closest to Emerson when we put ourselves in a position to see the charms of the later thinking and writing as qualifications of a message whose core remains at once simpler and broader, more absolute and more radical. For one thing —a crude but important point—the earlier belief is, at least potentially, *truer* than the later. This is particularly so of the two versions of the all-determining organic faculty. In Emerson's first account, this dimension of the Soul is directly and naturally available to each person. On behalf of this idea, one can always point out that each of us is always in some minimal sense alive; as long as he is capable of enjoying his life consciously, and of seeing it reflected from the particulars into which it is projected, he is free to find himself fundamentally inside the world, originally related to the universe. He can be ready to enlarge his sense of himself as a subject from this starting point. His organic consciousness provides a model for the more sophisticated actions of the self. The other faculties of the Soul, too, are always experienceable in specific moral and intellectual emergencies. Their congruence with each other and with the sense of life can be a possible faith for all who live in the world.

Emerson's latter-day belief in the beneficent forward motion of the total universe, on the other hand, seems less credible as a description of what is and might be. It is not merely an exteriorization of the organic faculty, but an elaboration of its mode of action into a myth. Like all myths, it bears the marks of its age, which is not ours. Subjective organicism is at least a permanent possibility for the human spirit; objective organicism involves a belief in an ameliorative evolution that cannot help but appear a Victorian illusion. The Emerson of the later doctrine therefore separates himself from our condition; he becomes the preacher of a myth about the Soul, instead of a prophet of the Soul itself.

The earlier Emerson continues, then, as a present witness for the total subject of action, for the potential interrelevance of all the faculties that are discoverable within our experiences of reality. Especially he stands for the possible coincidence of reliable insight and judgment with instinctive organic response. As such, Emerson's first doctrine of the Soul can still be useful, if not as a faith, then as a standard against which to evaluate the quality of experience in an age very different from his. The freedom to criticize our condition effectively is not the least of the gifts Emerson can give us. Matched against Emerson's faith in the subjectivity of significant action, all our tendencies to yield the theoretical initiative to outward forces can seem suspicious. We are painfully familiar with the assumption of "common sense" that enormous areas of our experience cannot be credited to any subjective agency at all. Theoretically and in practice, we like to think ourselves victims of exterior gods. The modern consciousness readily defines itself as an effect of irresistible "realities," whether these are psychic needs or political institutions, neuroses or nations. Rather little is easily felt to be *our own*. But is such a disposition necessary? Emerson can prompt us to ask, what makes it so?

Even within the sphere still habitually analyzed in terms of some formula of subjective action, one can use Emerson's belief in the unity of the Soul to become more conscious of a prevalent deterioration and separateness. For the early Emerson, the Soul is founded on a primitive sense of organic vitality, on our power to animate what we see. One could scarcely say of modern urban society that it neglects the organic satisfactions, in actuality or as fantasy. But few enjoy these satisfactions uncontaminated by anxiety, and fewer still "believe" in them, that is, connect the pleasures of life with the special motions of intellect and character. We have an underground culture that makes much of the pursuit of organic sensation, occasionally justifying this desperate endeavor in terms that interestingly echo Emersonian sayings. But sensual acts seem rarely to have moral resonance or intellectual implication. For many they exist and prevail to the degree that moral and intellectual concerns are repudiated, or at least kept safely at a distance. They can seem to stand rather as a kind of animal compensation for a pervasive inhibition of the other faculties, and not as a sacred source of life from which these may be renewed.

While discussing the moral sentiment, I raised some of the theoretical reasons why that portion of the Emersonian message can seem obscure or incredible. An observer of cultural fact may speculate that there are practical as well as historical reasons for finding it hard to believe in the inwardness and relevance of conscience. Moral action seems rare in our world even as something to pretend to. Few seem able to feel themselves moral agents; the self does not comfortably place its behavior in terms of this dimension. The frequently mentioned "crisis of identity" is presumably bound up with this condition. For a disbelief in the substantiality and efficacy of the self can be connected with the progressive weakening of the old belief in one's independent power to arrive at correct moral judgments. Without such a belief, a man subjects himself to ad-hoc systems of expectation generated by whatever group he happens to find himself in. To these expectations all responses are "role playing," not moral action. In such situations, there can be nothing categorical in the demands to which one accedes, and therefore nothing authentic and subjective about the forms of action through which they are fulfilled.

The best answer to such moral anaesthesia is probably implicit in the acts of those who have freed themselves from acquiescent routine and declared war on the evil in the world, like the civil-rights activists and the resisters to nuclear war. It is chastening and inspiring to observe that the rhetoric of these strugglers revives, as if it had never died, the idea that principle is available to individuals, who may find their manhood in obeying it. In such behavior the continuing relevance of the Emersonian belief can be made real again as a lively critique of habitual passivities and excuses.

Above all, Emerson's first faith can throw a critical light on the modern fortunes of intellect. The Understanding has triumphed with a completenes that would certainly have appalled those nineteenth-century prophets who made so much of the danger experience could suffer from unrestricted rationality. We live in a world increasingly dominated by separated Mind, the acts of which present us with problems solvable only by the application of still more Mind—solutions that will in their turn constitute still greater problems. And this Mind seems increasingly separated from the thinking of individuals. Yet a civilization racked by institutionalized technology seems able to think of no way out of its troubles except the further refinement of the agencies that caused them.

What would it take to create a new Emerson, who could throw affirmative light upon the old? It is worth speculating on, if only to confirm our understanding of our subject. One requirement would be a convincing idiom. Emerson could reargue the case for the Soul by using just that term—which, as I mentioned at the beginning of this book, is not now easily available. He could discover a full vocabulary in which to express his faith in that branch of the "perennial philosophy" that came to him and his readers through Coleridge, Cousin, and Swedenborg. The meanings of the master terms in this language happened, for reasons with which Emerson as an individual had nothing to do, to coincide with a certain stage in the Unitarian idiom, the stage represented, say, by the elder Channing. It was possible, that is, for Emerson to speak on behalf of the organic subject (my far clumsier term) by calling it "God" and "Reason" together. From the point of view of intellectual history, Emerson will appear a rare coincidence of a set of loaded words, whose interchange of energy could explode into vital meaning for himself and his readers.

In an age of intellectual dispersal like ours, a similar coincidence of major meanings, including among them some sacred term for vital energy, seems far to seek. "Mind," "imagination," "the self," retain their separate shades of useful connotation. It is hard, though, to anticipate anything but pedantic abstraction from their use together or apart. The idiom of psychoanalysis is (heavily qualified) available as a mode of description; but we must wait to see if its terms can have charismatic value outside of technical or casually social contexts.

What one wants, then, is not a criticism of Emerson but a continuation—or rather, a continuation that would make the criticism real. . . .

No work, life, or career from the past can appear deeply interesting to us unless it seems to contain within it an action which upon examination turns out to be something we are doing now, or would like to be doing now. Those elements of our experience that seem valuable but endangered can be strengthened by discovering for them an ancestry of articulate command. An eye that lacks vitality will search for visible evidences of life; a mind that distrusts its own thought will search for examples of thinking that have not lost the touch of life. Emerson's art can echo and sanction our most secret efforts to recover an inside for our multiple worlds.

I cannot leave the reader with a better instance of Emerson's potential serviceableness to this end than by bringing forward, once again, a singular passage. It might have been used earlier as a pendant to the discussion of the individual self and its local opportunities. I have reserved it to end with because its excellencies point the full moral of the Soul's potential in Emersonian language that requires no translation whatsoever for a modern mind. The passage in question is from the insufficiently praised essay, "Spiritual Laws." Emerson is talking about the way the Soul responds to the experience that belongs to it:

> He may have his own. A man's genius, the quality that differences him from every other, the susceptibility to one class of influences, the selection of what is fit for him, the rejection of what is unfit, determines for him the character of the universe. A man is a method, a progressive arrangement; a selecting principle, gathering his like to him wherever he goes. He takes only his own out of the multiplicity that sweeps and circles round him. He is like one of those booms which are set out from the shore on rivers to catch drift-wood, or like the loadstone amongst splinters of steel. Those facts, words, persons,

which dwell in his memory without his being able to say why, remain because they have a relation to him not less real for being as yet unapprehended. They are symbols of value to him as they can interpret parts of his consciousness which he would vainly seek words for in the conventional images of books and other minds. What attracts my attention shall have it, as I will go to the man who knocks at my door, whilst a thousand persons as worthy go by it, to whom I give no regard. It is enough that these particulars speak to me. A few anecdotes, a few traits of character, manners, face, a few incidents, have an emphasis in your memory out of all proportion to their apparent significance if you measure them by the ordinary standards. They relate to your gift. Let them have their weight, and do not reject them and cast about for illustration and facts more usual in literature. What your heart thinks great, is great. The soul's emphasis is always right.

That this is excellent, I hope need not be asserted—the arguments of this book make the best critical context I can provide for the appreciation I must presume. But the specific manner of the excellence can be brought more fully before the mind by attending to the changes Emerson's expression underwent as his statement shifted from journal to lecture to its final form in the essay. They are minor—that is the point. The work done is of a very simple kind, but it suffices to make art.

The immediate source of this passage can be found in a lecture called "The School." The lecture beginning was a good deal hazier: the second sentence started, "In the next place, this in its primary mysterious combination with the nature of the Individual makes what we call distinctively the genius of the man or the peculiar quality that differences him from every other." This fussy Coleridgizing, itself arrived at through a certain amount of deletion and insertion, has been neatly replaced in the essay by the succinct "A man's genius, the quality that differences him." Rhythm too has been improved throughout the passage, indeed created out of parenthetical clumsiness by a consistent substitution of a march of commas for original interruptive periods. The wordy independence of the lecture version, "and this evidently determines for each Soul the character of the Universe," is reduced to the modest, lower-case, smoothness of the essay's clause, "determines for him the character of the universe." A sermon-like seesaw, "as a man thinketh, so is he; & as a man chooseth, so is he, & so is Nature," proves too smug for effective alteration; it is dropped, and the passage continues directly with what was already good, the fine and simple, "A man is a method, a progressive arrangement."

Farther on much is dropped altogether, apparently because it is repetitious, diffuse, or weakly exemplary. In the lecture there is a sentence beginning, "Hence arises that mysterious emphasis which certain facts, thoughts, characters, faces, have." The single word "emphasis" is extracted to be used in a later sentence in the essay; except for this, the author's eye skips two whole paragraphs and resumes with "Those facts, words, & persons," a series that he rightly preferred to the looser catalogue he first wrote, "facts, thoughts, characters, faces."

In studying such transmutations of the passage from lecture to essay we have the advantage also of possessing a journal version. Emerson's first rendering of his idea took the form of two separate journal entries, one for November 27, 1837, and the other for November 25, 1838. The first is an independent note:

Expressiveness

I magnify instincts. I believe that those facts & words & persons which dwell in a man's memory without his being able to say why, remain because they have a relation to him not less real for being as yet unapprehended. They are symbols of value to him as they can interpret parts of his consciousness which he would vainly seek words for in the conventional images of books & other minds. What therefore attracts my attention shall have it, as I will go to the man who knocks at my door, & a thousand persons as worthy go by it, to whom I give no heed.

The second forms part of a longer entry not all of which is relevant. The section Emerson decided to use reads:

This is the reason why you must respect all your private impressions. A few anecdotes a few traits of character manners face a few incidents have an emphasis in your memory out of all proportion to their apparent significance, if you measure them by the ordinary standards of history. Do not for this a moment doubt their value to you. They relate to you to your peculiar gift. Let them have all their weight & do not reject them & cast about for illustration & facts more usual in English literature.

When he first made up his lecture, he brought these passages together, copying directly from the journal entries, but making a few changes, chiefly of omission, as he went. The lecture manuscript shows what happened. Thus he copied "I believe that those facts," but crossed out the first three words to improve emphasis and remove unnecesary egotism, and turned one of the original ampersands to a comma to formalize the series. The rest of the first entry he copied hurriedly, as a misspelling, "knows" for "knocks," proves, but he found time enough to superscribe a "whilst" over the original "and" to bring out a minor logical connection between clauses.

When he turned to the second journal entry, he composed a new transition: "It is sufficient that these particulars speak to me." This is a considerable sharpening of tone over the cozy banality of the old, "This is the reason why you must respect all your private impressions." A new voice is introduced, elevated and proud, consistent with the high sense of the idea it proposes. These "impressions," says the tone, are a man's noblest possession. (When he came to compose his essay later, he found opportunity for further improvement, changing the Latinate "sufficient" to the plainer "enough.") From this point on, he copied again as he wrote his lecture, adding commas to guide his reading emphasis, and dropping the otiose "of history" from the tail of the phrase "by the ordinary standards." This omission came to him as he wrote or rechecked his lecture text, for the prepositional phrase is first copied into the lecture manuscript and then crossed out. Similarly he concentrated "they relate to you to your peculiar gift" into "They relate to your peculiar gift." (Here too his later review for the essay led to a second change for the better. "Peculiar" was dropped, pointing the sentence still more intimately at the reader: "They relate to your gift.")

From this sentence on, the lecture version is an expansion of the second journal entry, apparently composed for the first time as he prepared his text for oral delivery. There are many deletions and interlineations. The pair of sentences that conclude the essay version are written on the lecture sheet in pencil, as if he had used that piece of paper as his rough copy for the essay. In making the final transfer from lecture to essay, he cut "all" and "English" from "let them have all their weight, & do not reject them & cast about for illustration & facts more usual in English Literature." Impatient at the unnecesary illustration from the history of botany he had gone on to use in the lecture, he leaps forward to his conclusion, dismissing some repetitive concluding sentences and replacing them with two phrases from the tangle of interlineations: "What your heart thinks great is great" becomes, with the addition of a comma for emphasis, the penultimate sentence, and "The soul's emphasis is the true one," with a new predicate to strengthen the affirmative tone and to create rhythm, becomes the fine ending, "The soul's emphasis is always right."

To attend to the local effect of these small acts of composition is to become engaged in the minute particulars of the Emersonian enterprise, of which the meaning of the passage is simply a rendering in terms of moral adventure. The stringency, the vital demand of this adventure, comes home to us as we follow the leaps of the pen from word to word, from phrase to phrase. Each rhetorical change is an enlargement of the imaginative authority from which the claims regarding the Soul are made. Literature—here in its most elementary form of rewriting, of changing the good word for the better—enacts the very mind to be advanced. As we compare texts, we move, as Emerson moved, in the direction of that unity of thought and tone which stood in his thinking as the best image for the Soul's proper style of engagement with experience. We are brought closer to the continuous presence of a simple truth, to whose imaginative reality every sentence wonderfully contributes.

And that truth is the one of all the truths respecting the Soul for which the least special argument should today be required. What Emerson is saying in this passage is still his old insight, but that insight put into modestly psychological terms, which should bring it especially close to our private sense of what is true, or ought to be true, about the rewards of consciousness. The paragraph —beautifully supported by the remainder of the essay—is elegant by virtue of its power to concentrate what might otherwise be a matter for trailing peripheral awareness. We all know our experience as progress through a universe of events that is charged with the quality of our minds and repeats the structure of our psychic constitution. But this cloudy motion is too often downgraded to a blur, an ineluctable static interfering with our perception of "objective," is inevitable until it becomes meaningful, Emerson answers in rebuke and encouragement. Examine what happens anyway, the stones on which we do in fact stub our toe—to these our line of vision is naturally perpendicular, and we can see, if the spirit wills, exactly what they are. The immediate reward is some small piece of that is, conventional, reality. But let us attend to the details of what knowledge; the consequent advantage is an insight into our own "method," our special mode of making "progressive arrangements" among our facts, and thence into the tendency of the Soul in us.

The center of the paragraph could even stand as an exact description of the theory of free association familiar from psychoanalysis: "Those facts, words, persons, which dwell in his memory without his being able to say why, remain because they have a relation to him not less real for being as yet unapprehended. They are symbols of value to him . . ." But one does not want to limit the bearing of the statement. Emerson is recommending an awareness that grows continually out of the sense of life, and his description of the knack of it holds because it fits the comprehensiveness, the undemanding alertness, the quick readiness to interpret what calls for interpretation, which should characterize free perception at all times.

A touch that renders the description an act of judgment as well as explanation is the word "value." They are symbols, these facts, words, persons, but symbols of value; they "mean," ultimately, the energies of the Soul whose unimpeded and accurate exertion is the core of life. "They relate to your gift," says another hinge sentence— to what you were given, to what you can give, to what is your particular genius. Let these facts have their "weight," treat them with awe and courtesy: "What attracts my attention shall have it." The ending is formed exactly to finish a passage where tone, the tone of confidence, awareness, tenderness, prevails so soberly and delicately, with a reminder of the transcendent importance of tone: "The soul's emphasis is always right."

THEODORE L. GROSS (1930–   ) is author of *The Heroic Ideal in American Literature* (1971), of which the essay that follows is chapter 1. He is chairman of the English Department of the City College of the City University of New York, and has written many books on American culture. The essay on Emerson argues that the author of "The American Scholar," the "Divinity School Address," *Nature,* and the two series of *Essays* was "significantly different from the aristocrat" who wrote *Representative Men* and Emerson's later books; that the religious idealist gave way to the practical pragmatist. The notion that there were essentially two Emersons, an earlier and a later one, is also expressed by Quentin Anderson in *The Imperial Self* (1971). In some important ways this line of criticism was anticipated and rejected by John Jay Chapman, whose essay on Emerson remains one of the most perceptive critical writings on Emerson.

Under the Shadow of Our Swords:
Emerson and the Heroic Ideal

THEODORE L. GROSS

"I wish you would take an American hero," Carlyle urged Emerson in 1845, "one whom you really love; and give us a History of him,— make an artistic bronze statue (in good *words*) of his Life and him!" This advice seems strange indeed, for in the previous decade Emerson had published essays whose specific intention was to characterize and define the distinctive hero in America—to create him, as it were, for the imagination of the people in the new world; and Carlyle himself was largely instrumental in the reprinting and circulation of Emerson's works in England. The Scotsman did add, in this same letter, that "No other voice in this wide waste world seems to my sad ear to be *speaking* at all at present"; but there remains Carlyle's dissatisfaction with Emerson's conception of the hero, his feeling that Emerson was somehow not forceful enough, not "concrete" enough. Carlyle, of course, was never completely reconciled to Emerson's mystical tendencies, as Emerson remained discontent with Carlyle's "defense of mere force," his attempt "to find a hero, and let [people] be his slave."

The two writers clearly perceived each other's strengths and limitations, but as we consider Emerson's achievement, his special contribution to the idealistic strain in American culture, we begin to sense that Carlyle did not fully recognize that the author of "The American Scholar" (1837) and the "Divinity School Address" (1838) was significantly different from the aristocrat who created

Representative Men (1850), *English Traits* (1856), and *The Conduct of Life* (1860), that the representative American hero projected in Emerson's early essays yields to the extraordinary, powerful man of the later work, that the youthful egalitarianism or freedom, to borrow Stephen Whicher's term, succumbs to a measured recognition of fate. There is a change in Emerson's concept of the hero, from that of an emerging idealist who challenges the "courtly muses of Europe" and the religious authority of his Puritan heritage to that of an exceptional man for whom power in the public world is paramount. This shift from a moral idealism to a social authority should be emphasized, not only because of its significance to the development of Emerson's own writing but because it suggests a similar tension in the work of his contemporaries—the transcendentalists, Thoreau, Hawthorne, and Melville—and it anticipates many of the problems that confronted Whitman and James, even though many of these other authors wrote in different forms. The clear conflict between Emerson's initial idealism and the authority of other cultures or past theologies became a conflict within Emerson himself. The Emersonian hero who spoke for all Americans ultimately speaks for only himself.

Emerson's decreasing faith in the potential heroism of the common American, his growing interest in the accomplished, fully finished man of all nations, suggests some of the reasons why the heroic ideal could not survive in nineteenth-century American thought. For it is one thing to speak of the democratic hero in the 1830's when one is thinking specifically in religious terms and only generally in social terms, when one is not challenged by the social fact. It is another matter to write, in 1850, of representative men who do not represent democratic Americans; to turn to the traits of Englishmen, in 1856, in search of an exemplary use of practical power; to speak, in 1861, of the conduct of life as though it has nothing to do with the power of God and everything to do with the power of man—in short, to write these later books, which concentrate on force and authority, precisely at the time (the period of abolitionism and the Civil War) when moral idealism is being tested in the actual world. The concept of idealism, so forcefully expressed in *Nature,* "The American Scholar," and "The Divinity School Address," surrenders to a social authority that encroaches upon the Emersonian hero; the balance is gone; and heroism, which is no longer evolving but is fully grown, becomes what we fear it has become in America today—success, power, and authority in the external world itself.

In concentrating upon Emerson's altered view of the hero—the ideal hero—we admit its central significance to his thought. We recognize that his theory of correspondences, his ideas about Nature and language and the Reason subserve his overriding concern with the perfectible man. From this point of view, Emerson's early essays form not only the history of the hero that Carlyle requested but a philosophical epic in which he defines the characteristics necessary for heroism in America. The Emersonian hero assumes the preternatural qualities of an epic figure; he emerges rather than appears, becomes rather than is; and he stands as an ideal in the mind of the American, representing the most complete embodiment of the American dream in our literature. "Our day of dependence, our long apprenticeship to the learning of other lands draws to a close," he announces in "The American Scholar," seeking to define a form of heroism that is peculiarly organic to America. And when he reminds his audience, in the same address, that they are different from the ancient Greeks, the Troubadours, and their contemporaries in Europe, that in fact they are unique in the history of man, he is attempting to specify the peculiar attributes of the hero in America. Indeed the famous early essays—*Nature*, "The American Scholar," and the "Divinity School Address"—define the essence of the American hero from the historical point of view: the secular man who ideally can establish a harmony between himself and Nature; the scholar who can be more than "a farmer, or a professor, or an engineer," who can become a transcendental egoist and include the Universe within himself; and lastly the servant of God who must discover personally the "one mind that is everywhere active" and thus be free of tradition, of society—of the constricting and crippling forces that reach out from the past. Each of these addresses is historically oriented and does battle with a past that inhibits the American from establishing his own originality; each is an affirmation of self-trust; each focuses upon one dominant philosophical aspect of Emerson's thought—Nature, the mind, the spirit—although each, inevitably, includes the concerns of the other two addresses. Taken together, the three statements constitute prolegomena to the essays in the first and second series.

In the conclusion to *Nature*, Emerson reminds the reader that "At present, man applies to nature but half his force. He works on the world with his understanding alone." Impatient with man's acceptance of himself as limited, Emerson exhorts him to the full use of his Reason and concludes by celebrating the need for self-reliance. "All that Adam had, all that Caesar could, you have and can do," he reminds his contemporary American. "Adam called his house, heaven and earth; Caesar called his house, home; you perhaps call yours, a cobbler's trade; a hundred acres of ploughed land; or a scholar's garret. Yet line for line and point for point your dominion is as great as theirs, though without fine names. Build therefore your own world." Self-trust also informs the final paragraphs of "The American Scholar" and the "Divinity School Address"; indeed, as we turn to the *Essays: First Series,* we discover that all of Emerson's statements—charged with confidence and affirmation, free of doubt and hesitation, fixed like individual maxims on the page—lead to the climactic assertion that "there are resources in us on which we have not drawn." He defies the past in his desire to champion the insurgent American hero. In "History," which begins *Essays: First Series,* Emerson conditions his argument with the proclamation that "there is properly no history, only biography"— history is "incarnate in every just and wise man"—and his expression of admiration for "the Heroic or Homeric age down to the domestic life of the Athenians and Spartans" leads inevitably, as he considers the great ages in which the great heroes have lived, to the present emergence of the American hero—an epic rather than a tragic hero.

Emerson seems to provide the conditions for tragedy in "Self-Reliance," the essay that follows "History," for he sees the confident hero in confrontation with "the unintelligible brute force that lies at the bottom of society"; he recognizes that "to be great is to be misunderstood." But his hero has no essential weakness because he is always in a state of possibility, of becoming. Society is rigid, in conspiracy against the manhood of the hero; the past intimidates the hero and makes him "timid and apologetic," a little man afraid to act instinctually in response to the moral idealism that is his most natural attribute. "Greatness appeals to the future," Emerson concludes, suggesting that whatever limitations man may presently suffer from will eventually lose their force in the process of evolutionary melioration. "Life only avails, not the having lived. . . . This one fact the world hates; that the soul *becomes.*"

Because he sees man evolving into greatness, Emerson does not seriously consider, in his first two books of essays, the ways in which man is limited; he knows very well, as he observes in "Compensation," that "there is a crack in everything God has made," but he refuses to define that crack, to take a complete account of tragedy. As Newton Arvin points out, in a persuasive consideration of Emerson's treatment of tragedy, Emerson is a thinker who is unwilling to offer "a steady confrontation of Tragedy, or a sustained and unswerving gaze at the face of Evil"; he is a writer who develops his ideas beyond tragedy and offers "perhaps the fullest and most authentic expression in modern literature of the more than tragic emotion of thankfulness."

Of all our significant nineteenth-century American authors, Emerson is most obsessed with greatness, with the heroic ideal; and if he does not see his hero in tragic terms—"there is no writer in the world," Mr. Arvin reminds us, "in whose work we are not conscious of missing *something* that belongs to experience"—he does see him as someone defending and representing the new world. In his essays of the 1840's he defines those characteristics necessary for the full development of the epic hero—spirituality, love, friendship, prudence, intellect, art, character, manners, and heroism—as if he is offering the kind of moral instruction that religious mentors gave young knights in the Middle Ages as an essential part of their education into life. And, in "Heroism," he defines explicitly the type of hero that he envisages for America: "The hero is a mind of such balance that no disturbances can shake his will, . . . There is somewhat not philosophical in heroism; there is somewhat not holy in it; it seems not to know that other souls are of one texture with it; it has pride; it is the extreme of individual nature. Nevertheless we must profoundly revere it. There is somewhat in great actions which does not allow us to go behind them. Heroism feels and never reasons, and therefore is always right."

In the hero the Reason finds its fullest expression as the intuition asserts itself and dominates human action. Emerson ascribes to the extraordinary man innumerable positive attributes—self-trust, virtue, naturalness, nobility, persistence, courage—until we realize that this man, in transcending the common person, in embodying ideal traits that are beyond the capacity of the common man, is in part mystically conceived, the idea of man rather than any actual man. We do not know the sources of the hero's greatness—"heroism is an obedience to a secret impulse of an individual's character"—and we follow Emerson's enumeration of the hero's characteristics in "Heroism" and the other early essays, always conscious that the author is suggesting what man ought to be rather than what he is.

Our present impatience with Emerson stems from Emerson's own impatience with man as he existed in his time. He is unwilling to view the human being as completely human, as he actually is; and the record of the intervening century, it would seem, has undermined and mocked many of his fundamental ideas. But if he has not proven to be historically or practically accurate, he does express an idealistic strain that is central to American life and culture, one that has recurred regardless of the bleak moment of history in which we have been living. When Emerson wrote his early essays the historical moment in America was, of course, not bleak, and much of his strength and self-confidence arise from a felicitious convergence of literary, religious, and economic revolutions that helped to liberate Americans. "The circumstances of man," he acknowledges in "Heroism," "are historically somewhat better in this country at this hour than perhaps ever before. More freedom exists for culture." The truth of the observation suggests why Emerson felt so free to demand ideal behavior from the people of his time. His attraction to scientific advancement; his awareness of the physical growth and industrial progress of the country; his nationalistic fervor; his success in promulgating transcendentalism—all of these factors buttressed his central desire to see an epic hero, absolutely unique in the history of the world, emerge in America.

After Emerson had written his early addresses and the essays of the first and second series, he focused less on the hero as representative of the common man than on the hero whom the common man should emulate. In championing the ordinary person—"I embrace the common," he had announced in "The American Scholar," "I explore and sit at the feet of the familiar, the low"—he found himself unable to use the language of the ordinary person; and as he came to analyze the hero in his essays he discovered, as early as 1842, that "the heroic cannot be the common, nor the common the heroic." The idealism that informs his vision of the average American, who is in the process of seeking heroic powers, yields to an altered vision in which the historical hero—Plato, Goethe, Shakespeare, Napoleon, the Englishman—has realized his ideals. The American is asked to watch this hero—to watch and to learn. Emerson's repeated conviction that "the only sin is limitation" leads to his rather aristocratic view of the hero in *Representative Men* and *The Conduct of Life;* his view that "we are born believers in great men," as expressed in "Character," leads directly to the opening statement in *Representative Men:* "It is natural to believe in great men. If the companions of our childhood should turn out to be heroes, and their condition regal, it would not surprise us. . . . The search after the great is the dream of youth, and the most serious occupation of manhood." Although Emerson was at odds with Carlyle's notion of the hero, although he emphasized the particular qualities represented by his heroes rather than the militant attributes of extraordinary men, he nevertheless grew more particular, more rigid, and more distant to the common man in the decade before the Civil War. In the thirties and forties, Emerson's works reflected the theological tensions then paramount in New England life; but the cultural break that he suggests in "The American Scholar" had not yet occurred, and when it developed in the 1850's and 1860's, Emerson was not prepared to adjust his thought or his style to the consequences—to the actualities of democracy that one sees reflected, for example, in the poetry of Whitman or in the political essays of Thoreau.*

Representative Men is Emerson's attempt to define those ideal aspects of human character in individual heroes. These men—Plato, Swedenborg, Montaigne, Shakespeare, Napoleon, and Goethe—represent us only in so far as they have achieved what we desire to achieve; it seems clear that Emerson is more interested in the heroes than in those common people whom they represent. In "The American Scholar," Emerson was a man speaking to men and his impatient attitude stems from his deep feelings about the individual's possibilities. In *Representative Men* he speaks of how the "imbecility of men is always inviting impudence of power"; and though he claims that "true genius will not impoverish, but will liberate, and add new senses," clearly he has greater faith in the representative man, the hero, than in "the victim" who gropes at minds of powerful method. "Mankind have, in all ages, attached themselves to a few persons, who, either by the quality of that idea they embodied, or by the largeness of their reception, were entitled to the position of leaders and law-givers."

In the opening chapter of *Representative Men*—"The Uses of Great Men"—Emerson approaches heroism from a utilitarian point of view. The basic use to which great men can be put, he believes, is their salutary influence on the common person. "We love to associate with heroic persons, since our receptivity is unlimited; and with the great, our thoughts and manners easily become great." But

---

*My intention is not to praise Whitman and Thoreau at the expense of Emerson, certainly not in this cursory a manner, but to point toward the differing forms that their work assumed as they lost a firm and idealistic faith in the common man. One may say—with all the excess that generalizations invite—that Emerson looked outwards, away from America, either in time (as in *Representative Men*) or in space (as in *English Traits*). Whitman and Thoreau faced the political facts of mid-nineteenth-century America more directly.

The response of these authors to the emerging Republic of mid-century presents many problems which it is not within my scope to discuss—F. O. Matthiessen and other critics have already written perceptively about the subject. Whitman's changing conception of the hero as the common American I discuss in a later chapter. Thoreau came to grips with actual social problems like slavery and, curiously, the literary development of his attitudes is analogous to Emerson's: from the general to the particular, from the ideal to the specific example. Compare, for example, the theoretical, idealistic quality of "Civil Disobedience" (1849) with the militancy of an essay like "A Plea for Captain John Brown" (1859).

as he attempted to define those characteristics that render Plato or Swedenborg or Montaigne superior, he confronts them personally, pitting them against himself in almost an exclusive way—and the average person is largely forgotten. In the early essays great men were genuine models, and Emerson stood between them and his audience—*he* represented his readers; but now the audience is absent, and the writer, fully developed and certain of his own artistic power, measures his chosen heroes in terms of himself alone—the dominant characteristics that each representative man exemplifies are characteristics which Emerson considers essential to himself. If he can sympathize with the "broad humanity" and "the patrician polish" of Plato, he can also find the strong will and democratic heroism of Napoleon attractive; if he finds the mysticism of Swedenborg significant, although excessively classified, he also values personally the skepticism of Montaigne. Philosophy, mysticism, skepticism, poetry, democratic heroism, and writing: these are aspects of Emerson, refractions of his total character, that he seeks to measure in a privative manner. In his conclusion to the introductory chapter he reminds us that "within the limits of human education and agency, we may say, great men exist that there be greater men. The destiny of organized nature is amelioration, and who can tell its limits?" Who can tell, that is, the limitations of Emerson as he measures himself in his full maturity against his chosen heroes of the past.

Of the six representative men only one is in fact a man exclusively involved in the democratic actualities of everyday life, and he, Napoleon, whom Emerson characterizes as "the man of the world," is a military hero. In an age of industrial growth, no hero of commerce is included; in an era of scientific development, no great scientist is represented; in a time of political tensions no political figure appears. These various heroes, again with the exception of Napoleon, are representative of the poetic or philosophic disposition —passive men, ultimately, who invoke the muse or the oversoul to inspire them. The entire volume is retrospective, general, impressionistic—safe, even tame, in a way that the early addresses and essays are not. The descriptions of Swedenborg and Montaigne are diffuse; the treatments of Plato, Shakespeare, and Goethe are effusive, hyperbolic—almost the tributes of an undiscriminating mind. Although F. O. Matthiessen is justified in stressing Emerson's achievement as part of a "literature for our democracy," *Representative Men* is not the text most illustrative of that achievement.

Emerson himself was aware that his representative men did not suggest the types of all mankind, to say nothing of the democratic

America in which he lived. He introduces the essay on "Sweden-borg; or, the Mystic" by asserting that "Among eminent persons, those who are most dear to men are not of the class which the economist calls producers"; they are the poets, the inspirational leaders, and not those who tend to govern or lead or live in any practical sense. This may be the reason that no chapter in *Represen-tative Men* is devoted to an American, for then Emerson surely would have had to draw upon a political or a military leader—or, as he wrote shortly after having finished the book, "the unexpressed greatness of the common farmer and laborer." The farmer or laborer would surely have been an adequate representative of America, but his presence would have jarred with the tone of the other chapters. Furthermore, it is difficult to conceive of Emerson approaching the common American as he treats Plato or Shakespeare or Goethe; these are particular heroes who are repersentative in only the most conceptual sense—they are heroes rather than representative men. The common man does not occupy the center of Emerson's thought at this stage of his career—he is, to use the term that Emerson em-ployed when he regretted his omission of "the common farmer and laborer" in *Representative Men,* an afterthought. It remained for Whitman to develop an heroic myth of the common American.

The absence of a contemporary American hero reflects, more precisely, Emerson's belief that the representative man who ex-hibited one dominant trait could not function in his time. In "Goethe; or, the Writer," Emerson acknowledges that Goethe

> appears at a time when a general culture has spread itself, and has smoothed down all sharp individual traits; when, in the absence of heroic characters, a social comfort and cooperation have come in. There is no poet, but scores of poetic writers; no Columbus, but hundreds of post-captains, with transit-telescope, barometer, and concentrated soup and pemmican, no Demos-thenes, no Chatham, but any number of clever parliamentary and forensic debaters; no prophet or saint, but colleges of di-vinity; no learned man, but learned societies, a cheap press, reading-rooms, and book-clubs, without number. There was never such a miscellany of facts. The world extends itself like American trade. We conceive Greek or Roman life,—life in the middle ages,—to be a simple and comprehensible affair; but modern life to respect a multitude of things, which is distracting.

Just a decade or so after Tocqueville, in his *Democracy in America,* had written of the American's concern with the future and with the multiplicity of democratic life, it is curious that the American who was most eloquent in urging a cultural as well as a theological revolution should be looking backwards, or, as in his next book, *English Traits,* looking away from his own country. But sensing that America would not yield the kind of hero whom Carlyle had called for in 1845 and whom he himself foresaw in his early work, Emerson turned to England, "the best of actual nations," and offered the "History" of the Englishman that Carlyle had wanted him to write of the American.

Still *English Traits* is a history of heroism and the great names fill the pages. The traits of the English people are really the traits of their heroes and when Emerson considers the people themselves he does so because he feels that they should become like their representatives. Furthermore, his eulogy of English culture—"the culture of the day, the thoughts and aims of men, are English thoughts and aims"—is meant to remind Americans whom they should emulate, for "the American is only the continuation of the English genius into new conditions." The aristocracy of talent that he emphasized in *Representative Men* is now attributed to English heroes and leads to the social aristocracy that one finds in *The Conduct of Life,* which is, as Stephen Whicher has suggested, a "gospel for patricians."

What impressed Emerson most about the English was their power. As he discusses race and character, wealth and aristocracy, he reminds us that the English "assimilate other races to themselves, and are not assimilated," that "the stability of England is the security of the modern world." He recognizes that the American system is more democratic, more humane; yet the American people "do not yield better or more able men or more inventions or books or benefits than the English." The English dominate the world, the most accomplished nation in modern European history, and Emerson's admiration is almost wholly devoted to those aspects of character that "have helped to make the English the leaders that they are." He does conclude, in a kind of afterthought, that the quality "which lures a solitary American in the woods with the wish to see England, is the moral peculiarity of the Saxon race—its commanding sense of right and wrong, the love and devotion to that—this is the imperial trait, which arms them with the sceptre of the globe"; but, in fact, as he notes early in the book, the English "are with difficulty ideal." His emphasis throughout *English Traits* is on the practical and not the ideal traits of the people, on their authority in the world and not their idealism. He is less concerned with what the English will become than with what they were and are. "The power of performance has not been exceeded," he reminds us finally, and the power of that performance is "the creation of value. The English have given importance to individuals, a principal end and fruit of every society. Every man is allowed and encouraged to be what he is, and is guarded in the indulgence of his whim."

Emerson's fascination with power and success becomes most manifest in *The Conduct of Life,* in which he asserts that life is, in effect, a search after power. The first two chapters, "Fate" and "Power," are in a mutual tension—"the antagonist of Fate is Power," Emerson states at the outset—and the reader recognizes the antipodal forces that Emerson conceives of as governing human nature. Although he admits that we are at the mercy of natural forces and that we are fated in many ways, Emerson insists that fate "can teach us a fatal courage," as long as we realize that the strongest power comes from Nature and that "There are sources on which we have not drawn. . . . For though Fate is immense, so is Power, which is the other fact in the dual world, immense. If Fate follows and limits Power, Power attends and antagonizes Fate."

The tone of these essays is patronizing, the attitude toward the common person condescending. Whereas the early work concentrated upon the moral virtues that stem from self-reliance, the later essays in *The Conduct of Life* are guides to practical success—and though they often use the same terminology, it now has a more secular, different purpose. Whereas self-reliance meant God-reliance in the early essays, now it means literally reliance on the individual self. Thought and the moral sentiment make us free so that we can transcend our fate and achieve a "sovereignty of power"; manners, whose basis is self-reliance, are a force and "impress us as they indicate real power"; power is what "men of esteem" want—"power to execute their design, power to give legs and feet, form and actuality to their thought"; man must learn not to spend but to "hoard for power." These statements, and they are representative of others in *The Conduct of Life,* reflect Emerson's conviction that "very few of our race can be said to be yet finished men"; and he concludes that man's purpose is now "to convert all impediments into instruments, all enemies into power" so that the organic effort of his human nature "to mount and meliorate" can be effected and "the corresponding impulse to the Better in the human being" can be achieved.

Emerson's work comes at a turning point in American culture. "The American Scholar" is one of the climactic expressions of nationalism and democratic idealism; the aristocracy of talent demanded in the early essay surrenders to a social aristocracy for whom Emerson prescribes the proper use of manners, behavior, culture, worship, and wealth—the proper conduct of life. The terms of this life, rooted as they are in power and force, have led to industrial, commercial, practical power and success—a pattern prefigured by the development of Emerson's own view. His waning interest in democratic idealism and his increased emphasis on the uses to which power can be put suggest the general direction that our society has taken; from a heritage of individualism we have developed into a centralized power state that reduces Emerson's early self-reliance to the realm of antiquated theory. Emerson's view is that only the "well born" can realize the self-reliance that he prescribes, and this view, which is increasingly pronounced in *Representative Men*, *English Traits*, and *The Conduct of Life*, is similar to the actualities of our so-called democracy today. Paradoxically, the individual whom he addresses in "Nature" and the "Divinity School Address" becomes the victim of twentieth-century literature, a victim to the kind of power advocated in *The Conduct of Life*—power in the political, commercial, and religious spheres or our life.

Emerson's concept of the hero as an emerging idealist struggling against the authority of tradition and conformity had a profound effect on his contemporaries and on Whitman. But the fusion of the early concept, with its concentration on morality, and the later concept, with its emphasis on manners, appears dramatically in the fiction of Henry James, F. Scott Fitzgerald, and other novelists. I do not mean to imply direct influence, but I would suggest that Emerson's shifting concept of the hero recurs in the work of these authors, embodying yoked and often irreconcilable opposites, and that it assumes a significant pattern in their writing. The idealist as wealthy and powerful man can be traced in one distinct portion of the literature since Emerson's time—from Christopher Newman of *The American* to Jay Gatsby of *The Great Gatsby*. There is a buoyant naïvety and self-reliance in the characters of James and Fitzgerald that is fused with their sudden acquisition of money or power—they are a little awkward with the money and the power, like Gatsby whose foot is never still. That awkwardness, which is still new enough to be decidedly idealistic, confronts the solid authority of European decadence (like the Bellegardes in *The American*) or the decadent rich in America (the Buchanans in *Gatsby*), and the larger conflict between idealism and authority is drawn. The hero of this fiction tends to be morally triumphant, even though he may end in defeat or death with his ideal yet unrealized;

but the real meaning of his experience lies in the unresolved tensions between his ideals and the sudden authority he possesses. After Gatsby's noble failure American writers begin to conceive of idealism as crushed by a mechanistic culture, by the very power it has helped to create. The hero then becomes the victim or the cripple or the idiot or the dislocated adolescent, receding inwards into private meditations, lonely introspection, fantasies, searching for that moment when the idealistic attitude of his country or his region, his family or his personal life began to turn into cynicism or bitterness: thus the work of Faulkner, Carson McCullers, J. D. Salinger, Truman Capote, Tennessee Williams, and Edward Albee. But then, as if a cyclical law is at work in the development of our literature, the ideal hero emerges in the work of some of these same writers and in that of other important contemporaries.

For the reader of modern literature Emerson's ideological dogmatism, unchecked by an ambiguity and irony so congenial to the present sensibility, is perhaps antipathetic and the concentration on force in his later work hardly attractive, given the events of twentieth-century history. But Emerson remains, as Newton Arvin suggested years ago, "in some sense our bishop." His vision was more profound than any single expression of it. In a fundamental way he assumed the posture that has become distinctly associated with the American writer: the assertion of the author's character throughout his work rather than the creation of a world of individual figures—comic or tragic—in which the creator's personality is largely absent. Thoreau, Whitman, and Emily Dickinson speak in the first person, and much could be made of this American obsession with self in the work of many twentieth-century writers. But most significantly Emerson expressed fully and profoundly that strain of idealism which is deeply embedded in the American consciousness. And if we have achieved the empirical power that he himself had come to admire, if we have sometimes abused that power—as he could not foresee we would—we have still the element of idealism that reasserts itself insistently.

No one would question the significance of the Gothic tradition as it has been traced by D. H. Lawrence, Malcolm Cowley, and Leslie Fiedler; but Gothicism is, in most cases, checked by an idealistic strain that finds its roots in Emerson's writing; and, of course, the tragic vision of Hawthorne and Melville, responsive as it is to the optimism of Emerson and his followers, cannot be fully understood without a knowledge of Emerson's work.

A Note on Bibliographical Materials

While there is no complete bibliography of Emerson, there are some bibliographic aids.

Of the older bibliographies, the following may be specially noted:

> Richard Garnett, *Life of Ralph Waldo Emerson* (London, 1888; bibliography follows the index).
>
> George Willis Cooke, *A Bibliography of Ralph Waldo Emerson* (Boston, 1908).

A "Selected Bibliography" is to be found in Konvitz and Whicher, eds., *Emerson: A Collection of Critical Essays,* Twentieth Century Views Series (Prentice-Hall, 1962). In addition to the items cited there, the following may be mentioned:

> Lewis Leary, *Articles on American Literature, 1900–1950* (Duke University Press, 1954).
>
> ———, *Articles on American Literature, 1950–1967* (Duke University Press, 1970).
>
> Jackson R. Bryer and Robert A. Rees, *A Checklist of Emerson Criticism 1951–1961* (Transcendental Books, Hartford, 1964).
>
> J. A. Robbins, ed., *American Literary Scholarship: An Annual,* for 1963 and successive years (Duke University Press).
>
> Martin Tucker, ed., *Moulton's Library of Literary Criticism,* Vol. IV (Ungar, 1966, pp. 3–26).

For the reception of Emerson in other countries, one may consult the following:

> William J. Sowder, *Emerson's Impact on the British Isles and Canada* (University Press of Virginia, 1966).
>
> Clarence Gohdes, "The Reception of Some Nineteenth-Century American Authors in Europe," in Margaret Denny and William H. Gilman, eds., *The American Writer and the European Tradition* (McGraw-Hill, 1950, especially pp. 117–119).